'Mark Leffert has shown himself to be the most creative analyst writing today. In this book, in keeping with his other innovative contributions, he demonstrates that modern psychoanalysis is intimately linked with developing knowledge in the fields of philosophy, neuroscience, psychology and existential thought. The new work extends and enriches our understanding of psychoanalysis as does none other in the contemporary literature. It is essential reading for anyone interested in the life of the mind.'

Theodore Jacobs, *training and supervising analyst at the New York Psychoanalytic Institute and the New York University Psychoanalytic Institute*

'Leffert elegantly guides us through multiple personal and social meanings to place contemporary psychoanalysis in the context of human evolution and development. He integrates phenomenology, existentialism, and confronting death. This book offers the reader a profound synthetic cognitive adventure and is strongly recommended for all clinicians and minds interested in modern psychoanalysis.'

Peter Loewenberg, *professor emeritus, University of California, Los Angeles*

Psychoanalysis, the Self, and the World

This book takes psychoanalysis into the 21st century, examining issues of existentialism, postphenomenology, social media, and death and death anxiety that have gone largely ignored in the psychoanalytic and psychotherapeutic literature.

Using an interdisciplinary perspective, Leffert explains that it is impossible to close the door of the consulting room. The therapeutic relationship is invaded by the outside world and its relationships for both patient and therapist and cannot be isolated from these influences. Drawing on richly detailed case studies, Leffert demonstrates how the internet, social media, and the metaverse have changed and expanded the self in ways that could not have been imagined in the last century. In turn, Leffert acknowledges recent advances in the neurosciences and addresses the lack of engagement with their implications for theories and practices of therapeutic action. Finally, the ways in which death and death anxiety impinge on the self, which have also gone mostly undealt with in psychoanalytic literature, become an important focus of this book.

As a novel exploration of interdisciplinary connections, this book will be of use to both scholars and practitioners of psychotherapy, psychoanalysis, social network theory, philosophy, and neuroscience.

Mark Leffert was educated in medicine, psychiatry, and psychoanalysis in New York and California. He has maintained a practice of psychotherapy and psychoanalysis in Del Mar, Minneapolis, and, currently, Santa Barbara. He has been on the faculty of five psychoanalytic institutes and has been a training and supervising analyst at four of them. He is the author of six prior books and several papers.

Psychoanalysis, the Self, and the World

Postphenomenology, Consciousness, and Death

Mark Leffert

Routledge
Taylor & Francis Group

LONDON AND NEW YORK

Designed cover image: Untitled, Mark Leffert, Mixed Media, 2005, Photo by Author

First published 2023
by Routledge
4 Park Square, Milton Park, Abingdon, Oxon OX14 4RN

and by Routledge
605 Third Avenue, New York, NY 10158

Routledge is an imprint of the Taylor & Francis Group, an informa business

British Library Cataloguing-in-Publication Data
A catalogue record for this book is available from the British Library

Library of Congress Cataloging-in-Publication Data
Names: Leffert, Mark, author.
Title: Psychoanalysis, the self and the world : postphenomenology, consciousness, and death / Mark Leffert.
Description: Milton Park, Abingdon, Oxon ; New York, NY : Routledge, 2023. | Includes bibliographical references and index. |
Identifiers: LCCN 2022029203 (print) | LCCN 2022029204 (ebook) | ISBN 9781032394008 (hardback) | ISBN 9781032394015 (paperback) | ISBN 9781003349556 (ebook)
Subjects: LCSH: Psychoanalysis. | Self. | Psychotherapy.
Classification: LCC BF175 .L446 2023 (print) | LCC BF175 (ebook) | DDC 150.19/5--dc23/eng/20220705
LC record available at https://lccn.loc.gov/2022029203
LC ebook record available at https://lccn.loc.gov/2022029204

ISBN: 978-1-032-39400-8 (hbk)
ISBN: 978-1-032-39401-5 (pbk)
ISBN: 978-1-003-34955-6 (ebk)

DOI: 10.4324/9781003349556

Typeset in Garamond
by KnowledgeWorks Global Ltd.

For my Grandchildren, Sarah and Adam

Contents

Acknowledgments

As my work has continued since the Millennium, I have relied on interactions with colleagues and their published work in ways that have become too numerous to mention. I would first like to thank my patients who have taught me most of the things that I have written about. I would like to thank Routledge and my editor there, Kate Hawes, for their ongoing support of my work, now stretching to include seven volumes. It has been a long journey that I hope to continue. I would next like to thank Kristopher Spring, my personal editor; we have worked together on each of my books, and I have trusted him to critique my ideas. Lastly, I want to thank my wife, Nancy Leffert, PhD, who has offered me unending support through difficult times.

Introduction

I began my formal medical education in the 1960s with the expectation that I would become first a physician and then a neurosurgeon. I found instead that, in medical school, what captured my interest was Psychoanalysis and neuroscience, which was then called neurophysiology. I did not at the time imagine that my youthful interests in archaeology and zoology would become relevant to the career I was setting out upon. They did.

This is the latest, the seventh, in a series of books (Leffert, 2010, 2013, 2016, 2017, 2018, 2021) exploring the way Philosophy, notably Phenomenology, Existentialism, and Postmodernism, and Interdisciplinary Studies have impacted Psychoanalysis as it is thought about and practiced in the early 21st century. It will take up, and we will have more to say about this shortly, Consciousness, Meaning and Absurdity, Phenomenology in the age of Social Media, the relations of Self and World, and the ultimate component of that relationship, Death and Death Anxiety. These subjects, arising out of the previous volumes, have shown themselves to require further thought and integration.

However, shortly after I began to write, in the winter of 2020, the world changed and the book was overtaken by global events on several fronts, a change that would echo down through the next two or three generations.[1] The topics to be covered, among them Existentialism, Phenomenology, and Systems Theory, are uniquely positioned to engage these changes. In addition, Death and Death Anxiety have taken a larger place in contemporary Being. Borrowing from Camus (1948/1991a), I would call what happened simply the *Plague*, rather than COVID-19[2] or any of its other scientific names. I do this because, as Camus' protagonist Dr. Rieux tells us, *it is a social disease*, and, as such, falls uniquely within the purview Existential Psychoanalysis, the disciplines we have been studying and *all* of the subject areas just listed. Epidemiology, we will see, is far closer to what we do as social practitioners than to virology.[3] The social context in which the Plague has unfolded includes global trends toward fragmentation—the January 6th rebellion at the Capitol and the Ukraine War are the latest symptoms of that fragmentation—best described by the term of rising anocracy (Walter, 2022), and growingly catastrophic climate change. These four elements—the Plague,

DOI: 10.4324/9781003349556-1

the global political fragmentation, and the rise of anocracies, and climate change—are mutually interreferential.

A Psychoanalysis that focuses primarily on the genetic past deploys a limited set of tools for viewing World (in Heidegger's terms (1975/1982), the *Mitwelt* and the *Eigenwelt*) and a therapeutic action offering only limited results in the best of times—it is particularly so in these dark times of Plague and War. The World crowds in on us and cannot be ignored. This is not to say that the genetic past and the psychodynamic responses to it have no place in Contemporary Psychoanalysis and Psychotherapy but, rather, that it is only a part of what we need to concern ourselves with.

In this volume, I plan to offer an interdisciplinary rereading of Psychoanalysis that includes standard psychoanalytic metapsychologies and the disciplines described above but goes beyond them. It is organized around an expanded, interreferential relationship between World and Self that has been called Postphenomenology (Idhe, 1995; Selinger, 2006). Its current focus is on the internet, but I have expanded it to include any relationship that the Self has with externally recorded information. This involves a history of writing and its uses.

Chapter 1 offers a brief history of 20th-century Psychoanalysis and its embeddedness in Phenomenology, Existentialism, and Postmodernism. In particular, it emphasizes Consciousness (as opposed to Unconsciousness and repression) and its relationship to World. Moving into Heidegger's (1975/1982) language this involves a shift in emphasis from the inner world, the *Eigenwelt*, and the two person aspects of the Mitwelt, the transference and countertransference, to the whole of the latter, and the surrounding sociocultural and physical world of the *Umwelt*.

In particular, Consciousness is by definition *about* something (Brentano, 1874/1995). It involves the *experiential subjectivity* of the Self in World, connected through *perception*. However, the Neuroscientists and the Postmoderns tell us, and this was missed by the Phenomenologists, that connections also interreferentiality involve unconscious mental activity (Figure 1).

The Unconscious connections to World and Conscious, in addition to Perception, involve the autonomic nervous system and the maintenance of

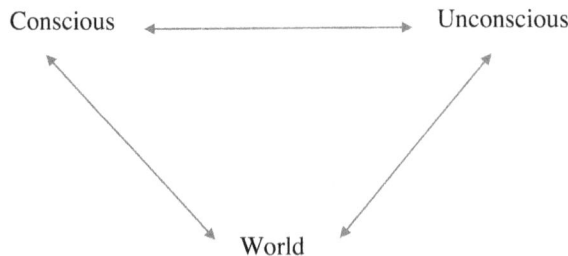

Figure 1 Relations of Self and the World.

homeostasis. The connections of both the Conscious and the Unconscious with World are *subjective*.

We will take up a particular thread of Husserl's massive opus that contemporary Phenomenologists (Idhe, 2012) call Experimental Phenomenology. It applies objective study via experimentation to document the subjectivities and intersubjectivities of Human Beings. Husserl introduces the concept of *Epochē* or "pockets," to document a "dropping out": putting an essential element aside for later consideration so as not to interrupt an ongoing argument. This is also the *defer* part of Derrida's *différance* (1978) (the other part being to *differ*). The concept is useful since it offers a way of putting aside theory or metapsychology echoing a recent trend (Rudden & Bronstein, 2017; Tuckett et al., 2008). Husserl offered a correlation between what is being experienced and its *mode* of being experienced. This is discussed in some detail and a clinical example is presented and considered in terms of Eissler's (1968) offering a distinction between understanding and explaining and Kahneman and Tversky's (Kahneman, 2011; Kahneman, Slovic, & Tversky, 1982) addressing uncertainty through their positing the use of heuristics. I constantly opt for an interweaving and re-interweaving of such diverse threads to maintain a whole greater than the sum of its parts.

Heidegger, while a controversial figure given his role in Nazi Germany (I have discussed this in Leffert, 2016), is, nevertheless, considered the foremost Phenomenologist of the 20th century. I posit that he (1975/1982, 1927/2010) is an ontologist rather than an epistemologist. He replaced the unproven psychoanalytic theory of psychic *depth* with the manifestly observable concept of *temporality*—bio-psycho-social history and development—and divided ontology into the three realms: the *Eigenwelt*, the *Mitwelt*, and the *Umwelt*. He also offered three modes of Being: the Thrown, the Everyday, and the Fallen. How COVID is expressed in these axes is discussed from the premise that it is a social as well as a virological disease. COVID must find a place in any clinical writing at least from 2020 to 2030.[4] Case illustrations are provided.

Existentialism is an interreferential discipline to Phenomenology. We will discuss the work of many authors here, but Camus and Sartre stand out here. They were concerned with Meaninglessness, Absurdity, and, influenced by the occupation of France and the Nazi presence during the Second World War, the way Death overshadowed life. Sartre's example of *Nothingness* (1943/2018) refers to the cafés of Nazi-occupied Paris where people who had come every day were, one day, just gone; a *Nothing* that was also a *Something*.

Phenomenology (Heidegger, 1975/1982, 1979/2009) and Existentialism (Kierkegaard, 1849/1980, 1846/1992) were the first branches of philosophy to turn away from Modernism—a position founded on a tight reading of science and rationalism—because of its inabilities to account for Human behavior, thought or decision-making. Husserl (1913/1983) and, later, Idhe (2012) made attempts to offer specific solutions, but this failing went otherwise unaddressed. It was taken up by the philosophical turn of the 1970s:

Postmodernism (Leffert, 2007a, 2007b). The chapter offers a brief review of the topic. In particular, I treat Postmodernism as a supplement to, *not* a replacement of, Phenomenology and Existentialism. It offers tools for dealing with multiple explanations and holding together seemingly contradictory ones. It also manages Uncertainty and Unknowability. Derrida (1978) is particularly relevant here as are Foucault (1980, 2000) and Lukes (2005) for new Postmodern considerations of Power. Latour (1991/1993) offers a singular reading of the interface between the scientific and the social.

The chapter also reviews and integrates problems that appear in decision-making under Uncertainty (Kahneman et al., 1982; Kahneman & Tversky, 1979/2000). The concepts of heuristics and biases and their relation to metanarrative are of particular importance in clinical psychoanalysis as they reveal both present day and historical pieces of character. Again, relevant case material is discussed.

Chapter 2 offers a new perspective on Phenomenology and Postphenomenology that focuses on their Evo-Devo. It presents an introduction to Postphenomenology and a new concept that I will term Prephenomenology. For these discussions, I require the use of the concept of Self (a Bio-psycho-social Self) as opposed to Mind. It also must deal with Pre-technical and Post-technical processes of Evo-Devo, which will take us back 3,000,000 years. Evo-Devo prefigured Postphenomenology in the evolution of the Brain-Mind with the addition ca. 9000 BCE of a particular kind of technological innovation producing devices and artifacts that supplemented or enhanced cognitive and emotional function.

I will consider Prephenomenology, Phenomenology, and Postphenomenology as linked ways of Being, that is, they make up the Existence of Dasein. What separates them is not that they are different ontologies but rather that *the apparatuses involved*—evolving biological brain, stable biological brain, and integrated bio-technological brain—*are different*. I'm going to novelly integrate Postphenomenology (which we will take up in the next chapter) into its Human prehistory.

There is another element to be considered, and that is Consciousness. Although I have discussed Consciousness a number of times in the past (Leffert, 2010, 2016, 2018), the present chapter and the one that follows convinced me that another, further evolved version, is required and it will be offered in Chapter 4.

Recent research summarized by Hofer (2014) has shown any separation of Evolution and Development to be artificial and led to the newly defined science of Evo-Devo. It involves, among other things, a reconsideration of Haeckel's previously repudiated premise "ontogeny recapitulates phylogeny" and the broadening of Development to include Embryology and Epigenetics. These are discussed as is the Evo-Devo of Human mental hardware, studied in the discipline of Paleoanthropology, going back 4–5 mya. The human brain, at 1300 cm^3, is a metabolically expensive organ to run. It uses 20% of the body's calories. To make Evo-Devo sense, it must convey enormous selective advantages to its possessor; its social and cognitive capacities explain its reason for Being (Dunbar, 2016), and this brings us back to the Prephenomenology-Phenomenology transition. Central to *this* is the evolving mother-child relationship and the evolving of Theory of Mind (ToM) (Baron-Cohen, 2000) in which the child learns that their caregivers are like them and have minds like them. This offers a theory of other minds. It entails the Evo-Devo of *Mentalization* which in turn entails the intersubjective experience of Intentionality (Brentano, 1874/1995).

There are three orders of Intentionality. *All* conscious organisms have some idea of the contents of their own minds. This is first order Intentionality. The ability to have ideas about what someone else has in their mind is second order Intentionality.[5] This involves a formal ToM. It is followed by a recursive sequence: I think that you think that I think (third order) and so on. Humans reach first order at +/− one year, second order (the stage barely reached by the great apes and chimpanzees) at age 5, and plateau at the fourth to the sixth level in our teens.

Dunbar (2016) posits four phase transitions in the Evo-Devo of Humans. The first is from apes to Australopiths with upright locomotion about 3 mya. The second is to genus *Homo* around 1.8 mya. These were the creatures that Louis Leakey, the noted paleoanthropologist, discovered in the Olduvai Gorge in Kenya in 1962. The social brain hypothesis tells us that brain size correlates with group size, and, for us, it is around 150. The third transition resulted in the appearance of archaic humans, *Homo Heidelbergensis*, around 600,000 ya with brains, at 1300 cm^3, the size of ours. The fourth and final transition was to Anatomically Modern Humans (AMH), *H. sapiens*, 200,000+/− ya in Africa. A fifth non-anatomical transition from *H. sapiens* to *H. sapiens, sapiens* occurred +/− 50,000 ya, resulting in what is called the Middle to Upper Paleolithic Transition (Mellars, 2005; Mithen, 1994). This involved the appearance of what we might call fully modern cognitive abilities and social behaviors. We do not currently have reasons for this comparatively sudden, qualitative change in us (from the intelligent *Homos* to the wise guys); whether it involved some change in the workings of the brain, perhaps due to changing climates, as a result of the Evo or the Devo side of things. This transition also involves the shift from what I have called Prephenomenology to Phenomenology. The chapter explores this change and changes in the nature of consciousness that seemed to be required by the transition.

Dunbar (2016) posits a sixth phase transition occurring roughly 12,000 ya at the beginning of the Holocene—the geologic epoch in which we live. In it, we began to settle in little villages in the Levant and the Fertile Crescent (the contemporary Middle East). He relates these transitions to evolving social practices, their correlations with brain size, and the increase in social group size that they made possible or followed from (we don't, perhaps can't, know). However, somewhere during this range of dates from 50,000 ya to 12,000 ya we became us and there was a shift from Evo-Devo to, for the present, Devo.

The shift from Prephenomenology to Phenomenology, from Existence to Meaning, also involved a shift in tools for study, from Paleoanthropology to Philosophy, survival to ontology. We, the Wise Guys are the only Phenomenal creatures who ask ontological questions about ourselves and other entities. Case material continues to be presented to illustrate what these changes are all about.

Chapter 3 finally brings us to Postphenomenology and its Evo-Devo. First described by Idhe (1995) in the analysis of human-technology relations, it entails the social and cultural roles of technology through a blend of empirical and philosophical research methods. This discipline endeavors to study the relations between Human Beings and the technology with which we surround ourselves. It focuses on the way technologies shape interactions between Human Beings and World. Technological artifacts are mediators of human experience and practice in the *Umwelt* and *Mitwelt*. They combine philosophical analysis with empirical investigations (Rosenberger & Verbeek, 2015, p. 9). Postphenomenology is inseparably bound up with Information Technology (IT): older one-way technologies (television, radio, film) and, contemporaneously, the two-way technologies of cellphones and the internet (taken together, they make up what we call the metaverse). This involves a split in Evo-Devo into the Evo of IT machines and the Devo of the way Humans make use of them.

We will consider Postphenomenology across a much wider span than Idhe does—from the Neolithic Period, 9000 BCE, give or take, to the present. It involves the creation of mental artifacts: devices created for mental, psychological, or cognitive purposes. This means that Phenomenology and Postphenomenology have existed for a time as parallel schools of ontology, rather than the latter replacing the former. They *supplement* each other rather than the shift from Modernism to Postmodernism that involves a *critique* of the former by the latter.

A dichotomy occurred, dating back to the Bronze Age, between artifacts developed for everyone's use, a house idol for example, to those developed for the use of specialists like cuneiform tablets for the use of accountants. Mathematics and alphabets evolved in this developmental line. The widespread appearance of books in the decades following the appearance of the moveable-type printing press and the Guttenberg bible showed a transition from specialist to generalist usage. The history of the invention of Postphenomenal artifacts, their evolution, and the Development of their users, is discussed.

There are three Postphenomenal milestones occurring over the course of human-artifact Evo-Devo. The first is the Development of language as a part of the Upper Paleolithic Package with written notations appearing around 10,000 ya. The second milestone involves the Evo-Devo of Human Beings into *Cyborgs*, human-technology mixtures. Idhe (2019) referred to the process as a "gradual accumulation of human-technology hybridization" (p. 34). The third milestone involves the growing representation of human cyborgs on the internet and in social media. We can put a working representation of ourselves, an *external* working model, onto the internet (best termed the *metaverse*) and, as we wish, operate it, or leave it unattended to interact with others.

Turkle (2008) posited a new Self State, a tethered Self, that had a life both on and off the internet. It results from a human-artifact connection. The quintessential Postphenomenal tool of the human-artifact is the Smartphone. It connects us with a different part of World—Cyberspace. Although I have set up my Smartphone and its connections to meet my particular needs, I do not imagine it as connected to me as I do my cardiac pacemaker. In Postphenomenal terms, they have become a part of our Everydayness. In Heideggerian terms they are "handy," ready-at-hand (*Zuhandenheit*) but *also* present-at-hand (*Vorhandenheit*) to be studied for themselves not just used. Smartphones can serve us in Throwness or Everydayness, but they can also lapse into Fallenness (mindlessly surfing the internet). Idhe contrasts hammers that act on the physical world with Smartphones that take us to different places in space and time.

It is a problem that although Postphenomenology has made inroads into every facet of our lives, it has hardly been mentioned in Psychoanalytic writings. It is only the advent of COVID that has forced Psychotherapists and analysts to the use of ZOOM, Facetime, and Smartphones, that has led us to think about these devices and their connections.[6] For some, it offers a new way of working with patients; for others, it just seems to confirm their criticisms. They seem to experience it as defensive rather than facilitative. Case material is again offered for purposes of illustration.

The social arena that is being created by Advanced Information Technology (AIT) is called Cyberspace. Smartphones, Personal Computers, and Tablets are portals from which to enter Cyberspace. It is an inhabited Space in the Postmodern sense first described by Bachelard (1958/1994). Its ontology is twofold. The first is that we individually furnish and customize it, just as we do with our homes: a space that others can enter or leave at will. The second is the wide world of Cyberspace that we can venture or travel in different ways. In the 21st century it has come to be called the Multiverse (Kim, 2021) and it is studied by an interdisciplinary community of Anthropologists, Philosophers, and Social Scientists. The multiverse allows us to present ourselves or journey into it in many ways (who we are there is plastic) with others being able to add to some of these presentations; these are our *avatars. In the multiverse we can be anyone we want to be.* The enforced isolation necessitated by the COVID Pandemic has enlarged our presence in the multiverse. These themes are explored at length.

We want to consider the place of Existentialism and Absurdity in the ontology of Cyberspace. Postphenomenology on its own does not do a particularly good job of addressing Meaning and Absurdity. I have struggled (Leffert, 2021), ultimately with little success, to combine the disciplines of Phenomenology and Existentialism with the latter being more concerned with individual issues than the former. There is an intersection of Meaning and Absurdity around the place of art and what constitutes art in Cyberspace that is discussed. The closest that Phenomenology can come involves the distinction between the ontologies of Thrownness and Fallenness as they pertain to Cyberspace. A clinical example is offered.

I would posit that, just as we have seen the Upper-Paleolithic package (ca. 50,000 ya) and a Neolithic package (ca. 11,000 ya), we are now seeing the appearance of a *Postphenomenological package* that is fully as game changing. It comes with its own *toolkit*, containing, among other things, a Smartphone, and a computer. Tools for medical treatments, with their benefits as well as their risks, are also discussed.

Chapter 4 offers a reappraisal of Consciousness and Unconsciousness, topics I have addressed a number of times (Leffert, 2010, 2018). While the latter has been of primary interest to Psychoanalysts, the former, termed "the hard problem," has been the purview of philosophers and neuroscientists. A series of turf wars have ensued among these three disciplines. The neglect of Consciousness by Psychoanalysts has been, I would posit, unjustified and, perhaps, clinically dangerous.

Consciousness is a *primitive*, it denotes a term that we use that neither requires nor benefits from further definition (Tarski, 1946). We may tend to employ intuition in attempting to define such a term, but it can easily lead us astray. Intuition brushes up against folk psychology and it can lead us, for example, to Descartes' (1641/1999) solution to the mind-body problem. I have come to conclude here that, in contrast to my earlier position, Neuroscience, its functional anatomy and chemistry, has only a limited contribution to make to understanding Consciousness, the mental property of the Self. I'll begin with a brief recap of the position I have taken over the past 20+ years.

In 2010, I did not attempt to offer a definition of Consciousness but limited myself to enumerating what such a definition should include. Psychoanalysis has treated repression and a System Unconscious as primitives that could be safely ingested without supporting evidence. As such, it is all too easy to confuse evidence with the Representativeness Heuristic (Kahneman & Tversky, 1979/2000) which tells us, in effect, "I recognize this, I've seen it before, *so it's true*." This is a restatement of the psychoanalytic arguments appearing in the later 20th century concerning Psychology versus Metapsychology (Gill, 1976; Gill & Holtzman, 1976).

We go on to look at three different kinds of Neuroscience Studies: what determines if a subject is conscious (Owen, 2017; Owen et al., 2006), split-brain studies (Sperry, 1969; Sperry, Gazzaniga, & Bogen, 1969), and studies of different kinds of Consciousness and Memory (Tulving, 1985/2003; Tulving, Kapur, Craik, Moscovitch, & Houle, 1994) to see what they can tell us *about* Consciousness.

Complexity bears directly on Consciousness. Complex systems, of which the Self is one, are very large. They change over time often via massive, sudden, and unpredictable shifts. Their behavior cannot be predicted from its antecedents or from the behavior of its parts. In other words, the whole of a complex system is both different from and greater than the sum of its parts. There is so much going on in complex systems such as the Self that they cannot be fully categorized and change while one is trying to audit them. Consciousness, I posit, is one of the *emergent* properties of the complex Self. In discussing its Evo-Devo, we go back to the Cambrian Explosion ca. 500,000,000 ya (Feinberg & Mallatt, 2016) and, perhaps, even farther back, to the age of one-celled organisms (Ogas & Gaddam, 2022). Evolution progressed to *sentience*, literally "capable of feeling," encompassing large, memory-enhanced systems that include emotion and involve the cerebrum. These are the beginnings of the systems described by Panksepp (2009). This is a move from sensory consciousness to subjective experience.

If Consciousness is a primitive, it does not mean that it is the same in all animals. Conscious, subjective experience exists in all vertebrates, ultimately evolving into sentience. Empathy, self-awareness, grief, consolation, and an awareness of Death when taken together—in us, Chimpanzees, Gorillas, Elephants, and Dolphins—as a package offer evidence of auto-noesis. Grief is particularly observable (King, 2014). Contrary to Koch (2019), elucidating the "mechanistic" basis of Consciousness, however interesting and seductive, does not further our inquiry into its subjective nature, the process that is Consciousness. In 2010 (Leffert), I believed it could be found in the reticular formation and its upstream and downstream connections to the rest of the Self. I now see that I (and many others!) was seduced by functional neuroanatomy. These studies (fMRIs, PET scans and the like) could cause areas of the brain to light up in the presence of various kinds of stimuli. While suggestive of the *presence or activity* of Consciousness, they cannot tell us much about what Consciousness is, its ontology, if you will. Consciousness is not, after all, identical to the brain image lighting up on the fMRI screen.

I am not, however, abandoning *physicalism* as it relates to Consciousness. Physicalism simply states that a process exists in the physical world and can be measured and studied, even if, at present, we do not yet possess the tools for doing so. It is tempting to equate the study of the sum of the electrical activity of the brain with the study and measurement of Consciousness. It did not help with the "hard problems" such as Consciousness and Human Being or Consciousness and Mammal Being. This led a number of authors (e.g., Koch, 2019) to make an implicit shift from the micro to the macro, from Neuroscience to Neurophilosophy; all I've done is to make the shift *explicit*. This leads us to a reassessment of Descartes' (1641/1999) formulation of a Mind-Body dichotomy with Mind being located in the Body-Self-Brain but ontologically different and incapable of being integrated. We have had some success in describing these Neural Correlates of Consciousness (NCC) — present when someone is Conscious, otherwise absent.

I discuss the Phenomenal basis of the new Integrated Information Theory of Consciousness (IIT) (Tononi, 2017). Briefly here, Consciousness is a complex property of mind that cannot be described in terms of the component properties of Mind and certainly not of Brain. Consistent with this are my suspicions that Consciousness is different for different individuals. While we can rely on the objective use of various neuroscientific instrumentation to determine if someone *is* Conscious, we are confined to subjective reports of human experience to determine just what consciousness is like (Nagel, 1970). The question involves different kinds of *ofs* and different kinds of *somethings*, which amount to different kinds of Being. They correspond to something being ready-at-hand, to use—*Zuhandenheit*—and present-at-hand, a subject for conscious study and reflection—*Vorhandenheit*. Roughly, the former is analogous to Everyday while the latter is Thrown. In the language of Tulving's Consciousness Studies they are analogous to Noetic and Auto-noetic Consciousness, respectively. Present-at-hand dominates intellectual and philosophical thought; it is a discipline of ontology.

I have consistently criticized S. Freud's (1915/1957) concept of a Dynamic Unconscious separated from Consciousness by a putative repression barrier. Those criticisms are summarized here. I have *not* criticized his concept of a Preconscious so long as it simply denotes a body of unconscious thought that freely moves in and out of Consciousness. There is what I would call the subjective fallacy of Consciousness in which it is experienced, due to the synthetic function of the Left Brain, as a continuous thread when it is in fact a series of rapidly unfolding discrete episodes. A stream of free associations is an example of such preconscious thought. The application of these ideas to Kahneman and Tversky's (Kahneman et al., 1982) decision-making under Uncertainty is discussed. Case material is discussed for purposes of illustration.

Interdisciplinary perspectives over the last four centuries position Consciousness at the pinnacle of Human experience. I offer a critique that, while acknowledging the richness of Consciousness experience, argues that it also is deeply flawed and that these flaws impact the success of a search for personal meaning. It takes us back to Existentialism (Camus, 1942/1989, 1942/1991b, 1942/1991c; Leffert, 2021) and the argument that *Consciousness is Absurd*. Absurdity involves a discrepancy between Self and World, involving both Meaning and Desire. We are seeking to explain, predict, and control, seeking to reconcile the physicality and the phenomenality of the Bio-Psycho-Social Self. If we want to differentiate our Consciousness from that of other animals, the one property that we *know* it has is that it *entails language*. The specific knowledge that we have that distinguishes us from other animals is the knowledge of our own approaching deaths and those of other Human Beings.

If we look for the single most important part of Human Being that Psychoanalysis and most Psychotherapies fail it consider, it is Death and Death Anxiety. We have limited ourselves to a consideration of grief, loss, and mourning and to the occasional patient who has or develops a terminal illness. Phenomenology and Existentialism can, however, be taken up to correct this failure. Despite what we might conclude as scientists and philosophers, it seems that roughly 80% of people believe in life after death and some sort of heaven. God is also involved in some fashion. Whether we, ourselves, are believers, agnostics, or atheists, it is *not* our place to correct or interpret a patient's beliefs, but only to make sure they are not deployed in destructive ways.

Death Anxiety is as old as Consciousness. Its roots lie deep in prehistory, even touching some of our hominin ancestors. Even vertebrates that do not possess Autonoetic Consciousness have at least an inkling of it. The transition from life to death perplexed our prehistoric and historic ancestors and still, to a degree, perplexes us. Yalom (2009) cites Epicurus as formulating three ontological statements that can serve as a treatment for Death Anxiety: the Mortality of the Soul, the Ultimate Nothingness of Death, and the Argument of Symmetry. Suicide, in particular, has not been considered in terms of Meaning and Absurdity.

If I want to consider Death and Death Anxiety from an Existential (that is, also a subjective) point of view, then an autobiographical account of my brushes with Death over the past half-century offers a mine of data. In choosing to take this route, I have taken a position on self-disclosure that is still controversial.

For Heidegger, Death is the Impossibility of Possibility. It is also, however, a prerequisite for Meaning. There are widespread disagreements among us, even today, about what Death is and what happens after. We scientist-philosophers easily slip into ignoring how much this is still the case. There *is* agreement based on observation that, in Death, the physical body becomes immobile and unresponsive and then decays. As to what happens to the Self, or the Soul, there are conflicting beliefs and points of view. It is clear that, for many millennia (or tens of millennia), we have tried to find our way around the inevitability of Death.

The COVID pandemic that unfolded as my writing of this chapter proceeded, made the external world, the *Umwelt* and the *Mitwelt*, a part of the conversation in ways not seen since the Polio epidemic of the mid-20th century and the Influenza pandemic a century ago.

Death is life's ultimate Absurdity. It offers both Meaning and Meaninglessness and, over the subsequent decades, *erases* our explicitness. It leaves us, at most, the *ripples* (Yalom, 2009) of who we were. The Phenomenology and the Existentiality of Death and Death Anxiety offer unique tools for their Deconstruction and understanding (Derrida, 1972/1991, 1974/1997) and are discussed. Case material is also presented.

Being-towards-Death has been fundamentally changed by the advent of the Metaverse (Kasket, 2012), which can offer us, for a time, a longer life, and, for some of us, even a kind of immortality. It is as yet unclear just how this will evolve in the decade(s) ahead. There seems to be no mention of the Metaverse in the psychoanalytic or therapeutic literature and Existentialism and Phenomenology have required the new discipline, Postphenomenology, to address it. These are discussed at some length.

The price of our self-reflectiveness, which has enormous evolutionary value, is that it brings us the awareness of our own eventual deaths and the Death

Anxiety that accompanies that awareness. Although an Existential engagement of Death may mitigate against Death Anxiety, it cannot entirely eliminate it. Experience of childhood trauma (PTSD) and a life that has gone partially unlived tend to intensify Death Anxiety. Irvin Yalom (Yalom, 1980, 2009; Yalom & Yalom, 2021) is the major contributor to the literature on the psychology of Death and Death Anxiety. Folk psychology acts to enhance the Denial of Death (Becker, 1973), alleging that, except when we lose a loved one or a prominent figure dies, we don't think much about Death until the final decade(s) of life. Yalom's work, in particular, has shown that this is blatantly false; he offers instead a Developmental Line (A. Freud, 1963) of Death Anxiety. This also involves the Evo-Devo of Death-awareness and Death Anxiety. I discuss the Evo-Devo of the two through Paleoanthropology, their evolution through Primary, Secondary, and, finally, Tertiary affects, and the prehistory from proto-religion, to polytheism, and to monotheism.

A great many researchers are now studying Death Anxiety; unfortunately, only a few of them are Psychoanalysts. As for the discipline as a whole, the tendency is still to treat it as a neurotic displacement from the usual anxieties we are comfortable with. Erikson, with his development of the concept of Epigenesis, and Yalom, May, and Frankl are our major contributors offering a base from which to consider Death Anxiety on its own terms. The Existentialists and the Phenomenologists look at the inevitability of Death and its Absurdity (Leffert, 2021). The Death Anxiety literature is discussed (e.g., Krieger, Epting, & Hays, 1979; Krieger, Epting, & Leitner, 1974; Lonetto, 1980; Lonetto & Templer, 1986; Templer, 1970; Thorson & Powell, 1988), including the use of the Threat Index (TI) to quantify and describe it. A case is discussed. Work on Death and Death Anxiety does not replace the standard clinical tools we employ but rather provides a necessary supplement to them. Yalom discusses the writings of the Greek philosopher Epicurus (Warren, 2009) as they illuminate our understandings of Death and Death Anxiety and offers us meaningful possibilities.

There is a clear *physical* boundary between Life and Death, but the *psychological* boundary is blurred by future travel (Schacter, Addis, & Buckner, 2008), religious belief, and denial. Phenomenologically, it is a matter for the Thrown and the Fallen, not the Everyday.

Suicide, for many, is very much a child of Existential issues that go unsolved in life rather than of untreated Depression. It is a surrender to the possibility of Death. It follows from an irretrievable loss of Meaning and can be taken up as a tool to address that loss. The prominence of Suicide in *fin de siècle* Vienna is discussed; it is both similar to and different from Suicide in 21st-century America with the internet playing a significant role. Camus' work bears on all facets of the Suicide problem and is discussed here.

In this chapter, I have offered an Existential and Phenomenological exploration into the nature of Death, dividing it into three categories, Death, Death Anxiety, and Suicide. The premise I hold to is that these such an inquiry needs to be a part of any analysis or intensive therapy, not just people in mourning or those suffering from a terminal illness. I am hoping that I have been able to convince the reader of this necessity.

Notes

1 Philadelphia was the epicenter of the Great Influenza (Barry, 2005), or the Spanish Flu of 1918–1920 that killed 50 million people, and perhaps as many as 100 million, worldwide. There are people alive in Philadelphia today who remember their grandparents' stories of sickness and death from those times.
2 Such a simple thing. My spell checker flags "COVID" as a misspelling; it has never encountered the word before. That will not be true ever again.
3 Again, but a moment's thought. If the novelly infected animal in the Wuhan fish market had been bought and eaten by a solitary shepherd he would have simply recovered or died, alone in his cabin or yurt: There would have been no Plague. *COVID-19 is a social disease and entails a Postmodern debate about the nature of reality.*
4 It is too soon to know how the war in the Ukraine will play out in our lives.
5 A narcissistic character disorder and Autistic spectrum disorders impair this ability: *Psychopathology impacts Intentionality.*
6 My own therapeutic experience with therapy at a distance dates back over 40 years (Leffert, 2003).

References

Bachelard, G. (1994). *The poetics of space* (M. Jolas, trans.). Boston, MA: Beacon Press. (Original work published in 1958).

Baron-Cohen, S. (2000). Theory of mind and autism: A fifteen year review. In S. Baron-Cohen, H. Tager-Flusberg, & D. J. Cohen (Eds.), *Understanding other minds: Perspectives from developmental cognitive neuroscience* (2nd ed., pp. 3–20). Oxford, England: Oxford University Press.

Barry, J. M. (2005). *The great influenza: The story of the deadliest pandemic in history*. New York, NY: Penguin Books.

Becker, E. (1973). *The denial of death*. New York, NY: Free Press.

Brentano, F. (1995). *Psychology from an empirical standpoint* (L. L. McCalister, trans.). London: Routledge. (Original work published in 1874).

Camus, A. (1989). *The stranger* (M. Ward, trans.). New York, NY: Vintage Books. (Original work published in 1942).

Camus, A. (1991a). *The plague* (S. Gilbert, trans.). New York, NY: Vintage Books. (Original work published in 1948).

Camus, A. (1991b). The myth of Sisyphus. In J. O'Brien (Ed.), *The myth of Sisyphus and other essays* (pp. 3–138). New York, NY: Vintage Books. (Original work published in 1942).

Camus, A. (1991c). *The myth of Sisyphus and other essays* (J. O'Brien, trans.). New York, NY: Vintage Books. (Original work published in 1942).

Derrida, J. (1978). *Writing and difference* (A. Bass, trans.). Chicago, IL: University of Chicago Press.

Derrida, J. (1991). Différance. In P. Kamuf (Ed.), *A Derrida reader: Between the blinds* (pp. 59–79). New York, NY: Columbia University Press. (Original work published in 1972).

Derrida, J. (1997). *Of grammatology* (G. C. Spivak, trans.). Baltimore, MD: Johns Hopkins Press. (Original work published in 1974).

Descartes, R. (1999). *Meditations and other metaphysical writings* (D. M. Clarke, trans.). New York, NY: Penguin Books. (Original work published in 1641).

Dunbar, R. (2016). *Human evolution: Our brains and behavior*. Oxford, England: Oxford University Press.

Eissler, K. R. (1968). The relationship of explaining and understanding in psychoanalysis. *Psychoanalytic Study of the Child, 23*, 141–177.

Feinberg, T. E., & Mallatt, J. M. (2016). *The ancient origins of consciousness: How the brain created experience*. Cambridge, MA: MIT Press.

Foucault, M. (1980). *Power/knowledge: Selected interviews & other writings 1972–1977* (C. Gordon, L. Marshall, J. Mepham, & K. Soper, trans.). New York, NY: Pantheon Books.

Foucault, M. (2000). *Power* (R. Hurley & Others, trans.). New York, NY: The New Press.

Freud, A. (1963). The concept of developmental lines. *Psychoanalytic Study of the Child, 18*, 245–265.

Freud, S. (1957). The unconscious. In J. Strachey (Ed.), *Standard edition* (Vol. XIV, pp. 166–215). London, England: Hogarth Press. (Original work published in 1915).

Gill, M. M. (1976). Metapsychology is not psychology. In M. M. Gill, & P. S. Holtzman (Eds.), *Psychology verses metapsychology: Essays in honor of George S. Klein* (pp. 71–105). New York, NY: International Universities Press.

Gill, M. M., & Holtzman, P. S. (Eds.). (1976). *Psychology verses metapsychology: Essays in honor of George S. Klein*. New York, NY: International Universities Press.

Heidegger, M. (1982). *The basic problems of phenomenology* (A. Hofstadter, trans. Rev. ed.). Bloomington: Indiana University Press. (Original work published in 1975).

Heidegger, M. (2009). *History of the concept of time: Prolegomena (Studies in phenomenology and existential philosophy)* (T. Kisiel, trans.). Bloomington: Indiana University Press. (Original work published in 1979).

Heidegger, M. (2010). *Being and time* (J. Stambaugh & D. J. Schmidt, trans.). Albany, NY: State University of New York. (Original work published in 1927).

Hofer, M. A. (2014). The emerging synthesis of development and evolution: A new biology for psychoanalysis. *Neuropsychoanalysis, 16*, 3–22.

Husserl, E. (1983). *Ideas pertaining to a pure phenomenology and to a phenomenological philosophy: Book one: General introduction to a pure phenomenology* (F. Kersten, trans.). New York, NY: Springer. (Original work published in 1913).

Idhe, D. (1995). *Postphenomenology: Essays in the postmodern context*. Evanston, IL: Northwestern University Press.

Idhe, D. (2012). *Experimental phenomenology, second edition: Multistabilities*. Albany: SUNY Press.

Idhe, D. (2019). *Medical technics*. Minneapolis: University of Minnesota Press.

Kahneman, D. (2011). *Thinking, fast and slow*. New York, NY: Farrar, Strauss and Giroux.

Kahneman, D., Slovic, P., & Tversky, A. (Eds.). (1982). *Judgement under uncertainty: Heuristics and biases*. Cambridge, England: Cambridge University Press.

Kahneman, D., & Tversky, A. (2000). Prospect theory: An analysis of decisions under risk. In D. Kahneman, & A. Tversky (Eds.), *Choices, values, and frames* (pp. 17–43). Cambridge, England: Cambridge University Press. (Original work published in 1979).

Kasket, E. (2012). Being-towards-death in the digital age. *Existential Analysis: Journal of the Society for Existential Analysis, 23*, 249–261.

Kierkegaard, S. (1980). *The sickness onto death* (H. V. Hong & E. H. Hong, trans.). Princeton, NJ: Princeton University Press. (Original work published in 1849).

Kierkegaard, S. (1992). *Concluding unscientific postscripts to unscientific fragments* (H. V. Hong & E. H. Hong, trans., Vol. II). Princeton, NJ: Princeton University Press. (Original work published in 1846).

Kim, S. (2021). The metaverse: The digital Earth—The world of rising trends. 1338 KB.

King, B. J. (2014). *How animals grieve*. Chicago, IL: University of Chicago Press.

Koch, C. (2019). *The feeling of life itself: Why consciousness is widespread but can't be computed*. Cambridge, MA: MIT Press.

Krieger, S. R., Epting, F. R., & Hays, L. H. (1979). Validity and reliability of provided constructs in assessing death threat. *Omega, 20*, 87–95.

Krieger, S. R., Epting, F. R., & Leitner, L. M. (1974). Personal constructs, threat, and attitudes towards death. *Omega, 5*, 299–310.

Latour, B. (1993). *We have never been modern* (C. Porter, trans.). Cambridge, MA: Harvard University Press. (Original work published in 1991).

Leffert, M. (2003). Analysis and psychotherapy by telephone: Twenty years of clinical experience. *Journal of the American Psychoanalytic Association, 51*, 101–130.

Leffert, M. (2007a). A contemporary integration of modern and postmodern trends in psychoanalysis. *Journal of the American Psychoanalytic Association, 55*, 177–197.

Leffert, M. (2007b). Postmodernism and its impact on psychoanalysis. *Bulletin of the Menninger Clinic, 71*, 15–34.

Leffert, M. (2010). *Contemporary psychoanalytic foundations*. London, England: Routledge.

Leffert, M. (2013). *The therapeutic situation in the 21st century*. New York, NY: Routledge.

Leffert, M. (2016). *Phenomenology, uncertainty, and care in the therapeutic encounter*. New York, NY: Routledge.

Leffert, M. (2017). *Positive psychoanalysis: Aesthetics, desire, and subjective well-being*. New York, NY: Routledge.

Leffert, M. (2018). *Psychoanalysis and the birth of the self: A radical interdisciplinary approach*. London: Routledge.

Leffert, M. (2021). *The psychoanalysis of the absurd: Existentialism and phenomenology in contemporary psychoanalysis*. London, England: Routledge.

Lonetto, R. (1980). *Children's conception of death*. New York, NY: Springer.

Lonetto, R., & Templer, D. I. (1986). *Death anxiety*. New York, NY: Taylor & Francis.

Lukes, S. (2005). *Power a radical view* (2nd ed.). New York, NY: Palgrave Macmillan.

Mellars, P. (2005). The impossible coincidence. A single-species model for the origins of modern human behavior in Europe. *Evolutionary Anthropology, 14*, 12–27.

Mithen, S. (1994). From domain specific to generalized intelligence: A cognitive interpretation of the Middle/Upper Paleolithic transition. In C. Renfrew, & E. W. Zubrow (Eds.), *The ancient mind: Elements of cognitive archaeology* (pp. 29–39). Cambridge, England: Cambridge University Press.

Nagel, T. (1970). What is it like to be a bat? *Philosophical Review, 83*, 435–450.

Ogas, O., & Gaddam, S. (2022). *Journey of the mind: How thinking emerged from chaos*. New York, NY: W. W. Norton & Co.

Owen, A. M. (2017). *Into the grey zone: A neuroscientist explores the border between life and death*. New York, NY: Scribner.

Owen, A. M., Coleman, M. R., Boly, M., Davis, M. H., Laureys, S., & Pickard, J. D. (2006). Detecting awareness in the vegetative state. *Science, 313*(5792), 1402.

Panksepp, J. (2009). Brain emotional systems and qualities of mental life: From animal models of affect to implications for psychotherapeutics. In D. Fosha, D. J. Siegal, & M. F. Solomon (Eds.), *The healing power of emotion: Affective neuroscience, development, and clinical practice* (pp. 1–26). New York, NY: W.W. Norton & Co.

Rosenberger, R., & Verbeek, P.-P. (2015). A field guide to postphenomenology. In R. Rosenberger, & P.-P. Verbeek (Eds.), *Postphenomenological investigations: Essays on human technology relations* (pp. 9–41). Lanham, MD: Lexington Books.

Rudden, M., & Bronstein, A. A. (2017). New educational approaches to the study of psychoanalysis. *The American Psychoanalyst: Quarterly Magazine of the American Psychoanalytic Association, 51*, 1, 21–22.

Sartre, J.-P. (2018). *Being and nothingness: An essay in phenomenological ontology* (S. Richmond, trans.). New York, NY: Routledge. (Original work published in 1943).

Schacter, D. L., Addis, D. R., & Buckner, R. L. (2008). Episodic simulation of future events concepts, data, and applications. *Annals of the New York Academy of Science, 1124*, 39–60.

Selinger, E. (Ed.). (2006). *Postphenomenology: A critical companion to Idhe.* Albany, NY: SUNY Press.

Sperry, R. W. (1969). A modified concept of consciousness. *Psychological Review, 76*, 532–536.

Sperry, R. W., Gazzaniga, M. S., & Bogen, J. E. (1969). The neocortical commissures: Syndromes of hemisphere disconnection. In P. J. Vinken, & G. W. Bruyn (Eds.), *Handbook of clinical neurology* (Vol. 4, pp. 273–290). Amsterdam, Netherlands: North Holland Publishing Company.

Tarski, A. (1946). *Introduction to logic and the methodology of the deductive sciences.* Oxford, England: Oxford University Press.

Templer, D. I. (1970). The construction and validation of a death anxiety scale. *The Journal of General Psychology, 82*, 165–177.

Thorson, J. A., & Powell, F. C. (1988). Elements of death anxiety and meanings of death. *Journal of Clinical Psychology, 44*, 691–701.

Tononi, G. (2017). The information integration theory of consciousness. In M. Velmans, & S. Schneider (Eds.), *The Blackwell companion to consciousness* (pp. 287–299). Malden, MA: Blackwell Publishing.

Tuckett, D., Basile, R., Birksted-Breen, D., Böhm, T., Denis, P., & Ferro, A., et al. (Eds.). (2008). *Psychoanalysis comparable and incomparable: The evolution of a method to describe and compare psychoanalytic approaches.* London, England: Routledge.

Tulving, E. (2003). Memory and consciousness. In B. J. Baars, W. P. Banks, & J. B. Newman (Eds.), *Essential sources in the scientific study of consciousness* (pp. 575–591). Cambridge, MA: MIT Press. (Original work published in 1985).

Tulving, E., Kapur, S., Craik, F. I. M., Moscovitch, M., & Houle, S. (1994). Hemispheric encoding/retrieval asymmetry in episodic memory: Positron emission tomography findings. *Proceedings of the National Academy of Science, 91*, 2016–2020.

Turkle, S. (2008). Always-on/always-on-you. In J. E. Katz (Ed.), *Handbook of mobile communication studies* (pp. 121–138). Boston, MA: MIT Press.

Walter, B. (2022). *How civil wars start; and how to stop them.* New York, NY: Crown.

Warren, J. (Ed.). (2009). *The Cambridge companion to epicureanism.* Cambridge, London: Cambridge University Press.

Yalom, I. D. (1980). *Existential psychotherapy.* New York, NY: Basic Books.

Yalom, I. D. (2009). *Staring at the sun: Overcoming the terror of death.* New York, NY: Jossey-Bass.

Yalom, I. D., & Yalom, M. (2021). *A matter of death and life.* Stanford, CA: Redwood Press.

Chapter 1

So Why Do We Need Philosophy Anyway?

Phenomenology, Postmodernism, and the Plague in the Psychoanalytic Workplace

Introduction

Psychoanalysis and Psychoanalytic Psychotherapy grew up around concepts surrounding development, infantile sexuality, and neurosis. They then moved on to examine adult relationships inside and outside of the Therapeutic Situation beginning with, of course, Transference and, later, Countertransference. We all know this but will shortly move on to more controversial matters.[1] Psychoanalysis began with pessimism, perhaps growing out the social declines of *fin de siècle* and, later, World War I Europe. Freud's famous goal, to replace neurotic misery with everyday unhappiness, perhaps sums up this pessimistic position. (He also suggested that the goal of analysis was to enable a patient to work and to love, *Arbeiten und Lieben*, without suggesting precisely *what* this entailed or how it was to be achieved. This was, as we will see, an entirely different sort of animal.) Perhaps until mid-century, Psychoanalysis was written, practiced, and taught as a cognitive sort of discipline, clinically as well as theoretically, with "insight" being pursued intellectually through verbal interpretation. It was largely taught by and to white, heterosexual men. (In the latter half of the century, it began to be recognized that emotion, albeit intellectually termed *affect*, needed to accompany this cognitive process if change were to occur.) Evolving analytic schools, organized around particular metapsychologies, developed and engaged in theory wars, fighting for the control of institutes, journals, and organizations (Leffert, 2010, Chapter 7).

Psychoanalysis had an ambivalent relationship with psychological symptoms. On the one hand, they were subjects of analysis, but, on the other, symptom removal and cure as a goal of therapy was frowned upon.[2] A reason for this position, I believe, was the fact that this kind of intellectual treatment often did not produce symptom improvement and to still seek it was thus to *critique the entire enterprise.*

These observations led to wider questions about just why patients[3] get better (or don't) when they come to see us. Stern and colleagues (Boston Change Process Study Group, 2005; D. N. Stern, et al., 1998) eventually came up

DOI: 10.4324/9781003349556-2

with the much-beloved term "something more" to try to define what was being left out in our clinical formulations of psychoanalytic technique but was necessary, like a fine seasoning, to yield therapeutic success. Something more does not seem to be singular. I have previously posited that some therapists do their own *something mores* either knowingly or unknowingly or, still another possibility, know they are doing something *without knowing* that it is a factor in Therapeutic Action. Taking this further, and addressing the limited analytic literature and much broader interdisciplinary literature available on the subjects, I introduced the controversial topics of *care* and *cure* in the Therapeutic Situation (Leffert, 2016) and included the Psychoanalysis of the Positive (Leffert, 2017) along with the Psychoanalysis of the Negative (that is, Psychopathology). From the beginning (Leffert, 2010), I posited that Interdisciplinary Studies must occupy a central place in the understanding of *all* psychoanalytic concepts. Neuroscience was the first of these studies to be included, albeit somewhat controversially (e.g., Pulver, 2003), in psychoanalytic writing. As I continued to work, I developed my own list, including Complexity, Science Studies, Network Studies, Subjective Well-Being, Evo-Devo, and Psychopharmacology. Meanwhile, the metaconcepts to come out of the Relational and Intersubjective Schools at the end of the last century were the Irreducible Subjectivity and Interreferentiality of human experience in relationships and in the world. As Renik (1993) argued in a widely cited paper, the two made it impossible to reliably assess the unfolding and progress of the Therapeutic Situation from *within* the Therapeutic Situation. He offered a controversial solution that the only way to dependably assess therapeutic progress was by monitoring a patient's life and the changes they were making in it.

Inevitably evoking controversy, I would observe that, taken as a package, the sum of these theories and procedures proved to be a *somewhat* effective therapeutic frame of reference, more helpful in removing or remodeling negative aspects of a patient's Self[4] and life than in adding new positive ones. Criticisms of the package date back as far as mid-century. As May (1958) observed,

> In recent years there has been a growing awareness on the part of some psychiatrists and psychologists that serious gaps exist in our way of understanding of human beings. These gaps may well seem most compelling to psychotherapists, confronted as they are in clinic and consulting room with the sheer reality of persons in crisis whose anxiety will not be quieted by theoretical formulae … Thus many psychiatrists and psychologists in Europe and others in this country have been asking themselves disquieting questions … Can we be sure, one such question goes, that we are seeing the patient as he really is, knowing him in his own reality; *or are we seeing merely a projection of our own theories about him?*
>
> (p. 3, italics added)

May's concerns could be equally applied to a 1960s Ego-Psychologist, or a 1990s Relational therapist, or a 2010s Bionian.

Twenty years later, Yalom (1980) offered an Existentialist response to May's concerns.

The existential position, he observed, emphasizes a different kind of basic conflict:

> neither a conflict with suppressed instinctual strivings nor one with internalized significant adults but *instead a conflict that flows from the individual's confrontation with the givens of existence.* And [he] mean[s] by "givens" of existence certain ultimate concerns, certain intrinsic properties that are a part, and an inescapable part, of the human being's existence in the world.
>
> (p. 8)

Just what these specific concerns might be, we will discuss in some detail below.

In the first decades of my own development as a therapist and later an analyst, I would describe myself as a Developmentally based Psychopathologist who operated out of an adherence to standard psychoanalytic theories—Freudian Ego-Psychology, Self-Psychology, and the British Schools—and later added the Relational and Intersubjective Perspectives as they came online. Although I didn't think in those terms at that time, I fell broadly into the group of therapists who was the subject of May's (1958) concerns. I did, however, think about why my patients were or weren't getting better, how I defined getting better, and how well I understood what was actually going on. Often, I felt that I didn't and, sometimes, felt a process was going on that I was making happen but didn't quite understand. Anticipating Renik (1993), I monitored how my patients were doing in their lives and what progress they were making in addressing the life issues that had motivated them to seek out treatment in the first place. As long as they were doing well in these areas I felt things couldn't be far off and, when they weren't, I studied the situation and adjusted my technique accordingly.

As we entered the new millennium, a number of ways of moving forward presented themselves. The most usual were elaborations and further development of existing theories. Often, authors who had made significant breakthroughs in the previous century were unable to continue to innovate and, instead of ceasing to write, offered repeated restatements of their original ideas. The ideas were good in their time but there was little to add to them. Although the bitter theory wars, also of the last century, had faded away, researchers clustered in groups around their theoretical beliefs and *largely talked only to each other.* This trend was also true for our journals, often publishing articles consistent with particular analytic frames of reference and rarely publishing papers outside of them. There were, however, other directions in which to go, directions that had been developing on their own for several decades but were not much adopted by mainstream Psychoanalysis.

One involved fundamental areas of human existence—Love, Death, Meaning, and Well-Being to name a few—about which standard psychoanalytic theories and theories of technique had very little to say. Explicitly or implicitly we went about our psychoanalytic work in the usual manner(s) and expected these things to take care of themselves. Another involved Philosophy: It was concerned with the nature of Being and the rules of Knowledge concerning it—that is, Ontology and Epistemology (Leffert, 2013). A number of analysts (e.g., Hoffman, 1998; Lear, 1990/1998; Stolorow & Atwood, 1992; Stolorow, Atwood, & Brandshaft, 1994) were already working in these areas but from the perspective of existing psychoanalytic theory and ego-psychology (see Hoffman, 1979/1998). Stolorow and his circle (Orange, Atwood, & Stolorow, 1997; Stolorow, 1990, 2002, 2011; Stolorow & Atwood, 1992; Stolorow et al., 1994; Stolorow, Orange, & Atwood, 2002) were drawn from Intersubjectivity to Phenomenology while a group of analysts and psychotherapists (Frankl, 1959/2006; May, 1958, 1977/1996; May, Angel & Ellenberger, 1958; Yalom, 1980, 2009, 1989/2012) were working Existentially, largely unnoticed by the mainstream of American Psychoanalysis.

What I have been offering in a series of works is a critique of the position that Psychoanalysis could ever be considered a free-standing, independent, discipline; that it is rather a sub-category of the study of Human Beings and their Existence. Further, it must be an interdisciplinary undertaking. Looking at how Human Beings exist in the world also must involve the study of the Being of Human Beings, a part of the wider study of Being known as *Ontology*, dating back to the Greek philosopher Parmenides in the sixth century BCE. It is this Being of Self and the Being of World that we are studying (that Psychoanalysts should study), always from the perspective of Human Being observers. (The fact that animate and inanimate machines, particularly digital machines have a complex and important role in all of this will be discussed in Chapters 2 and 3.) Being of Self became the provenance of the linked schools of Phenomenology and Existentialism while Being of World had to make the journey from Rationalism to Postmodernism. What is also involved here is the study of the rules governing the acquisition, deployment, and remodeling of knowledge, rules that have changed and will continue to change over time. This is the field of *Epistemology*. An understanding of Ontology and Epistemology, although requiring considerable effort on the part of otherwise busy clinicians, pays off therapeutically. Problems in, literally, how one *exists* are common but poorly conceptualized by standard Psychoanalytic theories (the British Middle School comes closest), yet patients often tell us about them using everyday language describing their relationship to World. A more encompassing way of describing such things as conflicts, inhibitions, and anxiety is that they involve *systematic errors in how information about Self and World is processed.* Anxiety, for example, can arise out of a confusion of rules of knowledge that were valid in the past of a traumatic childhood but are no longer valid in the present. This, as we will discuss, involves a subset of Epistemology called the *Archaeology of Knowledge* (Foucault, 1969 & 1971/1972; Leffert, 2013).

I am now faced with the task of telling you a story, a story about Phenomenology, Existentialism, and Postmodernism, fields that have led, since mid-century, to new ways of engaging the Psychoanalytic enterprise. It is a story I have told a number of times (Leffert, 2007a, 2007b, 2010, 2013, 2016, 2017, 2018, 2021). I need to offer a version of it yet again because the material that follows will not be comprehensible to a reader who has not already been exposed to it. At the same time, I don't want to be overly rep-etitious for readers who have already exposed themselves to the philosophy. In the way that no two narratives of the same event are ever identical (being able to engage the difference between narratives and events is one of the tools that Postmodernism brings to the ontological "table"), I've had something not quite the same to say each time and will do so again here. I would fur-ther posit that the COVID Plague has introduced permanent changes into both our ontology and our epistemology that we will have to consider. The Epistemology of Death, for example, has fundamentally changed from some-thing that affects us individually to something that effects our entire social network, our *Superorganism* (Christakis & Fowler, 2009) if you will.

In my discussions of Phenomenology/Existentialism and Postmodernism, I have treated them as independent, separate domains. Postmodernism devel-oped initially in France, beginning in mid-century when philosophers grew tired and critical of Existentialism and Phenomenology. Both disciplines sought a singularity and a certainty that could not be critically defended. Postmodernism addressed the failings of such ontologies and the related fail-ings of structure, prioritizing instead plurality, uncertainty, and *différance*. It appeared as a discipline discrete from Phenomenology and Existentialism and I treated it as such. I have recently found it necessary to question this distinction. As we will see, they both concern themselves with Ontology and Epistemology but, more importantly, their accounts are complementary and synergistic rather than at odds with each other.

Phenomenology and Existentialism have faced a different sort of problem. Authors are usually particular about identifying themselves with one term or another, yet the distinction between the two disciplines has not been gener-ally agreed upon.[5] The distinction that I make between them *seems* sensible to me, but I am reluctant to claim standing for it; instead, I will treat it as simply a *convention* I will apply for the purposes of this volume (and the others I have written). I will base it on the definitions of the two terms I would put forward; definitions I would not consider exhaustive but at least unobjectionable. I consider Phenomenology to be a kind of hard social sci-ence (and I apprehend a lot by this) that studies Human existence (*Existenz*), the Being *there* of Human Beings. It is wrapped up in Heidegger's difficult term Dasein.[6] Human Beings can be in the world in three ways: Everyday, Fallen, and Thrown (I make a sharper distinction between the first two than I find in my reading of Heidegger). Existentialism is first taken up with the subjective ability of a person to *be* in the world and the feelings that accompany such being. It involves a search for personal, subjective *Meaning* in this Being. Camus (1944/1958, 1942/1989, 1942/1991) added the concept *Absurdity* (Leffert, 2021) to the failure to find Meaning.

A further difference between Phenomenology and Existentialism exists in the nature of the texts that their adherents use to put their ideas forward. Phenomenology tends to involve dense and often lengthy texts that engage ideas. While some of that is to be found in Existentialism (e.g., Sartre, 1943/2018), its ideas are more likely to appear in texts conveying the human condition: novels, plays, music, art, the cinema, and, in the case of therapy and analysis, individual case studies.

I have never been happy with how I've handled the two terms. I've tried putting them together with a slash or just using one or the other to stand for both of them. What I will try here is to use one or the other when it most closely fits my meaning or use both when both apply.

I don't know if I've fully addressed the question of why we, as Psychoanalysts and Psychotherapists, need this philosophy in our work. Many will feel it's unnecessary and have said so. The philosophy, however, accomplishes a number of things. One is that it deals with topics, such as Death or Absurdity to name just two, that aren't really addressed by any of the Psychoanalytic Metapsychologies, and another is that it offers an umbrella that integrates much of the Metapsychology we do try to deploy. Most importantly it addresses May's critique (May et al., 1958) and offers a way to *stay with the patient's experience rather than the analyst's theories*. The path it provides stays with Husserl's "the things themselves" and avoids certain problems with the analyst's use of clinical theory or theory theory. We will step outside of Psychoanalysis to see how Kahneman and Tversky's (1979/2000) work on decision-making under uncertainty illuminates these problems. Their work also bears directly on Postmodernism's exploration of plurality and uncertainty. Let's begin chronologically with Phenomenology and Existentialism and then move on to Postmodernism.

Phenomenology

Phenomenology and the Problem of Consciousness

As Phenomenology developed over the course of the 20th century, the fact that it referred exclusively to mental processes that were *Conscious* was treated as a given. The problem with this position lay with the pre-Neuroscience definitions of consciousness that existed in the first part of the century but changed over time. They were not reexamined by the Phenomenologists as developments in neuroscience changed our understanding of mental processes and their nature over the course of the century. Their position contained a critique of the existence of what was not conscious but was treated as synonymous with unconsciousness in the sense of a Freudian Unconscious. The problem the Phenomenologists had (appropriately) with such an Unconscious was twofold: that it was isolated from World (by the so-called repression barrier)[7] and that it manifested systematic distortions of reality and its perception (neurotic psychopathology) *not* present in Consciousness. It should be noted that while what the Existentialists wrote about were implicitly Conscious mental events involving World, they were not explicitly concerned with the problem of Conscious versus Unconscious processes and gave little thought or interest in the existence of a singular, dynamic Unconscious separated from the rest of the mental apparatus by Repression.

Phenomenology was built on Intentionality (Brentano, 1874/1995), then the Self's *Conscious* connection with World. Consciousness was always Intentional; to be conscious was to be conscious *of* something, to be *about* something or someone. (Consistent with our *current* understanding, it is also possible to be *Un*conscious about something.) It involved the connection and distinction between the *experiential subjectivity* of the Self and the World and its objects, with connections made through *Perception*. But the problem is, the problem *is*, that the Neuroscience tells us that there are many such relationships that have nothing to do with what we now call Left Brain Consciousness (Leffert, 2010). For example, one such connection is that of the Autonomic Nervous System to World around temperature regulation, the maintenance of Homeostasis. It passes all the requisite tests of Phenomenology except consciousness. Or, let's take the Consciousness of the Right Brain (Leffert, 2010). The Left Brain knows little about it, yet *its* subjectivity is equally connected to World and receives perceptions that it monitors and is influenced by. Intentionality, then, is about *all* mental activity, not just the Left-Brain Consciousness. We have also come to understand that the kind of experiential and logical purity that Phenomenology would want to attribute to what we now know to be the Left Brain is equally subject to distortions. Cleaning up some of the distortions present in both cerebral hemispheres is another way of describing what we seek to achieve through Psychotherapy and Psychoanalysis.

Husserl

If we are going to talk about Phenomenology, the place to start is with the work of Edmund Husserl (1937/1970, 1925/1977, 1913/1983, 1931/1999, 1913/2001, 2005), its founder. This is the first of many instances in which we are dealing with a body of work so large that it is beyond my ability to summarize it in the space I have available. I will discuss the threads of his work that are a necessary part of the story I am telling. The particular thread I want to pick up involves what contemporary Phenomenologists (Idhe, 2012) have come to call Experimental Phenomenology. It involves the *objective study* via experimentation of Phenomenology, an attempt to document the Subjectivities and Intersubjectivities of Human Beings. Referring back to Brentano (1874/1995), Husserl insists that these are, almost by definition, *Intentional.*

Husserl distinguishes between an "I" that is World-conscious and an "I" that is Self-conscious (Self-reflective). To the extent that it is possible, in World-consciousness the "I" drops out of the picture. To express this "dropping out," a putting aside of an element for later consideration in order to allow for an uninterrupted focus on a particular argument, Husserl (1913/1983, 1931/1999) introduces the use of brackets, drawn from the Greek *Epochē*. Hence, the notation for "I" is [I]. There are two points I want to make here. Husserl is making a distinction about [I] that prefigures Heidegger's (1927/2010) onto-logical concept of Everydayness (*Alltäglichkeit*) in which one is totally present, Being-in-the-World, focused on what is about, athandedness. (An Everyday hammer is something to pick up and hit a nail with, not a member of a class of tools that exist to pound on different kinds of things with.) It is a lesser form of Being that includes husbandry and the rendering of care or service. Unlike Heidegger, however, Husserl does not treat this as any sort of diminished state of being; as contrasted with Heidegger's [higher] state of being, thrown-ness (*Geworfenheit*), it is a *different* state of Being. If we take into account the Neuroscience perspective (Tulving, 1985/2003) on these different states of Being it is that they pertain to Autonoetic (*Self* knowing) Consciousness and Noetic (knowing) Consciousness. There is a lot to unpack in this paragraph that we will take up in subsequent chapters.

A more basic question, perhaps, is why do we, as early 21st-century Psychoanalysts, need to concern ourselves with bracketing at all? The answer is that it would improve both our clinical and theoretical writing and help us to see past our own theory-based arguments if we simply bracket the the-ory in our clinical discussions. This mirrors a recent and beneficial trend to keep theory out of clinical discussions (Rudden & Bronstein, 2017; Tuckett et al., 2008) and trying instead to stick to what is happening for the patient and the therapist. There is a long-forgotten psychoanalytic root to this kind of thinking that goes back to the work of Kurt Eissler (1968), a very ortho-dox Psychoanalyst who described a clinical distinction between a psychology of *understanding* and a psychology of *explaining*. Understanding involves an unstructured grasping of the material as a whole, what our patient is telling us combined with what we think about it on a moment-by-moment basis. Explaining, however, involves the application of some formalized theory to the material that is being understood. Although Eissler saw the latter as inev-itable (I'm no longer so sure of that), he recommends delaying it as long as possible because *explaining terminates the open-ended process of understanding.*

Explanations impose rigid limitations on the analyst's thought. They involve, in Postmodern terms, the deployment of *Identity Categories*. As Eissler describes the process of therapy or analysis two generations ago, after an explanation is proposed new material that in part contradicts the explanation continues to build up (if the analyst is still able to hear it). This imposes a mounting tension in the explanation until it finally breaks apart and a new phase of understanding begins.

Husserl (1913/1983) introduces his thinking in this area in *Ideas Pertaining to a Pure Phenomenology and a Phenomenological Philosophy*. In most philosophies, a distinction—called a *correlation*—is made between the object and the subject that knows the object. Husserl transmuted this distinction into a correlation between what is being experienced and its mode of being experienced. He termed this correlation *Intentionality*. That is, all experience is experience of something, and the thing that is experienced and its mode of being experienced are *relational*. Husserl[8] gave the thing that is being experienced the name *Neoma* and the mode of experiencing *Noesis*. Idhe (2012, p. 26) diagrams this state of affairs as

$$\textbf{noesis} \rightarrow \textbf{noema}$$

where there is that which is experienced, a mode of experiencing and a necessary third term: the *experiencer*. To take this piece of World (which is a part of what Heidegger will call Dasein) and to separate out everything else is to perform, in Husserl's terms a Phenomenological reduction and this makes up a lot of what his phenomenology is all about. But there is more. He further distinguishes the experiencing that is what one does as one goes about one's business of doing things, an *everydayness* of an experiencing Self, from that of reflection *about* what one is experiencing, performed by a Self who is reflecting on what it's experiencing. This is a transcendent Self and Husserl calls the process a *transcendental reduction;* it is the mark of Intentionality. This gives us an appended diagram

$$\textbf{Transcendental Self}$$
$$\downarrow$$
$$\big[\,\textbf{Experiencing Self}\,\big]\textbf{noesis} \rightarrow \textbf{noema}$$

Heidegger and others will take Husserl's thinking further: from Knowing to Being to knowing Being. Husserl was offering a science of *Epistemology*, explaining rules of knowing or knowledge while Heidegger and the Existentialists who came after offered a science of *Ontology*, taken up with the study of Existence (*Existenz*) and Being (Dasein). But, so far, is this of any use to us as analysts and therapists?

It is, because it forces us to think consistently about the different kinds of knowing that we make use of in the Therapeutic Situation. Let me offer a clinical illustration of this.[9] First the story. Steve, a married endocrinologist with two daughters, was in his 40s when he came to me suffering from chronic depression. Successful in his work at an Academic Health Center, he loved his wife, a warm, intelligent woman, and his daughters, but felt that he emotionally isolated himself from them. After seeing me for a month or so, he observed with surprise that he had been talking to me not about his present unhappiness but rather about his parents and childhood.

An only child, raised by a warm, depressed Irish mother who doted on him, he grew up attending Catholic parochial schools that offered him both a sound academic education and an inherent sense of guilt. Shortly after his birth, his mother began showing symptoms of what was eventually diagnosed as a pituitary adenoma. It required a neurosurgical procedure, a difficult recovery and a subsequent opiate and alcohol addiction. His father, a passive and childish man who blamed Steve for his wife's chronic illness, helplessly deserted the family when Steve was eight, but not before conveying to his son that he was responsible, through his birth, for his mother's pituitary disorder. The result was that, with his father's departure, Steve became his mother's caretaker and she in turn showered him with overstimulating closeness; both overwhelmed him. Traumatic experiences ensued. At night, his mother would, on occasion, pass out under the influence of sedatives and alcohol, come crashing to the floor suffering broken glasses, cuts and bruises and leaving the little boy to try to somehow drag her to bed. He would frequently lie in bed listening for the sound of her getting into bed while fearing the crash of a fall.

Steve had thought he was the product of a nurturing childhood, admired by his mother and her large family. As we talked about it, however, it became clear that he was the subject of significant neglect, often left to fend for himself. He was solitary and at the mercy of debilitating social anxiety, suffering from many poorly diagnosed and treated illnesses of childhood and adolescence: among them at times debilitating childhood migraines, massive, brutally treated dental caries, severe cystic acne, anemia, and various orthopedic problems. In Phenomenological terms, the analysis here involved a shift from an Experiencing to a Transcendental Self. What Steve already knew and understood was that repeated childhood strep throats treated with penicillin injections, had led to an incapacitating needle phobia and a tonsillectomy accompanied by traumatically induced anesthesia (he was held down and forcibly given ether). The parents had taken him to the hospital without telling him anything about what was going to happen or what would be done to him. (The needle phobia and the social anxiety were both ameliorated during the first years of his analysis.)

Always one to get ahead of the curve, Steve decided in childhood to become a physician, a career choice that delighted his mother and was supported (ultimately financially) by her family but *not* his father. His father experienced this as an abandonment (it involved study in the distant city where his mother then lived) and eventually came to hate him for it. Perhaps amazingly, Steve had not made anything special of his choosing to become an endocrinologist, saying he enjoyed the study of homeostasis; he met my observation that he seemed to want so very much to cure his mother with shocked acceptance. (There will be more to say about Steve and his analysis but, for the moment, let's return to Husserl.)

In this Phenomenological Reduction, Steve is the noema I am experiencing and I am trying very hard to keep that experience in these terms, free of transcendent metapsychologies.[10] This is very hard to do and we must forgive ourselves for (sometimes systematically) failing at it. We have two ways to understand this. The first is Eissler's (1968) dilemma of trying to *understand* rather than *explain* for as long as possible. The second has to do with how we deal with *Uncertainty* (see Kahneman, 2011; Leffert, 2016) in the Therapeutic Situation. In life we regularly encounter situations where we lack sufficient knowledge with which to make judgments free of uncertainty. The solution (Kahneman, Slovic, & Tversky, 1982) is to have developed families of rules, called *Heuristics*, that aid us in decision-making. Although Heuristics often aid us in navigating the world, they sometimes get things wrong. One of those heuristic families is *Representativeness*. In it, if we encounter something that strikes us as having something in common with a class of things that we have come to know and understand we simply treat it as a member of that class, resolving our uncertainty. A second prominent family is *Availability*. In it, we are more inclined to treat something as a member of a class if we have recently experienced examples of that class. It is important to realize that Heuristics operate *Unconsciously*, but they can be *made* Conscious by reflection; that is, they can be made *Transcendent*.

With Steve, for example, I cannot think about his mother without thinking about his unresolved Oedipal feelings for her (and, certainly, hers for him). I can, though, catch myself doing it (making use of Representativeness) and the notation I can use for doing so is brackets. So we would [mother], a very important kind of therapeutic knowing of Steve. This is not to say that there mayn't be Oedipal issues that are problematic for him in his feelings for his wife, but that we will defer considering them until later. Similarly, we would [father] and the intense ambivalence Steve felt for him. We would also [narcissism] and [phobias]. I would consider the possibility of a hostile, competitive [Oedipal] paternal counter-transference, an idealizing [narcissistic] transference, or a relative absence of [defensive] transference. Husserl is thus offering us a usable epistemology that we can carry forward.

Heidegger

Heidegger (1975/1982, 1927/2010) is an ontologist rather than an epistemologist. I would also [Phenomenologist] because he abjures the term: Idhe

(2012) deals with this by substituting the term Existential Phenomenology. That is to say Heidegger studies Human Being and Being-in-the-World. He does so across three axes. I have written about Heidegger extensively in the past (Leffert, 2016, 2018, 2021) and, since my thinking about him has not changed, will do so more briefly here. The simplest of these is Temporality: Being is different at different times in the Existence of a given Human Being. This includes Bio-Psycho-Social Development and the history of changes in World. Temporality in phenomenology replaces the unprovable concept of psychological depth, positing instead the position that the Self is always fully deployed, although some parts of it may be kept hidden or secret.

The next not-so-unfamiliar axis involves the different kinds of relationality manifested by the Self. The most familiar of these involves the relations of the Self to other Human Beings, the world of Being with (the *Mitwelt*), the Relational Self of the psychoanalytic discipline by the same name. Another involves the Self's relations with and focus on itself, the *Eigenwelt*, one's *own* world; Self-Psychology and Ego-Psychology loosely fall here. Finally, we have the Self's physical and mental relationship with the physical world in which it dwells, the *surrounding* world, the *Umwelt*. Phenomenologists treat these as discrete zones of Being but they cannot be truly separate. Postmoderns can use dialectical constructivist tools to describe how these zones are connected, documenting their *interreferentiality*. What one does in the *Umwelt* will be affected by human relationships in the *Mitwelt*. These three categories offer a way of clinically monitoring how a patient is functioning (or not functioning) Heidegger, as we have said, coined a difficult term to describe the manners of the Self's Being-in-the-World, Being-*there*: Dasein.

The advent of Plague in the winter of 2019–2020 changed the Self's Being on this axis. If the virology of the Plague lies in the *Umwelt*, you must realize that every other aspect of it involves the *Mitwelt*: Like all Plagues, it is a social as well as a virologic or bacteriologic disease. Most, but not all, of what I have seen in my own practice involves *my patients' reactions to these realities, not neurotic distortions of them*. The reality largely overshadows the reactions that exist solely on an internal basis, that is, reactions centered on the *Eigenwelt*. Contagion became *the* issue in the world of things and of relationships. Space became dangerous and contact with people other than those we shelter together with became a source of fear. Whatever might have been the past meanings of these things were overshadowed by the reality of the danger of meeting illness or death in World. While this is what I saw in my practice, I also knew, as of September of 2020, that some portion of the population did not believe this and did not follow social distancing guidelines.

There were exceptions. I have two patients suffering from moderate to severe OCD. One of them is symptomatically unchanged; he has reacted with depression to how the Plague has realistically interfered with his taking steps forward in his life. The other has seen her obsessions run wild with magical thinking rampant and ideas of infecting the people she is close to or being infected by them (she and they seem not to have contracted the virus). The relevant difference between them seems to be that where he has done several years of work on himself in therapy, she is just starting out.

Josh, a businessman in his 60s, had spent much of his time fighting to be in control of his life by which he meant getting the people around him to behave in the ways he wants them to and to participate with him in events he finds meaningful. Failure on their part to do so was met with equal parts of grief and rage. This problem had been the focus of some years of therapy with considerable success that paralleled the realization that he wasn't experiencing them as *people*, with their own centers of motivation but rather as two-dimensional cardboard cutouts who should want just what Josh wants. When the need for social distancing made it impossible for a social gathering he wanted very much to take place in just the way that *he* wanted it too, the *rage and grief flared up again but became subject to interpretation*. Feelings that would have lasted for weeks resolved over a span of hours.

The final (and strangest sounding) axis refers to the manner of one's (that is, Dasein's) Being-in-the-World. We have already mentioned two of these— Everydayness and Thrownness. Everydayness involves going about the daily business of living. It manifests *Unreflective* Consciousness (more about this in the next chapter) on the part of the Self that is *there*: Dasein. Thrownness, to the contrary, involves a total reflective engagement with life. In particular, it manifests an awareness of Death and its inevitably; the commitment as a result of this awareness is to a life lived moment-by-moment to the fullest. The third way of Being is *Fallen*. In a Fallen state, one is less engaged with living life than in seeking pleasure that is more empty than not and fear of Death. That fear is accompanied by a corollary that it is possible to stave off Death for a very long time and the conscious or unconscious fantasy that one can live forever. It can manifest dietary strategies, including the vitamin supplement du jour, exercise regimens, and plastic surgeries (woman in their 20s and 30s are now consumers of Botox injections to smooth out facial wrinkles). Fear of Death, called Death Anxiety (we will discuss this in Chapter 6) can be prominent. These anxieties can be normative as well as signaling the presence of a Fallen state. (The pandemic has changed the way we have to regard Death Anxiety.) There is nothing theoretical or metapsychological about these ways of being; they are descriptive and you can go out and find them in your own *Mitwelt* right now. The presence of Death Anxiety or the failure of the first two (Everyday and Thrown) is evidence of psychopathology and leads patients to seek us out. Most of us are accustomed to think about and discuss these problems in terms garnered from our various theoretical (or at times biological) orientations; I would posit that these are unnecessarily divisive.

How does the Plague play out along this axis? Plague raises the immediate presence of Death in the equation of living. Its very presence lessens the part of life lived in the Everyday where Death is *not* a factor. With social isolation the rule for many of us and continued, now essential work for the rest of us, a lot of the Everyday drops out of our lives and we are left mostly with the Thrown and the Fallen. How we deal with Death and the Death Anxiety we experience depends on who we are psychologically and socially.

For the Fallen, with Death a constant fear and prolonging life and youth to a fantasied immortality an ever-present Desire, the Plague brings the reality of a universal risk of Death and an attempt at its denial into their present. The fear of Death as an unspecified future event is replaced by its presence on the nightly news. Its tangible closeness increases as degrees of separation from infected and Dead others decline. It is a different experience when everyone knows someone who knows someone who is infected and worsens still more as people begin to know someone who knows someone who has died.[11] Where the Fallen stay fallen, the Plague Throws more people into dealing with and accepting the inevitability of Death. In the best Heideggerian fashion, it makes life more precious. The first of these are the medical "soldiers" on the front lines of the Plague. They are there to care for the ill and the suffering (Leffert, 2016) because they took an oath, formally or implicitly. This does not mean that the experience is relished, only that it becomes compelling and the risk is accepted. Nor does it mean that Death is not feared or that life is any less valued.

The existence of this choice highlights the worsening social divide present in our society in the early 21st century. Many people must choose to work and risk Death not out of some moral calling, but rather because they must work to feed and shelter their families (and themselves). *Many more* people would make this choice if they were permitted to do so in our society, shut down as it was during the early months of the Plague.

Let's add Existentialism to this package and then talk about Therapeutic applications and Steve in these terms.

Existentialism

Here too, space limitations require a much abbreviated presentation of material I have previously (Leffert, 2021) discussed at length. I'm going to do so by limiting my arguments to two rather different authors—Sartre and Camus. They have things in common. They wrote about the fictional lives of Human Beings in order to describe their philosophies of Existence. They were both concerned with Meaninglessness and the way Death overshadowed life. Their work matured in the Nazi era, the German occupation of France, its restrictions of personal liberty, and the risks of individual suffering and death. The Nazi occupation was certainly a kind of Plague that offered the same choice of stepping out into the storm because of one's moral beliefs: here a fight for freedom from oppression rather than fulfilling an oath to care for the suffering. Where Sartre was a conscientious objector to the Occupation, Camus was an active participant in the Resistance.

Sartre also produced over seventy works, including a number of philosophical texts, while Camus' short oeuvre of a number of novels, plays, essays, and his posthumously published notebooks was cut off by his untimely death in 1960.

On October 29, 1945, a bit over a year after the liberation of Paris, Sartre gave a lecture under the auspices of *Club Maintenant* (Club Now) on Paris' Left Bank entitled "Is Existentialism a Humanism?" (Judaken, 2012). Hundreds of people attended, thousands had to be turned away, and Existentialism erupted on the world stage of thought as the philosophy of *now*. The lecture, and its written version (Sartre, 1947/2007), offered a crisp short statement of the 20th-century Existentialist assertion "existence precedes essence" (*l'existence précède l'essence*) in contrast to the very hard text *Being and Nothingness* (Sartre, 1943/2018). Sartre's point was that we are *first* randomly thrown into existence (a critique of Kierkegaard for whom God *first* provided our essence, our soul) and then must make of it what we will by *defining and constructing* our essence. This *creation* involves the continuous making and remaking of choices and, in parallel, the continuous making and remaking of the Self. Perhaps surprisingly, the advent of the Plague does not really change that.

In *Being and Nothingness*, Sartre (1943/2018), following Heidegger, contrasts the Being of World, Being-in (*en-soi*) with the Being of Human Beings, consciously[12] and intentionally (Brentano, 1874/1995) Being-for (*pour-soi*) something. Human Beings, Daseins, are free; they exist as Human Beings through being Conscious. Nothingness always had some *specific* quality for Sartre as is illustrated by an old Existentialist joke. Sartre walks into a café and orders coffee without cream. The waiter returns shortly and says, "I'm sorry, M. Sartre, we are all out of cream, will coffee without milk do?" He and De Beauvoir both believed that philosophy was lived not just written about. (Camus (1962/1963) similarly observed that if you wanted to do philosophy you should write novels.) They both refused academic appointments or prizes (Sartre refused the Nobel Prize; Camus accepted it). Prizing freedom and rebellion, Existentialism became a cultural movement in a way that Phenomenology never could.

The Plagues

The enforced social distancing and sheltering in place that came with the Plague in the early Spring of 2020 became a kind of imprisonment— necessary, but imprisonment nonetheless—that people metabolized as a loss of freedom and led to defiant rebellions. Not surprisingly, those rebellions occurred most among two groups: students/millennials and the population of middle-aged, white, mostly males who experienced themselves as disenfranchised and supported the Trump presidency. This imprisonment occurred in an atmosphere of Death that we were all Thrown into and left to try to come to terms with. It is reminiscent of that faced by the three protagonists in Sartre's play *No Exit* (1946/1989) who are dead, although they appear to be very much alive, and are incarcerated in a room we conclude to be a room in hell with a "Room-Valet," a door with a handle that turns but does not open, and a doorbell that does not ring. This is also a Plaguelike isolation experience in which we struggle with the play's two themes of Existence: Being and Death.

Our patients (and us) experience a profound shift from being tormented by inner, neurotic constraints that limit our lives and our Being to new external constraints, risks, and fears imposed by the Plague. My clinical experience has been that while some of my patients process the Plague in their own [neurotic] ways, the majority do not, engaging it as a piece of at times overwhelming external reality.[13] When Society had shut down in March and April of 2020, the population of the United States fell into a number of groups, differing in their situations vis-à-vis the Plague. There were people who were largely housebound and not working because their jobs had disappeared. For them, finding the financial resources to maintain a basic, minimal life style became their primary concern and a source of traumatic anxiety, greater than any fear of contracting COVID. Then there were the people working from home who were contending with fear of the Plague, housebound children, and painful isolation. A diverse group was working out in the world providing essential services, keeping society running by providing essential services and the medical workers on the front lines, often lacking all but minimal PPE. These included the doctors and nurses but also the larger group of support staff that kept our hospitals functioning. The mortality rate in this group was unconscionably high; a result of the failure of the federal government under the Trump presidency to manage the Plague. Finally, there were the older, sometimes retired, people confined at home, often living alone or isolated from their families in nursing homes. Many of these suffered from chronic illnesses that raised their risk of death if they contracted the Plague to as high as 80%. The ontological risks facing Human Beings then included disabling illness and Death, possible hunger, homelessness, and financial ruin. The psychological risks included anxiety, depression, and traumatic stress.

We also have to discuss the large group of COVID deniers who saw the Plague as a semi-hoax and rebelled against mask-wearing or anything they experienced as constraining their freedom or their "rights." Trump, instead of being a cheerleader for battling the pandemic, actually *encouraged* their behavior supported by governors, senators, and congressman who were beholden to them. He repeatedly denied both the seriousness of the Plague and its probable duration, recommending treatments without any scientific basis. This occurred even though, as we now know, he was informed about these things by February (Woodward, 2020) *at the latest*.

In the fall of 2020, as some K-12 schools, colleges, and universities attempted a return to in-person classes a new at-risk group was created, one in which children could also return home to infect parents and grandparents.

We often saw these programs having to shut their doors, necessitating a prompt return to distant learning.

My patients at that time did not suffer financially because of the Plague. They mostly practiced social isolation (as did I) with rare contacts with similarly isolated family and friends. All lived in areas with low case numbers. They experienced the Plague as a kind of presence, a darkness inhabiting their physical and psychological space (Bachelard, 1958/1994). Periodic depressions lasting several days were common, and I experienced them myself. Some continued to work on the intrapsychic issues that had brought them to seek treatment, but the majority focused on how the pandemic had changed their lives; a new entity with its attendant, frightening unknowability (it requires a move into Post-Structuralism to engage this issue). I conceptualized my therapeutic role as changing, to include talk about the pandemic as well as my patients' intrapsychic responses to it. As a physician as well as a psychotherapist I felt able to do this—one of the uncommon situations in which, over the years, I have found my medical training particularly important. (I'm not sure how psychotherapists without this training have dealt with the Plague.)

Steve was torn. At a time when office visits to medical specialists were limited to urgent matters, he was seeing few patients. Yet he felt a calling to enter "the trenches" with colleagues risking their lives to fight the virus and save lives. There were few to none of such patients to be seen in our quiet county, and his working with patients in acute care settings was decades in the past. He thought about volunteering elsewhere in California or even New York City but his family would have none of it. He found himself struggling with a sense of guilt yet doubted the care COVID patients were receiving. Steve's Duty of Care was a complex matter. While it undoubtedly had infantile roots in his relationship with his mother, it had, over the years, developed Existentially, becoming, if you will, a part of his *essence*, of who he was. I felt pulled in similar ways while my age and a couple of chronic illnesses pretty much guaranteed my death if I were to contract a case of the disease. Based on this assessment, I intervened, not by referring back to his mother, but rather by validating his feeling and I did that by sharing with him that I felt drawn by the same obligation to *do* something.

A therapist whose work is informed by an understanding of developmental psychopathology *and* Existentialism recognizes the necessity of choosing paths of Therapeutic Action that emphasize one or the other or, sometimes, both. These choices can vary from patient to patient but, more often, they refer to different clinical issues in the same patient. A failure to address both and to correctly tailor one's response to particular issues in the same patient can (and often does) lead to an incomplete therapy.[14]

I continued to educate myself about the unfolding Plague, spending about an hour a day researching the various medical websites that had come online about it. A major issue was that the popular press had emphasized that social distancing and mask-wearing were the most important tools available for fighting the plague (true!). What they did *not* stress and what I told my patients over and over again was that if they social distanced, having unprotected contact only with the people they lived with—loved ones and roommates—then they could expect not to become ill. This intervention has remained therapeutic. My physician patients—Steve among them—whose work put them in harm's way, went to great (successful) lengths to disinfect themselves.

Camus offers a unique perspective (Leffert, 2021) on Existentialism that is particularly relevant to the clinical practice of Psychoanalysis. It turns out that his work is also singularly applicable to the situation that society and its members (that is, us) now find ourselves. Camus' individual contribution to the body of Existential thought is the concept of Absurdity he formulates in the texts—*The Stranger* (1942/1989), *The Myth of Sisyphus* (1942/1991), and *Caligula* (1944/1958)—that he referred to as his "three Absurds."

Absurdity describes a basic discrepancy between the existence of World and the Being of Self. If we want to consider it in Heidegger's terms—something Camus did not attempt—we would say that it involves a fracture in Dasein, between the Being and the "there"—between the *Da* and the *sein*. *World* involves both the Mitwelt and the Umwelt; the fracture is in the world of relationships and the world of physical objects. The discrepancy involves two states of human being: Meaningfulness and Desire (Leffert, 2017). Absurdity is the condition that results when they fail to connect. There can be a failure to find Meaning, or its sudden loss into meaninglessness, or a change in World with Desire no longer constituting a tool for successful living leading to Meaning. Another way of saying this is that Self and World part company.

If we think of *Absurdity as the outcome of a failure of Meaning and Desire*, it offers us a reformulation of what leads people to turn to mental health treatment (of whatever sort),[15] psychoanalytic psychotherapy, or psychoanalysis. None of these treatments require any *particular* metapsychological framework to offer therapeutic action; the therapist's/analyst's conviction (explicit *or* implicit) that the process must involve a search for meaning (Frankl, 1959/2006) *is*, however, essential.

The advent of the Plague has changed our conversation with World in fundamental ways. Plagues add a whole new element to the Absurdity of our relations with World, to *Existenz*, to Dasein. At least many, if not most or nearly all, of the ways in which we find Meaning or satisfy Desire in World were disrupted by the Plague by April of 2020. For some, they have been replaced by various forms of personal disaster. Others have found new ways of Being and new sources of Meaning (for myself, caring for my patients has intensified the meaning of being a Psychotherapist). The Plague is *psychologically* Absurd, living in its presence has a subjective absurdity, but for anyone with a knowledge of epidemiology or virology it makes all too much sense.

Such individuals find Meaning and Desire in its pursuit, as do the medical personnel on the front lines of the pandemic. Existential fulfillment does not necessarily carry happiness with it, whether Thrown, Everyday, or Fallen; it can instead bring unhappiness, sadness, fear, or numbness.[16] Some of us find a shared risk of a common Death in the picture as we have not otherwise experienced in our lives. It can bring with it terror or numbing indifference. Others do not—as of July, 2020—experience the Plague as having a biological reality. They see it as a mild flu-like illness whose presence, mortality, and crippling sequelae *have all been exaggerated* for political purposes. To them, social distancing and mask-wearing represent unnecessary and at times maddening intrusions on their personal liberty (I have heard "I have my rights" and "you can't make me" in grocery stores). The distinctions between Thrown, Everyday, and Fallen very much apply to peoples' responses to the Plague.

Camus' "Three Absurds" find their protagonists seeking Meaning in an Absurd world. None of them seek or find it in their connections to or Care of others (Leffert, 2016). This is a problem faced by the Existentialist school in general; it is not Relational. Indeed, Caligula (1944/1958) and Meursault (1942/1989) search for Meaning through murder and its ramifications, while Dr. Rieux (Camus, 1948/1991, a fourth Absurd) does not find it in his work with patients, whom he "cares for" by rote. Sisyphus (1942/1991) is a different character entirely. In Camus' formulation, Sisyphus is seeking Meaning in an Absurd world (in this way he casts Sisyphus as a representative of Everyman). For Camus, the corollary to the search for Meaning is the question, "Is life worth living?" a, perhaps *the*, foundational question for all philosophy.

World, as the Existentialists find it, is Absurd; in the face of Absurdity there are three ways for us to go forward. First, if there is no way out of Absurdity, no Meaning to be found, then the only rational alternative, Camus (1942/1991) posits, is suicide, to in effect *end the Self*. (Robin Williams suicide as a result of undiagnosed Lewy Body Dementia offers, I think, an example of this.) Another choice is Kierkegaard's (Ferreira, 1998; Kierkegaard, 1843/1983), to make a *leap of faith*; to wit that God exists and he [sic] knows what he's doing. It is the position that all those who cleave to religion must take (*The Plague* constitutes Camus' further exploration of the fallacy of this argument and the root of his personal atheism). It leads Kierkegaard to the inevitable conclusion that essence precedes existence, a position that Sartre (1947/2007) has shown to be an ontological failure.

The third possibility is to accept, even *embrace*, the absurdity of the objective world of the *Mitwelt* and *Umwelt* and instead to seek, to *construct*, Meaning in the Subjective. And this is precisely what Sisyphus (in Camus' (1942/1991) retelling of the myth) does. Where Sartre prescribes changing the world to find Meaning (just as his protagonist Roquentin does in *Nausea*, 1938/2013), Camus sees the Absurdity of World as fixed and that we are left to find our own meaning in it. Sisyphus grasps his rock and roles it to the top of his mountain only, at the very last, to have it slip from his hands and role back to the bottom. He walks down the mountain to face his torment again. But in that "hour" he is *conscious*, he is free. He experiences sadness, but also joy. He accepts and finds meaning in his task as all working people must do, the Everydayness of an Absurd world we must accept.

"Sartre views Absurdism as a collapse into a pathological state, and the problem is for the individual to regain meaning, while Camus posits that there are things in life that cannot be changed and it is our task to, like Sisyphus, find meaning *in* them" (Leffert, 2021, p. 63). (This is quite consistent with classical psychoanalytic formulations of outcome and Therapeutic Action.) I have argued for these as clinical positions for some time (I think we all do, at least implicitly). The Serenity Prayer, recited at the beginning of all Alcoholics Anonymous meetings is about the same thing.

Plague Narratives

With this in mind, let's return to the Plague. I found four surprisingly similar Plague narratives spread over the past 400 years. The first is "our" Plague that is evolving as I write. The second is Camus' (1948/1991) fictional Plague described in *The Plague*. The third is the influenza pandemic of 1918–1919 described by Barry (2005) in *The Great Influenza: The story of the deadliest pandemic in history*. Last is Defoe's almost contemporaneous account (1722/2003), *A Journal of the Plague Year*, of the Plague that struck London in 1665.

The Plague of Camus' novel (1948/1991), struck the Algerian port city of Oran, arriving mysteriously in 194_. With one exception, it is Absurd to each of the characters caught up in it. The exception is the priest, a father Paneloux, who at first finds Meaning in the Plague. As he preaches to his parishioners, God has sent them the Plague as a [meaningful] punishment for their sins and they must atone and repent. As the Plague progresses and Paneloux accompanies Dr. Rieux, the narrator, on his rounds, he is present at the agonizing death of a child; an event that must be seen as God's will *even though the child must be innocent of sin or wrongdoing*. Here too, Meaning is lost, and Paneloux eventually contracts a disease of "doubtful diagnosis" and dies. Camus, as he describes the horrors of the Plague, its sickness and death, uses a distant and emotionally neutral voice, as he does in his other works. It is as if we are made to note the absence of emotion and make of it what we will. The Plague and its effects on the people of Oran are portrayed as lacking *any* meaning; they are Absurd.

Barry's (2005) epidemiological rendering of his narrative of the great influenza pandemic of 1918–1919 is quite different; yet in describing pandemics as social as well as epidemiological and virologic entities, it underscores the similarities between the great influenza and our own COVID-19. It is set against the background of a developing American medical establishment in the 19th and first part of the 20th centuries that went from the near non-existent training of incompetent physicians and the apprenticeship system to the appearance of premier hospitals, medical schools and research facilities that became the best in the world. We find a cast of medical heroes and crass incompetents much as we have today and a political establishment bent on pursuing its own power agenda (in this case, Woodrow Wilson and World War I) and treating the reality of viral pandemics as if they were events that could be controlled and shaped politically.

The great influenza or the Spanish flu[17] that we now know to be caused by a version of swine flu (Influenza type A H1N1) that seems (Barry, 2005) to have appeared on a hog farm in central Kansas in February of 1918. From there it travelled to a large, nearby army base, Fort Riley. Woodrow Wilson, who had opposed US entry into the war for its first 2½ years, switched to actively favoring it (the United States formally entered the war in April of 1918) and set in motion a huge buildup of US armed forces to make that possible. This entailed the rapid movement of large numbers of young men among expanding military bases around the country and overseas. This was a human pathogen's dream; it mimicked the effects of globalization on the spread of COVID-19 a century later. The initial responses of national, state, and local governments then were surprisingly similar to our own governments' today. It was, at all levels, an inconvenient truth. Wilson did not want anything to interfere with our entrance into the war and simply avoided the pandemic, much as Trump has done. Local governments did not want it to interfere with the lives and economies of their states and cities.

Then, as in the opening days of COVID, treatment was of limited value. What was known was that people, mostly young people, were getting sick and many of them were dying, sometimes after only hours or days. The disease was seen to be highly contagious; then as now, social isolation and distancing were known to be the only ways to curtail its spread. Then[18] as now, social isolation was often not practiced. Then as now medical staff, doctors and nurses, particularly nurses, often sickened and died from the disease. Unlike now, the cause of "their" Plague was unknown.[19] Unlike now, *there were no treatments for infectious diseases in 1918.*[20] (Attempts of limited success *were* made, as they have been now, to treat the disease with convalescent serum.) Research focused on trying to isolate and identify the pathogen, whereas with our Plague, the pathogen, SARS-Coronavirus-19, was identified in days, and research focused on repurposing other anti-viral agents (President Trump suggested, Hydroxychloroquine, an anti-malarial, injections of bleach and exposure to ultraviolet light) and developing a vaccine.

Eventually, as with other plagues, the Great Influenza (1920) went away on its own. Whether this was simply a result of so-called "herd immunity" or something to do with the comings-and-goings of viruses and bacteria is not really known. (Presumably, we can expect something of the same with COVID, although, as with Influenza, it will probably recur.) What was previously not much considered or studied were the social and psychological sequelae to the plagues. These affected those who contracted the illness and recovered, their families, the families of those who died, and the people, both professional and lay, who, often helplessly, cared for them and frequently presided over their deaths. Psychologically these sequelae involved grief and mourning, both acute and chronic, Post-traumatic Stress Disorder, and the social and economic damage the various Plagues did to people. Instead, what we had was a rather simplistic notion that there was mostly just psychological relief when Plagues were over and people then went on with their lives.

Certainly, the psychological sequelae to the Great Influenza went unnoted and unstudied in the 1920s. COVID, *our* Plague, is already different. Grief over lost loved ones is very much in the national press and the evening news, as is shared mourning. Burnout of healthcare workers treating hospitalized Plague patients and the lay staff that supports them is well known and efforts were made to offer PTSD-centered brief psychotherapy to help with burnout (how systematic these efforts are remains to be seen). The suicide of a highly respected Emergency Department physician in the spring of 2020 that seemed to relate to her only partially treated depressive and guilt feelings that she couldn't do enough for her patients—in spite of a brief psychiatric hospitalization that preceded her suicide—suggests that we are not adequately caring for our wounded warriors.

This brings us to the oldest (1722/2003) of the Plague narratives, Daniel Defoe's *A Journal of the Plague Year*. Defoe describes the Great Plague of London of 1665, the last major occurrence of bubonic plague in that city, in which 97,000 died. Defoe wrote it in 1722, hoping it would be of interest when the plague broke out in Marseilles in 1720. In providing a more or less contemporary account, he offers us a chance to see what people thought of a pandemic 400 years ago. Our first question is, exactly what sort of narrative is this? It is very fully researched and, in signing it HF, Defoe refers to his uncle Henry Foe, a saddler who stayed in London through the plague and kept a journal (Defoe was 5 in 1665 and must have grown up hearing his uncle's stories about the plague). The *Journal* appears to be a well-researched history in which short fictional narratives of people were interspersed to lend human meaning to the experiences.

The cause of the plague was then unknown.[21] It was thought to come from "distempered air"; it was known to be highly contagious, that people who were still well could carry the contagion, but it was not known just how it was transmitted. This state of knowledge magnified peoples' anxiety and led to all kinds of useless forms of treatment or protection. People desperately believed in the efficacy of procedures like the surgical lancing of bubos or the application of medicated plasters to the body, or untold numbers of droughts and medicines to be ingested; people did sometimes recover, and who was to say that the putative remedy was not the cause?[22] What was known and practiced was the benefit of social isolation for containing the illness.

When someone contracted the plague, they and their entire family were sometimes quarantined in their home; most usually died.

In the absence of modern treatment, Bubonic Plague has a Case Fatality Rate (CFR) of 5%–60% with the lower number being doubtful. It comes in three forms: the Bubonic form characterized by lymphatic swelling and a course of days; the Septicemic form which, approaching 60% is the deadliest; and the Pneumonic form that is spread as a respiratory illness and can kill in days or even hours with a CFR approaching that of the Septicemic form. The Plague shattered lives and families within a few days.

The emotions that accompanied the plague were terror and hopelessness. Defoe describes a woman shouting out of her window *"Oh! Death, Death, Death!"* (Defoe, 1722/2003, p. 79), but he is helpless to do anything and rides on. Shortly thereafter, another woman screams out of her window and when asked what is the matter says that her master, a rich and successful man, has just hung himself. It is unclear if his motive was that he had just discovered the signs of plague on himself or if he was simply overwhelmed. Five months into *our* Plague, things are quite different. There is anxiety, certainly, and there is grief and sadness among those who have lost loved ones or friends (as there would be for anyone who has suffered such loss). But now there is mostly a reaction among people of how COVID disrupted their lives and capacity to care for themselves and their families (certainly true), economically and socially, but also varying degrees of denial of the personal threat to life and limb. People do not seem to fully comprehend *our* virus until someone they know is sickened by it. The strongest feelings today are about children and grandchildren with parents being torn between work and family. (Since infant and child mortality were relatively high in 17th-century London to begin with, this danger of Plague may have been less of a focus for people who already viewed their children's fate as uncertain.)

As "our Plague" wore on into the Fall of 2020, there was a growing sense that, like the Great Influenza, it was gathering itself, with the approaching cold season for a more massive continuation or second wave. Numbers of cases were rising exponentially and, although we had become more adept at treating severe cases, case fatalities were also on the rise.

In Defoe's Plague, "It [was] scarcely credible what dreadful Cases happened in particular Families every Day; People in the rage of Distemper or in the torment of their swellings … oftentimes laying violent hands upon themselves … mothers murthering (sic) their own children … and some dying of mere grief" (Defoe, 1722/2003, p. 79). Physical and emotional agony drowned out Meaning and people's very *Being*. Therapeutically, these experiences, past and present, are best understood in terms of trauma and Existential crises, sometimes effecting whole societies.[23]

What all of these Plagues have in common is that they render life Absurd. It is only when *effective* care is possible that this is not the case and then, sort of by definition, you don't have a Plague. What I have tried to show here is that they could only be approached psychologically in Existentialist terms as the things themselves and needed to be treated in the world and later if psychological signs and symptoms persisted, in the Self.

The Postmodern Turn

It should be obvious by this time that Postmodernism was not the first school of philosophy to turn away from Modernity; that Existentialism, if not Phenomenology as well, had already done so in offering an objective assessment of the Subjective and Intersubjective. Within these earlier disciplines, the result was an irreducible Subjectivity and Intersubjectivity under which we all, including therapists and patients, curate our own reality. This was, if you will, an *anti*-Modern concept. Beginning in the 19th century, at least with the work of Kierkegaard (1849/1980, 1843/1983, 1846/1992), it had become clear that the arguments of Modernism, founded in a tight reading of Science and Newtonian Physics, failed to adequately account for the human condition. In particular, Rationalism could not account for human decision-making, thought, or behavior (although attempts to use it to do so extended at least into the mid-20th century); this failing was not specifically addressed by either Phenomenology or Existentialism.

Postmodernism is a term that became prominent in the 1970s. It is as hotly contested a term as *Existentialism* and *Phenomenology* and I can only offer my own reading of it, somewhat tailored to the present volume. It has been used to refer to a historical period, to schools of art, architecture, and literature, and to a detailed critique of Modern Epistemology; it is in this sense that I will use the term. I have previously written (Leffert, 2007a, 2007b, 2010, 2013) on the subject, organizing my ideas around the work of specific contributors (although it is worth noting that Lyotard (1979) summarized these critiques in *The Postmodern Condition: A Report on Knowledge*); I do not plan to take that approach here.

In contrast with Modernist Epistemologies that attempt to reduce knowledge to singular statements of fact (sic) and singular histories (sic) of events, Postmodern discourse either—depending on the practitioner's point of view—glories in or makes lemonade out of their irreducible plurality. Postmodern discourse strives to take into account, to represent, ambiguity, difference (*différance*), and interreferentiality. To these, I have added, in my own work, uncertainty (Leffert, 2016; Tversky & Kahneman, 1974/1982) and complexity (Leffert, 2010). This discourse is both intersubjective and relational. Psychoanalysts have either incorporated these ideas into their thinking or violently rejected them. The unique tool that Postmodernism brings to the tasks of Psychotherapy and Psychoanalysis is *deconstruction*. Deconstruction is of particular use in freeing knowledges from metanarratives[24] (or "grand narratives"). (Psychoanalysis has been singularly limited (Leffert, 2010) by its reliance on metanarrative and has benefited from Phenomenologically based, atheoretical observation.)

When Postmodernism, in particular Post-structuralism (a critique of binary reasoning), appeared, it was to offer a further critique of Modernism, without taking into account those already offered by Phenomenology and Existentialism. In treating them all in a single chapter, I am implicitly arguing that Postmodernism offers a supplement and an extension, not a replacement, to both the ontologies and epistemologies offered by these earlier 20th-century philosophies. A criticism of this position would revolve around the fact that Existentialism and Phenomenology are fundamentally concerned with the search for personal Meaning and its antithetical failure, Absurdity (Leffert, 2021), and a superficial reading of Postmodernism as a critique of Meaning.

Neo-pragmatism (Rorty, 1979, 1982)—an extreme branch of Postmodernism[25]—does offer a critique of meaning, insisting that it has no existence within the Self. What Rorty and the other Neo-pragmatists were really talking about was rather that there is no *objective* Meaning (or Meanings) that the Self necessarily subscribes to. Phenomenology and Existentialism had already replaced it with a Human, irreducibly Subjective Meaning that can be Intersubjectively validated.

Postmodern architecture preceded its philosophical writings by a decade. It emerged as a critique of Modernism, adding ornamentation and freedom to the latter's battle cry of form follows function. Robert Venturi, its founder, saw it as an architecture of complexity and contradiction, attempting to embody the richness and ambiguity of modern experience. It was able to contain such apparent contradictions as the Piazza d'Italia in New Orleans by Charles Moore, a kind of collection of slabs of architectural wedding cakes stacked side by side and the Guggenheim Museum in Bilbao by Frank Gehry, an undulating form of concrete, glass, and titanium scales displaying both synthesis and fragmentation. Various works integrate humor and irony, pluralism, and *trompe l'oeil*. These architects sought meaning and at times offered buildings that embodied a kind of deconstruction-in-action, holding opposites in creative tension. Postmodern architecture takes *account* of function but does not limit itself to an *expression* of it.

This might seem like a digression, far removed from clinical work. I included it because looking at these buildings for a bit offers an intuitive grasp of what Postmodern thought is all about in much the same way as novels and plays (e.g., Camus, 1942/1989, 1948/1991; Sartre, 1946/1989, 1938/2013) are primary texts of Existentialism. They offer us an entrance into the philosophy of multiplicity and deconstruction and then their clinical ramifications.

Multiplicity and Interreferentiality

Postmodern Epistemologies offer ways of dealing with multiple explanations, at times contradictory ones, without losing any of them. With the exception of the concept of multiple function (Waelder, 2007), classical psychoanalysis was based on the assumption that, while multiple interpretations of an action or association were *possible*, there was, at a particular time, a *single, best one*. These Postmodern concepts were adopted by Relational (Fairfield, Layton, & Stack, 2002) and Intersubjective (Stolorow & Atwood, 1992) clinicians (Leffert, 2007b) producing a somewhat contested (Eagle, 2003) and classically ignored turn in Psychoanalysis. For some authors (e.g., Hoffman, 1998; D. B. Stern, 1997) this adoption was implicit rather than explicit but nevertheless involved multiplicity and interreferentiality. More than a decade ago (Leffert, 2007a, 2010), I offered an integration across these multiple perspectives.

McGowan (1991) describes a heterogeneity of Postmodern discourse, observing that "within the configuration of postmodernism, two (or more) incompatible things are desirable and … different strategies are involved in the effort to think these incompatibilities together" (p. 89). Other authors (e.g., Leary, 2002) argue that Postmodernism (Post-Structuralism) is not a theory in its own right but "rather … involve[s] critiques that are meant to destabilize existing constructs" (p. 227). Postmodernism argues for plurality and the various forces—uncertainty, unknowability, complexity, interreferentiality—that make single-solution thinking untenable. The Modernist solution to this problem is the premise (and it is just a premise) that we exist in a concrete reality that can be grasped through perception and objectively assessed and measured free from bias: It is *knowable*. To illustrate the difference between the Modern and the Postmodern I am reminded of the story of the three umpires. It seems that there are three umpires having a drink together—when, in the pre-COVID world, such things were possible—who fall into discussing how they call plays. The first umpire says that he carefully measures the distances involved between players and bases and looks at the instant replay if he is still unsure. The second umpire asserts he has found he doesn't need to do that and just "goes with his gut." (So, we have logic and intuition.) But it is the third umpire who moves the discourse into the Postmodern. *He* says, "The play *doesn't exist* until I call it."

Latour (1991/1993), in his seminal work, *We Have Never Been Modern*, takes this further, arguing that epistemology can describe ontology only in terms of large, branched chain hybrids including both the scientific and the social; it is impossible to separate the two. For a current example we need to look no further than the wearing of masks in social situations. In spite of hating it, we find it impossible to separate the *science* of its epidemiology from the social of its *politics*.[26] The *science* of Epidemiology cannot be separated from the mind of Donald Trump.

Interreferentiality argues that it is impossible to separate the knowing of something from the thing that is known or the Human Being who knows it. (Husserl's Transcendental Reduction is fully consistent with this.) It speaks to uncertainty and complexity. Uncertainty involves the fact that the knowing of something can change the thing that is known and that we Human Beings have developed ways of figuring things out in situations that are irreducibly uncertain (Kahneman et al., 1982; Kahneman & Tversky, 1979/2000). Complexity (Leffert, 2008) is a property of ontological systems. It involves the dual observations that the behavior of a complex system cannot be understood or predicted based on the sum of the behavior of its components and that the point at which change occurs in a complex system, while sudden and massive rather than gradual, is not predictable (hurricanes, earthquakes, and change in psychotherapy come readily to mind). A corollary to this premise is that attempts at prediction (beyond probabilities of occurrence over time) will always fail.

Heuristics and Metanarratives

Postmodernism takes cognizance of these many facets of plurality, uncertainty, and knowability. However, to actually *live in* such a world as a Human Being is extremely dysphoric; uncertainty can also be dangerous. In Phenomenological terms, it is dysphoric for Dasein to Be-there. We use two tools to simplify, to solve this problem. The first we have already discussed: the shortcuts for decision-making under uncertainty (Kahneman et al., 1982; Kahneman & Tversky, 1979/2000), Heuristics and Biases. These are "shortcuts" that we all employ *unconsciously* to decide how we will act or think. They can, depending on the situation, work fairly well or produce systematic errors. Patients come to us when they make such systematic errors using Heuristics and Biases that were developed as a response to particular traumas (we saw this with Steve). *We* make use of these as psychotherapists, for good or ill, when, for example, a patient offers a series of associations that reminds us of a class of conflicts, or a kind of attachment issue, or …; we *unconsciously* make use of the *Representativeness Heuristic* to ascribe that meaning to it. The best strategic tool we have to manage our own Heuristics is to employ a light scrutiny when we find ourselves drawing theoretical conclusions about therapeutic content or process. This brings Representativeness into Consciousness where we can consider it.

When we think about our lives, reflecting on memory and unfolding events, trying to piece them together, we tend *to serially string them together into discrete narratives*. Once they are formed, they tend to stand as filing cabinets of a sort that *organize experience*. They are not necessarily accurate, nor do they necessarily manifest optimum utility. Phenomenology and Existentialism provide no tools for addressing these emotional-cognitive activities. But we also take things further than that, often unconsciously. Using Representativeness and Availability, we seek commonality among our narratives with which to abstract higher "truths" about life. Postmoderns call such truths *Metanarratives*[27] and are much troubled by them. They view them critically as unnecessarily constricting meaning and, once formed, they are highly tenacious.

Sarah, an attractive, divorced attorney who sought analysis in her mid-40s because of repeated experiences dating in which men at first seemed very interested in her but dropped her after a couple of dates, showed a continuity between her narratives and her metanarratives. She would repetitively offer up narratives of experiences that she seemed unaware of having spoken of many times. One such story told of a time that her young daughter seemed ill to her. When, after several visits, urgent care and her pediatrician found nothing, Sarah insisted on her being seen again and again. An x-ray eventually showed a bronchial pneumonia. This at first seemed simply like an instance of attuned mothering. But as Sarah combined it with other narratives and used it to narrowly guide her life, it became an instance of a metanarrative, something like *triumph in the face of adversity*. It told Sarah that when she thought something or had a hunch she should stick to her guns no matter what *and never change*. She would turn out to be *right* in the end. While this actually served her fairly well as an attorney conducting a cross examination, it spelled disaster in relationships and, along with other such metanarratives, significantly restricted her life. Sarah organized much of how she lived her life with such metanarratives and she clung to them tenaciously. It took years of work to get her to actually question her metanarratives while first only paying lip service to my interpretations of them.

Metanarratives, I have found, are not particularly subject to interpretation. People readily acknowledge them but don't find them problematic, indeed, they find them, as Sarah did, *comforting*. Since they also don't readily appear on the standard psychoanalytic radar, they are usually not even noticed by analysts or therapists. In order to deal with them we have to first create an index of suspicion for Metanarratives within ourselves. To address them, as we will see below, we will have to have recourse to the Postmodern toolbox.

Meaning and Différance

We have already encountered Meaning and Human Beings' search for it in Existentialism[28] and, to a lesser extent, in Phenomenology (e.g., Frankl, 1959/2006). Postmoderns are also very concerned with Meaning, but more from the perspective of how it is narrowed and lost through particular epistemological practices. (The *Existential* outcome of such narrowing is Absurdity.) Metanarrative formation is a singular example of such practices. Another is the construction of serial, linear narratives as opposed to narratives containing multiple, simultaneous elements. (Since the world is not like this, elements of Meaning must be discarded along the way to construct such a narrative.)

> These areas are ultimately concerned with postmodern responses to questions of meaning, ranging from attempts to grapple with it, to regarding it as infinitely plural, individual and irreproducible, created new each

time. Similarly, dealing with questions of meaning either does not, can or does require dealing also with all prior discourse on a particular subject. Most extremely, meaning is seen as a hopeless prisoner of language, described as a surface with nothing underneath it.

(Leffert, 2010, p. 7)

Perhaps the most powerful Postmodern response to Meaning is *Différance* as it was deployed by Derrida (1978, 1972/1982). *Différance* is a complex term of Derrida's creation. It combines, interreferentially, two meanings: *differ* and *defer*. Although unnoticed (and unacknowledged by Derrida), *defer* offers a continuation of Husserl's Phenomenological concept of bracketing or *epoché*, a tool used to continue an argument without fully resolving or completing a piece of it. Finally, to further set the term apart from the usual term (in French) *différence*, Derrida changes the second *e* to an *a*, resulting in *différance*.

So, what, exactly, does one do with *différance* after unwrapping it from the packaging it comes in? I have to offer a rather complex and, of necessity, condensed argument here that summarizes some of my previous work (Leffert, 2010, 2016, 2021). It solves the problem of limiting discourse to single strands of meaning. *Différance* allows for multiple strands of meaning that differ. Their linearity is critically addressed by interreferentially braiding them together, deferring their meaning until they form a sheaf of *différance*. These braided chains, in Latour's (1991/1993) terms, contain elements of the social and the scientific, the "objective" and the subjective. I set *objective* apart in quotes because Being in the World, Dasein, Being-*there* if you will, is not so objective, not really. Our judgments about World and what is present in it are plagued by uncertainty and unknowability. We usually tend to see precision rather than accuracy and, when we speak about the human condition (as we must as therapists) we can never see beyond our own irreducible subjectivity. The answer to this, again dating back to Husserl, is that we can *Intersubjectively* validate our Subjectivity. The idea of a sheaf of *différance* can serve to clinically formulate complex ways of Being, of Dasein. In practice, we don't often explicitly formulate this multiplicity but a sheaf is always implicit in whatever we have to say (or think) about meaning. The creation of a sheaf is a Post-Structural, dialectical constructivist enterprise (Hoffman, 1998). An enactment is an example of such a sheaf. It combines multiple elements of a person's Being (drawn from the Self and its relations with World) in a way that offers integration and allows for contradiction; it is, in a word, interreferential.

Psychoanalysis *does* have a theoretical tradition of exploring the multiple meanings of a single psychological event. Waelder (2007), in a now classic 1936 paper described how such events mobilized elements from multiple psychological systems that could be explored in Psychoanalysis. As he put it, "We see accordingly that an aspect of enormous many-sidedness of motivation and meaning of psychic occurrences results from psychoanaly-sis" (p. 92). In keeping with the times, however, he discussed motivation and meaning in terms of structural theory—the ego, the id, and the superego. In the decades that followed, relational elements were added, along with limited considerations of the external world, but with no systematic way of consider-ing how the various elements influenced each other. The Postmoderns offered an Epistemology of *différance* that allowed for a simultaneous consideration of all of these elements and their interrelations (the *sheaf*). The only theoret-ical limiting factor[29] in their use in the Therapeutic Situation was how many of the elements a clinician could formulate and keep in mind.

To Sum Up

So what should you take away from this opening chapter? The first thing is that the more different kinds of psychological and physical material that a therapy can encompass, the better. If, however, they are to truly make sense together, one has to have ways of stringing them *all* together. The concept of a sheaf of *différance* offers the epistemological way of doing so. The *potential* to construct such sheaves as a way of making sense of Being exists whether or not a clinician makes use of them; depending on the degree of one's particu-lar therapeutic and theoretical orthodoxy, one can recognize the presence of few or many threads in a given sheaf.

The major point of the chapter is the hypothesis that Existentialism/Phenomenology and Postmodernism are complementary, that the latter did not *replace* the former as it was posited to do by its proponents. It is perhaps true that Existentialism and Phenomenology are more of an Ontology while the Postmodernism is more of a pluralistic Epistemology.

Let's return to Steve, the patient we have discussed intermittently over the course of this chapter. Steve suffered from a sheaf of mother and wife that he had unconsciously woven together. While he thought of them as separate, he could not formulate that separateness. Although we frequently encounter such situations clinically, we don't think of them in this way and rather inter-pret what we think of as a transference problem. How clinically successful such interpretations ultimately prove to be has not, to my knowledge, been systematically studied (the efficacy of different kinds of interpretations—separation anxiety, denial, oedipal phase, etc.—also seem not to have been discretely studied).

A particularly difficult example involved his inability to emotionally dis-tinguish his wife's warm and at times *appropriately* seductive behavior toward him in the present from his mother's inappropriate, overtly seductive behav-ior that occurred in the past when they lived alone together. This failure, and the distance it produced in his marriage was one of the factors that contributed to his depression. Clinically, it seemed most useful to observe to him that there were times when he *was* (not seemed) unable to tell them apart.

This did not produce any immediate effect, nor did I expect it to do so. Steve's intellectual knowledge of the blurring of wife and mother did not lead him anywhere. What I thought was important was not that Steve knew about the blurring of the two threads but rather that he knew that *I* knew about it. What gave this Meaning (remember Meaning?) was the context, the relationship with me, an older man, in the present, that gave him the things he had never gotten from his father. Steve's insight was of no use in checking up on how we were doing. What *was* of use was when, after a year and a half or so, he began to notice and enjoy his wife's sexuality. This outcome was the result of Deconstruction that restored *différance*, that freed up cognitive and emotional knowledges of the two women in Steve's life.

As my work has evolved over the last two decades, I have come to see that what Existentialism/Phenomenology and Postmodernism have to tell us about Being and Knowing (Existence and Knowledge) need to be taken up and used together in the Therapeutic Situation (Leffert, 2013) if we are to maximize Therapeutic Action. Let's carry this forward into the subsequent chapters of this book.

Notes

1 I am offering here only a sweeping survey of the history of our discipline that does not pretend to do it justice. I do so for purposes of orientation and ask the reader to bear with me.

2 In the 1970s, a very qualified senior analyst was refused appointment as a Training Analyst at an East Coast institute because he was thought to be overly concerned with treating patients' symptoms.

3 I use the term *patient* to refer to the sick or unhappy Human Beings who come to us seeking to be healed rather than insight and would suggest that other analysts and therapists do the same, whether or not they have a medical degree. *Client* simply does not convey what they are seeking or why they come to us.

4 I use the term *Self* not in any of the familiar psychological senses of it, but rather to signify a Bio-Psycho-Social Self that includes the wider frame of reference of Mind in Body in World.

5 Heidegger, for example, called himself a Phenomenologist until he broke with Husserl in the 1920s, after which he dropped the term but did not take up another. I, and most authors, I believe, still think of him as a Phenomenologist; he certainly wasn't an Existentialist.

6 By convention, it is capitalized but not italicized.

7 I have offered repeated (e.g., Leffert, 2010, Chapter 5) neuroscience-based criticisms of the existence of a dynamic unconscious in the Freudian sense of the term.

8 Within Phenomenology, there is considerable controversy concerning the meaning of these terms; I am offering my own reading of them here.

9 The clinical illustrations that will be offered throughout this book (as they were in my previous books) are case composites. I have chosen this mode of presentation because it is the only way I can truly protect the confidentiality of my patients. Many authors, in offering clinical vignettes, talk about actual patients in the belief they are offering something of evidential value; they are not, such accounts are subjective and cannot have *evidential* value. In asserting only an *illustrative* purpose, I make no such claims.

10 I use the term *metapsychology* as a shorthand for the kinds of differing metanarratives that we are encouraged in our training to apply to our work. A critique of the metanarrative concept is inherent in both the Phenomenological/Existential and Postmodern traditions, with the latter offering the tool of *Deconstruction* with which to deal with it.

11 The experience of the Plague, as I am told by those who have experienced both, is thus radically different in New York City as compared to my little city of Santa Barbara.

12 As I have argued, current neuroscience has made the conscious-unconscious dichotomy far more complex than it was a half-century ago. What the Existentialists and Phenomenologists were calling simply consciousness, is, more accurately, Left Brain and Right Brain Consciousness with a complex multifaceted relationship to things unconscious. We will deal with this in Chapter 4.

13 I believe the stance of the analyst/therapist is crucial here. If one attempts to continue the therapeutic process in the usual manner pursuing, Therapeutic Action in the usual ways, and remaining silent or interpreting resistance in the face of a patient's bringing up the Plague, then one can force compliance and an iatrogenic regression. If, however, one maintains an Existential approach to the patient's Being, equally open to past *and* present, one can pursue the central themes of Meaning, Absurdity, and Death that will lead to a patient's own unique experience of them.

14 Of course, there is no such thing as a "complete" therapy What I'm referring to here is simply work that *could* have been done, *should* have been done, but *wasn't* done.

15 In some circumstances an antidepressant might be the treatment of choice, in others any of the various forms of psychotherapy.

16 In the care narratives of frontline medical workers, we see ample evidence of this.

17 The name is, for our purposes, interesting. For purposes of "morale" accurate newspaper reporting of the flu was suppressed. Spain proved to be the exception, hence giving its name to the pandemic.

18 The worst example was the Philadelphia war bond parade of September, 1918. It was held despite the pleading of medical authorities and attended by 200,000 people. As a result, the city became the worst "hot spot" of the pandemic.

19 It was originally thought to be bacterial in nature and a hard-to-culture, the eponymously named coccobacillus, *Haemophilus influenzae*, was thought to be its cause. There *was* a suspicion that a much tinier causative agent that would, in the next two decades, be understood to be a virus, was involved. It became known as the Influenza virus and it came in many varieties.

20 The first antibiotics, the sulfa drugs, did not come on the scene until the mid-1930s.

21 Koch's four postulates for the identification of the origins of a disease were still two centuries away. In addition, they represent scientific knowledge; even today there are many people who cannot understand or don't believe in scientific knowledge.

22 Such remedies for *our* Plague have included bleach, UV light and Hydroxychloroquine.

23 When Plague struck Europe in the 14th century, the Tuscan cities of Florence and Sienna were similarly struck. It turned out that Florence came back rather quickly, even hiring foreign workers to replace those who fell to the Plague. However, Sienna really didn't; it remained socially and economically damaged and, to this day, has something of a dark, depressive character.

24 Lyotard (1979) defined postmodern as simply "incredulity toward metanarrative" (p. xxiv).

25 The other branches being Neo-Marxism, Post-Structuralism, and a group of disciplines focusing on otherness of race, gender, and LGBT studies, originally termed Queer Theory.

26 This is true for all of what we call *science*; it is just sometimes harder to grasp.

27 One is struck by a similarity with a term we are otherwise familiar with, *metapsychology*, that refers to our own, often dubious and highly controversial attempts (see Leffert, 2010) to seek higher levels of abstraction in clinical meaning.

28 Camus' (1942/1989) anti-hero in *The Stranger*, Meursault, finds only Absurdity through his search for meaning in the anticipation of his public execution.
29 The practical limit is the number of clinicians who simply don't think in this way.

References

Bachelard, G. (1994). *The poetics of space* (M. Jolas, trans.). Boston, MA: Beacon Press. (Original work published in 1958).

Barry, J. M. (2005). *The great influenza: The story of the deadliest pandemic in history*. New York, NY: Penguin Books.

Boston Change Process Study Group. (2005). The "something more" than interpretation revisited: Sloppiness and co-creativity in the psychoanalytic encounter. *Journal of the American Psychoanalytic Association*, *53*, 693–729.

Brentano, F. (1995). *Psychology from an empirical standpoint* (L. L. McCalister, trans.). London, England: Routledge. (Original work published in 1874).

Camus, A. (1958). Caligula. In S. Gilbert (Ed.), *Caligula and 3 other plays* (pp. 1–74). New York, NY: Vintage Books. (Original work published in 1944).

Camus, A. (1963). *Notebooks 1935–1942* (P. Thody, trans.). Chicago, IL: Ivan R. Dee. (Original work published in 1962).

Camus, A. (1989). *The stranger* (M. Ward, trans.). New York, NY: Vintage Books. (Original work published in 1942).

Camus, A. (1991). The myth of Sisyphus. In J. O'Brien (Ed.), *The myth of Sisyphus and other essays* (pp. 3–138). New York, NY: Vintage Books. (Original work published in 1942).

Camus, A. (1991). *The plague* (S. Gilbert, trans.). New York, NY: Vintage Books. (Original work published in 1948).

Christakis, N. A., & Fowler, J. H. (2009). *Connected: The surprising power of our social networks and how they shape our lives*. New York, NY: Little, Brown and Company.

Defoe, D. (2003). *A journal of the plague year*. New York, NY: Penguin Books. (Original work published in 1722).

Derrida, J. (1978). *Writing and différence* (A. Bass, trans.). Chicago, IL: University of Chicago Press.

Derrida, J. (1982). *Margins of philosophy* (A. Bass, trans.). Chicago, IL: University of Chicago Press. (Original work published in 1972).

Eagle, M. N. (2003). The postmodern turn in psychoanalysis: A critique. *Psychoanalytic Psychology*, *20*, 411–424.

Eissler, K. R. (1968). The relationship of explaining and understanding in psychoanalysis. *Psychoanalytic Study of the Child*, *23*, 141–177.

Fairfield, S., Layton, L., & Stack, C. (Eds.). (2002). *Bringing the plague: Toward a postmodern psychoanalysis*. New York, NY: Other Press.

Ferreira, M. J. (1998). Faith and the Kierkegaardian leap. In A. Hannay, & G. D. Marino (Eds.), *The Cambridge companion to Kierkegaard* (pp. 207–234). Cambridge, England: Cambridge University Press.

Foucault, M. (1972). *The archeology of knowledge & the discourse on language* (A. M. S. Smith, trans.). New York, NY: Pantheon. (Original work published in 1969 & 1971).

Frankl, V. E. (2006). *Man's search for meaning* (I. Lasch, trans.). Boston, MA: Beacon Press. (Original work published in 1959).

Heidegger, M. (1982). *The basic problems of phenomenology* (A. Hofstadter, trans. Rev. ed.). Bloomington: Indiana University Press. (Original work published in 1975).

Heidegger, M. (2010). *Being and time* (J. Stambaugh & D. J. Schmidt, trans.). Albany: State University of New York. (Original work published in 1927).

Hoffman, I. Z. (1998). *Death anxiety and adaptation to mortality in psychoanalytic theory Ritual and spontaneity in the psychoanalytic process* (pp. 31–67). New York, NY: The Analytic Press. (Original work published in 1979).

Hoffman, I. Z. (1998). *Ritual and spontaneity in the psychoanalytic process.* Hillsdale, MI: The Analytic Press.

Husserl, E. (1970). *The crisis of European sciences and transcendental phenomenology* (D. Cairns, trans.). Evanston, IL: Northwestern University Press. (Original work published in 1937).

Husserl, E. (1977). *Phenomenological psychology: Lectures, summer semester; 1925* (J. Scanlon, trans.). The Hague, Netherlands: Martinus Nijoff. (Original work published in 1925).

Husserl, E. (1983). *Ideas pertaining to a pure phenomenology and to a phenomenological philosophy: Book one: General introduction to a pure phenomenology* (F. Kersten, trans.). New York, NY: Springer (Original work published in 1913).

Husserl, E. (1999). *Cartesian meditations* (D. Cairns, trans.). Dordrecht, Netherlands: Springer. (Original work published in 1931).

Husserl, E. (2001). *Logical investigations* (J. M. Findlay, trans.). London, England: Routledge. (Original work published in 1913).

Husserl, E. (2005). *Phantasy, image consciousness, and memory (1898–1925)* (J. B. Brough, trans.). Dordrecht, Netherlands: Springer.

Idhe, D. (2012). *Experimental phenomenology (2nd ed.): Multistabilities.* Albany: SUNY Press.

Judaken, J. (2012). Sisyphus's progeny: Existentialism in France. In J. Judaken, & R. Bernasconi (Eds.), *Situating existentialism: Key texts in context* (pp. 89–122). New York, NY: Columbia University Press.

Kahneman, D. (2011). *Thinking, fast and slow.* New York, NY: Farrar, Strauss and Giroux.

Kahneman, D., Slovic, P., & Tversky, A. (Eds.). (1982). *Judgement under uncertainty: Heuristics and biases.* Cambridge, England: Cambridge University Press.

Kahneman, D., & Tversky, A. (2000). Prospect theory: An analysis of decisions under risk. In D. Kahneman, & A. Tversky (Eds.), *Choices, values, and frames* (pp. 17–43). Cambridge, England: Cambridge University Press. (Original work published in 1979).

Kierkegaard, S. (1980). *The sickness onto death* (H. V. Hong & E. H. Hong, trans.). Princeton, NJ: Princeton University Press. (Original work published in 1849).

Kierkegaard, S. (1983). Fear and trembling (H. V. Hong & E. H. Hong, trans.). In H. V. Hong, & E. H. Hong (Eds.), *Fear and Trembling/Repetition.* Princeton, NJ: Princeton University Press. (Original work published in 1843).

Kierkegaard, S. (1992). *Concluding unscientific postscripts to unscientific fragments* (H. V. Hong & E. H. Hong, trans. Vol. II). Princeton, NJ: Princeton University Press. (Original work published in 1846).

Latour, B. (1993). *We have never been modern* (C. Porter, trans.). Cambridge, MA: Harvard University Press. (Original work published in 1991).

Lear, J. (1998). *Love and its place in nature.* New Haven, CT: Yale University Press. (Original work published in 1990).

Leary, K. (2002). Response to Layton. In S. Fairfield, L. Layton, & C. Stack (Eds.), *Bringing the plague towards a postmodern psychoanalysis* (pp. 225–231). New York, NY: Other Press.

Leffert, M. (2007a). A contemporary integration of modern and postmodern trends in psychoanalysis. *Journal of the American Psychoanalytic Association, 55,* 177–197.

Leffert, M. (2007b). Postmodernism and its impact on psychoanalysis. *Bulletin of the Menninger Clinic, 71,* 15–34.

Leffert, M. (2008). Complexity and postmodernism in contemporary theory of psychoanalytic change. *Journal of the American Academy of Psychoanalysis and Dynamic Psychiatry, 36,* 517–542.

Leffert, M. (2010). *Contemporary psychoanalytic foundations.* London, England: Routledge.

Leffert, M. (2013). *The therapeutic situation in the 21st century.* New York, NY: Routledge.

Leffert, M. (2016). *Phenomenology, uncertainty, and care in the therapeutic encounter.* New York, NY: Routledge.

Leffert, M. (2017). *Positive psychoanalysis: Aesthetics, desire, and subjective well-being.* New York, NY: Routledge.

Leffert, M. (2018). *Psychoanalysis and the birth of the self: A radical interdisciplinary approach.* London, England: Routledge.

Leffert, M. (2021). *The psychoanalysis of the absurd: Existentialism and phenomenology in contemporary psychoanalysis.* London, England: Routledge.

Lyotard, J. (1979). *The postmodern condition: A report on knowledge* (G. Bennington & B. Massumi, trans.). Minneapolis: University of Minnesota Press.

May, R. (1958). The origins and significance of the existential movement in psychology. In R. May, E. Angel, & H. F. Ellenberger (Eds.), *Existence* (pp. 3–36). New York, NY: Simon & Schuster.

May, R. (1996). *The meaning of anxiety.* New York, NY: W.W. Norton & Co. (Original work published in 1977)

May, R., Angel, E., & Ellenberger, H. F. (Eds.). (1958). *Existence: New directions in psychiatry and psychology.* New York, NY: Simon & Schuster.

McGowan, J. (1991). *Postmodernism and its critics.* Ithaca, NY: Cornell University Press.

Orange, D., Atwood, G. E., & Stolorow, R. D. (1997). *Working intersubjectively: Contextualism in psychoanalytic practice.* Hillsdale, MI: The Analytic Press.

Pulver, S. E. (2003). On the astonishing clinical irrelevance of neuroscience. *Journal of the American Psychoanalytic Association, 51,* 755–772.

Renik, O. (1993). Analytic interaction: Conceptualizing techniques in the light of the analyst's irreducible subjectivity. *Psychoanalytic Quarterly, 62,* 553–571.

Rorty, R. (1979). *Philosophy and the mirror of nature.* Princeton, NJ: Princeton University Press.

Rorty, R. (1982). *Consequences of pragmatism: Essays 1972–1980.* Minneapolis: University of Minnesota Press.

Rudden, M., & Bronstein, A. A. (2017). New educational approaches to the study of psychoanalysis. *The American Psychoanalyst: Quarterly Magazine of the American Psychoanalytic Association, 51,* 21–22.

Sartre, J.-P. (1989). No exit. In *No Exit and three other plays* (pp. 1–46). New York, NY: Vintage Books. (Original work published in 1946).

Sartre, J.-P. (2007). *Existentialism is a humanism* (C. Macomber, trans.). New Haven, CT: Yale University Press. (Original work published in 1947).

Sartre, J.-P. (2013). *Nausea* (L. Alexander, trans.). New York, NY: New Directions. (Original work published in 1938).

Sartre, J.-P. (2018). *Being and nothingness: An essay in phenomenological ontology* (S. Richmond, trans.). (Original work published in 1943).

Stern, D. B. (1997). *Unformulated experience.* Hillsdale, MI: The Analytic Press.

Stern, D. N., Sander, L. W., Nahum, J. P., Harrison, A. M., Lyons-Ruth, K., Morgan, A. C., et al. (1998). Non-interpretive mechanisms in psychoanalytic therapy: The 'something more' than interpretation. *The International Journal of Psychoanalysis, 79,* 903–921.

Stolorow, R. D. (1990). Converting psychotherapy to psychoanalysis: A critique of the underlying assumptions. *Psychoanalytic Inquiry, 10*, 119–130.

Stolorow, R. D. (2002). From drive to affectivity: Contextualizing psychological life. *Psychoanalytic Inquiry, 22*, 678–685.

Stolorow, R. D. (2011). *World, affectivity, trauma*. New York, NY: Routledge.

Stolorow, R. D., & Atwood, G. E. (1992). *Contexts of being*. Hillsdale, MI: The Analytic Press.

Stolorow, R. D., Atwood, G. E., & Brandshaft, B. (1994). *The intersubjective perspective*. Northvale, NJ: Jason Aronson.

Stolorow, R. D., Orange, D., & Atwood, G. E. (2002). *Worlds of experience: Interweaving philosophical and clinical dimensions in psychoanalysis*. New York, NY: Basic Books.

Tuckett, D., Basile, R., Birksted-Breen, D., Böhm, T., Denis, P., & Ferro, A., et al. (Eds.). (2008). *Psychoanalysis comparable and incomparable: The evolution of a method to describe and compare psychoanalytic approaches*. London, England: Routledge.

Tulving, E. (2003). Memory and consciousness. In B. J. Baars, W. P. Banks, & J. B. Newman (Eds.), *Essential sources in the scientific study of consciousness* (pp. 575–591). Cambridge, MA: MIT Press. (Original work published in 1985).

Tversky, A., & Kahneman, D. (1982). Judgment under uncertainty: Heuristics and biases. In D. Kahneman, P. Slovic, & A. Tversky (Eds.), *Judgment under uncertainty: Heuristics and biases* (pp. 3–20). Cambridge, England: Cambridge University Press. (Original work published in 1974).

Waelder, R. (2007). The principle of multiple function: Observations on over-determination (originally published 1936). *Psychoanalytic Quarterly, 76*, 75–92.

Woodward, B. (2020). *Rage*. New York, NY: Simon & Schuster.

Yalom, I. D. (1980). *Existential psychotherapy*. New York, NY: Basic Books.

Yalom, I. D. (2009). *Staring at the sun: Overcoming the terror of death*. New York, NY: Jossey-Bass.

Yalom, I. D. (2012). *Love's executioner: And other tails of psychotherapy*. New York, NY: Basic Books. (Original work published in 1989).

Chapter 2

The Evo-Devo of Phenomenology and Prephenomenology

Introduction

This second chapter was originally going to be about Postphenomenology. *Very* briefly (we will have *all* of Chapter 3 to talk about it) Postphenomenology is a rather new discipline (Idhe, 1979, 1995, 2012) that deals with, as its disciples would say, the way that technology and the devices it has produced have become integrated with Mind. I would say (e.g., Leffert, 2018), instead, that it involves how these devices have become integrated into the *Self.* I will also want to posit that these devices become *parts* of the Self, that they are constantly becoming more advanced, and that this advancement is what we would call an *Evo-Devo* of Postphenomenology.

This Postphenomenological Evo-Devo has replaced the biological Evo-Devo of us, *Homo sapiens sapiens*, the primates whose name I loosely translate as the *Wise guys*. Postphenomenological Evo-Devo is a much, much faster process: A Human Being with a personal computer in 2020 is a vastly more powerful and competent creature than one with a television set in, say, 1970 or a ledger or a map in 1700, or a Sumerian with a clay tablet and a stylus in the Mesopotamian city of Uruk during the fourth millennium BCE. (In saying this, I am positing a new definition for Postphenomenology.) We are, however, also left with further questions of how to think about the pretechnological biological process of Evo-Devo.

I believe that, in order to answer these questions, we need to posit the existence of what I will call Prephenomenology—an area that predates Phenomenology and Postphenomenology and the creation of mental artifacts. It involves, instead of technology, neurobiology. It encompasses the study of Hominin[1] Paleoanthropology with a biological back story (Leffert, 2018) dating back roughly 3,000,000 years. Technology, to be sure, exists during this period, but it is not a technology of Mind-Brain enhancement but rather a technology that acts directly on and is used by Selves to make their way in the world. Although there is a temporal, or at least an Evo-Devo component to the relations of Prephenomenology to Postphenomenology no such component exists for Phenomenology. *It* refers to the study of the Existence

DOI: 10.4324/9781003349556-3

of Human Beings, defined as *H. sapiens sapiens*. Although it does not refer to our hominin ancestors, it is present in parallel with Postphenomenology. This all will become clearer over the course of this chapter and the next.

To conceptualize the difference between Postphenomenological technology and the kinds of technology used by our various ancestors, we need to understand that we are dealing with two sorts of processes—discovery/management-refinement and invention. There does exist some degree of overlap between these two sorts of processes. Prephenomenological examples of the first sort are fire and the ability of sharp stones to cut; a Phenomenological example of the second sort is the atlatl javelin.[2] The Postphenomenological subset of this latter group encompasses inventions that involve the acquisition, creation, processing, and storage of *information*.

I want to recast Postphenomenology as a further iteration of the new science of Evo-Devo. Evo-Devo (e.g., Carey, 2012; Carroll, 2005; Leffert, 2018) integrates the disciplines of Evolution and Development, heretofore artificially separated, into a single, interreferential science. Development includes Embryology and involves a reappraisal of Ernst Haeckel's previously discarded aphorism, "Ontogeny recapitulates Phylogeny." Following Erikson (1950/1963), it continues through the life cycle as Self-World interactions continue to change one another. We will confine ourselves here to Hominin Evo-Devo. I am positing that, prior to the existence of technology (the invention and production of mental artifacts), neurobiological Evo-Devo prefigured Postphenomenology where the evolution and development of the Brain-Mind resulted in the changes in Hominins that would, beginning slowly ca. 9000 BCE, be accomplished by technological innovation. This technological innovation was of a particular kind: It produced devices and artifacts that supplemented or enhanced cognitive-emotional function.

In talking about our Existence as Human Beings, I believe we have to take Prephenomenology, Phenomenology, and Postphenomenology as linked processes, all related to the Being of Human Beings, that is, to Dasein. What separates them is not that they are ontologically different processes but only that the *apparatuses involved*—evolving biological brain, stable biological brain, and brain with integrated technology—*are different*. As long as all we had was Phenomenology and Postphenomenology we could elide the difference but, once we add Prephenomenology and Evo-Devo, that no longer works.

We are going to consider Postphenomenology in the next chapter, but first we are going to novelly integrate it into its Human prehistory. I am assuming (always a dangerous undertaking) that the bulk of my readers are largely unfamiliar with Postphenomenology and, in contrast with those who are knowledgeable about it, are unaware of just how complex and *novel* (taken in its original sense of new and unusual, not as a euphemism for wonderful) the juxtaposition in these two chapters really is. There are a number of reasons why this integration is necessary, but before laying out the plan for this discussion, we will need to define some terms. The first is the *Self.* I do not use the term in its usually constrained psychoanalytic manner or as a particular mental function but rather to refer to the Bio-Psycho-Social-Self that is embedded in World: the World of objects, of other selves, and the inner world of the microbiome (Leffert, 2021). I am going to describe the [Mind-Brain] as an aspect of the Self, much but not all of which is to be found located in the physical brain (the brackets denote my uncertainty concerning this term—considering it only as the best available). Finally, as only a *metaphor* for describing what the mind-brain consists of, I'm going to choose two terms—hardware and software. Unlike what the terms represent in computer science, the hardware and software of the mind-brain are inter-referential; the latter modifies the former. Again, I don't want to put much stock in any of these terms, except that they are necessary for discussing Postphenomenology and Neurobiology.[3]

Let me illustrate the hardware-software paradigm as it refers to the straight-forward Phenomenological statement, "I see." It involves bilateral biological hardware—two eyes, retinas, optic nerves, visual cortex, etc. But let's go on to the "*I* see" part, which is more complex. It seems that some people are born with congenital cataracts, a whitening of the lens of the eye that makes vision impossible and results in blindness. Cataracts usually appear late in life, affecting people who have had otherwise normal vision. Although the surgical removal of cataracts is quite ancient (Ascaso, Lizana, & Cristóbal, 2009)—cataracts were described in ancient Egypt ca. 2500 BC and their surgical removal is mentioned in the Babylonian Code of Hammurabi in 1750 BC—widespread cataract surgery and insertion of a synthetic lens did not come into practice until the 20th century. (The lens implant takes us into Postphenomenology.) The removal of cataracts in an older adult who was blinded by them results in the immediate return of normal vision. The surgical removal of bilateral congenital cataracts began in the early 20th century. The procedure (von Senden, 1932/1960) resulted in a curious finding. It seems that, if the surgery was performed on a child prior to the age 11 or 12, they could learn (and learning *was* required) to see for the first time. If, however, the surgery was performed later, the individual was unable to learn to see and only perceived patterns of shifting colors, the effect of which was highly dysphoric. The capacity to learn vision is very much a function of the visual cortex and it was lost at a certain point in Development.[4] In other words, vision is the product of upstream information about perception coming from the retina and downstream information about vision coming from the cerebral cortex. I am going to metaphorically treat activities like the former as hardware and those like the former as software. To put it a little differently, the Cerebral Cortex is hardware. A Smart Phone is hardware. Language is software. An App is software. The neurobiological distinction between hardware and software is a softer one than the technological one.

For example, although we know that people with intact visual apparatuses see very similar things, we cannot know if what they see is exactly the same and have good reason to suspect that it isn't. People from different cultures or vocations may very well have *Developed* different ways of perceiving particular things and *different languages* for describing what they see. Evo-Devo results in a hardware-software interaction during childhood and early adolescence that produced differing Brains. (For example, native American tribes of the Southwest and the Inuit in Alaska and Canada have developed ways of perceiving and languages to describe weather, water, rain, and snow, that are far more complex than what would be seen by the average New Yorker.)

Making sense of all of this can only follow from an interdisciplinary approach that combines empirical research—including biology, neuroscience, psychology, Phenomenology, anthropology, paleoanthropology, physics, and computer science, and deploying a much broader pallet than is customarily used by orthodox Postphenomenologists (or Psychoanalysts for that matter).

There is another element that we will have to consider, perhaps reconsider is more apt, and that is Consciousness. I have previously discussed Consciousness at length in prior volumes (Leffert, 2010, 2016, 2018), critiquing the standard psychoanalytic approaches, considering the neurobiology and the neuroscience, and updating the Phenomenology of Consciousness. It did not at first seem that still another chapter on the subject would be required. This present chapter and the one that follows changed my mind. Contrary to the considerations of authors writing in Phenomenology and Postphenomenology, it *is* necessary to consider Unconscious and Conscious relationships with experience, perception, technology, and, specifically, with mental artifacts. Also, the latest research (e.g., Nieder, Wagener, & Rinnert, 2020) suggests that Consciousness in birds and animals is not so easy to distinguish from Consciousness found in us and our Hominin ancestors. We have, for decades, relied upon Tulving's (1985/2003) tripartite model of Human anoetic, noetic, and auto-noetic Consciousness that has also had to be fleshed out to include the newer neuroscience research. We will draw on this chapter and the next one (on Postphenomenology) in a further discussion of the topic, also called "the hard problem." That said, let's get on with the present task.

Evo-Devo

Psychoanalysis has, from its infancy, awarded pride of place to "the" Unconscious and to psychological Development (the Genetic point of view in Metapsychology (Freud, 1905/1953, 1915/1957)). Only much later was physical Development and, even later, Developmental Neuroscience (Schore, 1994), added to the mix. Both Development and Evolution (Hofer, 2014) were present at the birth of Psychoanalysis and were of much interest to our founding father. We have now come to understand that any separation of the two is artificial. Development includes Embryology and Epigenetics. The hard distinction between us (*H. sapiens sapiens*) and everyone else further down the evolutionary tree is artificial and what we have referred to as *instincts* is a misnomer. Panksepp's (Panksepp & Biven, 2012) cross-mammalian studies of primary, secondary, and tertiary emotional states have shown them, "instincts," to be present in all mammals and, perhaps, in all vertebrates. In addition, the Mirror Neuron System (Gallese, Fadiga, Fogassi, & Rizzolatti, 1996), which functions as the engine of Attachment for Human Beings, was first described in Macaque Monkeys where it operates in much the same fashion as it does in us.

We are now able to say that Development *did not exist* prior to the Cambrian Period (540–485 million years ago (mya)). Until that point, all organisms were unicellular; they formed via cell division or budding and only Evolved new intracellular structures or properties. Then during a 20–25 million year period termed the Cambrian Explosion[5] (Gould, 1989), multicellular organisms burst on the scene and, and by its end, the ancestors of all living Phyla had appeared. There *had* to be a process, then, by which what started out as a single cell (or a fertilized egg) became a complex multicellular organism. This process, Development, had to subsume Embryology, Epigenesis, and postpartum growth and change. An organism that started out as a single cell had to grow into a whole collection of specialized cells that fit together nicely. That meant that cells needed to divide, become specialized in different ways, and then move around in the developing organism or embryo. "Development and its capacity to generate variation is seen as a major participant and *even a cause of Evolution*" [emphasis added] (Hofer, 2014, p. 15). The goal is plasticity, *not* the production of physically and genetically identical individuals; plasticity *makes* Evolution possible.

Until quite recently, Development was seen as an innate sequence arising out of a fully evolved genome with "no molecular/genetic mechanism for interactions with the environment to affect the course of [that genetic] development" (Hofer, 2014, p. 13). Epigenesis is, essentially, the opposite of this: We now know that just such a molecular/genetic mechanism interacts with the genome to mediate environmental effects, in the broadest sense of the term, on intrauterine (in the case of class *Mammalia*) and subsequent extra-uterine Development. Areas within a chromosome interact with the cellular environment to turn on and off other (usually adjacent) areas of the chromosome that engage in protein synthesis.

It turns out (Carroll, 2005) that mammals and birds all have roughly the same amount of DNA with much of it held in common: There is only a 5% difference between our DNA and that of the great apes. Of our DNA, only 1.5% of it codes *all* of our proteins and 3% of it is regulatory, turning the synthesis of particular proteins on and off. (The remaining 95.5% consists of redundancy and "genetic noise.") These regulatory genes are largely held in common across Phyla, with us, for example, sharing 99% of them with fruit flies and yeast cells. Evolution is not so much a product of heritable mutation as it is changes in the sequence and timing of the activation of regulatory genes: that is, Evolution occurs both as a result *of* and results *in* Development. Diverse anatomical structures are assembled from relatively few component proteins whose synthesis is turned on and off at crucially different times. Development is not, as it was first thought to be, a process designed to produce uniform adults. It (Devo) rather "operates to produce transgenerational *variation* in organisms (humans too) in response to individuals' interaction with their environment that ultimately results in evolution (Evo)" (Leffert, 2018, pp. 65–66).[6] For our purposes here, the particular point is that *Evo-Devo is the engine of Prephenomenology* in us and our hominin ancestors.

Paleoanthropology, the Evo-Devo of Human Mental Hardware: An Archaeology of the Self

How we got to be us is an exciting story. Our direct ancestor, some unknown *Australopithecus* species (literally Southern ape), appeared in Africa 4–5 mya. There is a species of *Australopithecus* that we *do* know, *A. africanus*, (African Southern Ape), that either split off from the line to become genus *Homo* 2.5–3 mya[7] (Reardon, 2012), or is our direct ancestor (Falk et al., 2000). But to backtrack for a moment: In 1924, a fossil skull fragment of what was first thought to be a baboon was found in the northern Transvaal of South Africa by Raymond Dart. What was so very unusual about the fragment was that the inside of it offered an endocast of the creature's brain and that Dart realized that he was looking at, not a baboon, but some young hominin ancestor, one that walked the earth around 2.6 mya ago; this individual had died at age 3 or 4. They named him "Taung." The fragment revealed a cast of Taung's Right Cerebral hemisphere. The position of its foramen magnum (where the spinal cord exits the skull) also strongly suggested that Taung was bipedal (Falk, 2011). One of the sutures of the skull remained unfused; fusion of skull sutures is a developmental process that happens in the great apes shortly after birth. This incomplete fusion at age 3 or 4 was consistent with the needs of what would become the evolving genus *Homo*, whose brains continue to grow and develop during childhood.

Around 3.4 mya, a gene, SRGAP2, that drives and then shuts off the growth of the Neocortex, unusually doubled (adding a slightly different daughter gene), and 2.5 mya, in an even rarer event, *it doubled again* (adding a slightly different granddaughter gene). As Reardon (2012) put it, "the stage was now set. Around 2.5 million years ago, *the erroneous duplication of a single gene* changed the course of our brains' evolution forever" (p. 10, italics added).[8]

The story gets more interesting. The SRGAP2 is conserved in all mammals with changes occurring *only* in the human lineage. The new doubled (daughter) and redoubled (granddaughter) genes inhibited the SRGAP2 shutoff, allowing for an increased period of neoteny and the continued growth and development of the brain, producing a larger, more complex cerebral cortex. The human brain, 500 cm^3 at birth, doubles in size to 1,000 cm^3 at the end of the first year of life and, ultimately, reaches 1,300 cm^3. We are talking here about the evolution of hardware. This adult brain uses 20% of the body's calories, so this 1,300 cm^3 brain is an evolutionarily expensive appliance to possess. It would not have been selected for and conserved if it wasn't important. So why do we need it? Answering this question involves a combination of informed speculation and the archaeology of neuroscience. What we know is that for such an expensive organ (its possessor requires an increased caloric intake necessitating increased foraging or hunting in order to feed it) to be evolutionarily conserved, it must convey significant survival benefits on its possessor. Were this not true, it would have been selected *against* and our brains would have evolved to be smaller than our ancestors'.

It is thought that around 3.5 mya significant climate change occurred in Southern Africa, with retreating jungles giving way to open savannas. There would have been an advantage to walking upright and being able to see farther; life would have become more complex with the need to sort out prey and predators. But the general sense is that what an individual got for the extra calories and the 1,300 cm^3 of neural tissue was a much more complex and effective social brain (e.g., Woolf, 2020) that ultimately made possible social systems, first groups of individuals and, much later, towns and cities. Social systems promoted individual and species survival.

Transitions

Let's take a step back for a moment. Falk (2016) describes three trends in the Evo-Devo of Human Beings from our primate and hominin ancestors. These changes led to delays in Development; Neoteny as compared to our primate ancestors. The first trend involves the change to upright posture and bipedal locomotion. Feet exclusively became appendages of locomotion allowing upper appendages freedom to develop more complex functions— grasping, foraging, toolmaking, etc. The second trend involves the obvious fact that human babies do *not* like being set down by themselves and make their displeasure known. This must have also been true of their ancestors as well. They sought comfort through the evolving use of signals, first through cries that adult humans reportedly find incredibly irritating or disturbing as well as a range of appealing and happy-making sounds that reward those same adults (endorphin and oxytocin release) for taking care of them. We're talking here about the Evo-Devo of the mother-child bond from secure base (Bowlby, 1988) to autonomy (Bowlby, 1973). The third trend in Evo-Devo is the marked increase in brain size during the last trimester of pregnancy and the first year of life, allowing our brains to grow to 3 to 4 times the size of those found in the *Australopiths*.

Dunbar (2016) in turn describes these trends as taking place through four phase transitions. (As we will see, I think there are more.) He is looking at a number of variables beginning with the physical situation: Skeletal remains, presence of tools, dating the site, and the paleoclimate of the time and place. He then looks at skull and hence, brain size, as it relates to that of living and extinct primates and our hominin ancestors. He uses this information to infer social group size and time budget models: the amount of time *that must be spent* in foraging, resting, social grooming, and then, later, the role of language.[9]

The first transition is from the apes to the Australopithecines occurring around 3 mya. The *Australopiths* evolved bipedal locomotion and stood erect. This was, as we have said, useful in navigating the climate change occurring in Southern Africa from jungle to open savannahs. There was little change in brain size from that of Chimpanzees (from 400 cm^3 to maybe 450 cm^3 in the Australopiths) and little change in social group size. If anything, what was noteworthy was how similar to the apes they were, rather than how different. We do know, however, that the unfused skull suture that Taung manifested at age 3 or 4 suggested the appearance of Neoteny, and that means, even if we don't know precisely how, that this Prephenomenological brain was already different from that of the old-world monkeys. It may have been roughly the same size as a chimp's brain, but it *developed differently* and, presumably, worked differently. Its development occurred through, and during, interaction with the environment. One would suspect, because of the Neoteny, that the nature of mother-child bonding had evolved and that changes in the right orbito-prefrontal cortex of the brain (Schore, 2002, 2009) had occurred. Over the course of time one of the *Australopith* species evolved into a *Homo* species that became our first hominin ancestor.

Mother-child bonding requires a particular mental function that is very important to evolving hominins: Theory of Mind (ToM) (Baron-Cohen, Tager-Flusberg, & Cohen, 2000; Main, 1991). ToM contains a description of what an individual perceives and experiences about their own Mind but also what they understand about the nature of Other Minds. Particularly, it contains an understanding that Other Minds are similar to their own. Dunbar (2016) describes how both increase as we ascend Evo-Devo through our various ancestors from the *Australopiths* to ourselves. He uses the inter-subjective experience of *Intentionality* (Brentano, 1874/1995), the experience of our own and others' capacity for intentions, for thinking, for believing, for wanting—for in other words—*mentalizing*, as a gauge of this. Mentalizing as a neural activity has been shown to require more neurons, more work, and more calories as compared to mental activities such as simple factual memory tasks. As a kind of confirmation of this hypothesis, it has also been shown that people who work at higher levels of Intentionality have larger orbital prefrontal Cerebral Cortexes.

All conscious organisms have *some* idea of the contents of their own minds (we will talk about what *kind* of Consciousness in Chapter 4). We know to include here most if not all mammals. This is first order intentionality. The ability to have ideas about what someone else has in their mind is second order intentionality. This means that someone has an idea about what someone else has in mind (formal ToM). This is followed by a recursive sequence: I think that you think that I (or someone else) am thinking (third order) and so on. Human Beings develop first order intentionality at around the first year of life, reach second order intentionality (a stage that the great apes and chimpanzees grasp for and barely reach) at age 5, and plateau at the fourth to sixth levels in their teens.[10] Although as Psychoanalysts, we never think in these terms, the Development of Intentionality can be individually or culturally impaired as a result of psychopathology. Narcissistic Personality Disorder, Narcissistic Character Disorder, and, of course, Autism (Baron-Cohen, 2000; Baron-Cohen, Leslie, & Frith, 1985) are all examples of such Developmental Psychopathology. Empathy correlates with Intentionality and, conversely, these diagnoses can limit an individual to primary Intentionality. Although this is something we can successfully treat, sometimes partially treat, we usually don't name it as such.

Given what we know about great apes and chimps, we are well within our rights in positing that the *Australopiths* with their upright gait and neoteny were at least well within second order Intentionality. Just how ascending orders of intentionality played out across hominin evolution we are unable to say beyond positing that increasingly large social brains would ascend that ladder, with Anatomically Modern Humans (AMHs) having reached four or five.[11]

The second transition is to genus *Homo*, approximately 1.8 mya. This involved a group of early hominins including Louis Leakey's *H. habilis* (handy man), the first hominin found with accompanying tools in the Olduvai Gorge in Kenya in 1962, *H. rudolfensis*, and finally the clear break with the *Australopiths* that was made by *H. ergaster*, all around the same time. In a couple of hundred thousand years, these species would come to dominate Africa and colonize Eurasia. *H. ergaster* had a larger brain and a modern long-legged human form adapted for a striding gate. They also invented the Acheulian handaxe, the crude but iconic tool that would serve humans essentially unchanged until the appearance of more modern tools around 500,000 ya. If we turn to the Prephenomenology—the change in the neural hardware as opposed to the change from cellphone to smart phone— *H. ergaster's* brain had grown to roughly 760 cm^3. Let's consider just what the extra 280 cm^3 of brain tissue bought *ergaster* and what they had to pay to get it.

We know that they were able to mount the first exodus out of Africa: *H. ergaster* remains dating from 1.8 mya were found in Georgia near the Black Sea. We don't know how this was achieved, or how long it took or how many individuals were involved. It would seem unlikely for it to have been some sort of large continuous migration: some large batch of them heading north in some kind of Long March or Biblical Exodus (many stayed behind). So, what do we know socially about *ergaster*? The social brain hypothesis tells us that brain size correlates with basic group size and that for us, it repeatedly circles 150 individuals.[12] Following the equation, ergaster's 760 cm^3 of brain tissue gets them a social group of around 75 or 80, what we understand to be, anthropologically, similar to an aboriginal *Band*. We know about Bands. They offer protection from predators, from raids from other hostile bands, and, perhaps, information exchange. I would posit that 760 cm^3 would not get them a language with syntax. If, however, they were able to sustain a multi-generational move North, they must have had, if not grammar and syntax, then names for things, nouns, proper nouns, adjectives, verbs, and adverbs. But these terms were not just *names*, they must have had *meaning*. And, absent the formal language, we locate such Meaning squarely in Prephenomenology.

Bands also associate loosely with other bands, and individuals can come and go between them. It seems that some of these *ergaster* social units, Bands, began drifting[13] North about 1.6–1.8 mya. What needs to be accounted for is the large increase in the latter's brain volume and the smaller but significant subsequent increase in *H. erectus* (first an increase of 280 cm^3 or 52% from *Australopith* to *H. ergaster*, then another 170 cm^3 for a total of 930 cm^3 in *H. erectus*: remember, we are at 1,300 cm^3). These increases required a substantial increase in caloric intake. Given that the *Australopiths'* time budgets were already stretched, how did these early *Homo* species evolve to make this possible, bearing in mind that the exodus out of Africa required even more calories and more time that had to be drawn out of their time budgets? *H. ergaster* busted the time budget of the *Australopiths*. In order to exist, a number of things had to change. We know that the larger the Brain, the larger the social group, and the larger the amount of time it was necessary to spend each day in social grooming to maintain the group. Primates rely on the endorphin release triggered by social grooming to maintain social bonding, maxing out at about 20% of the time budget equation. For *ergaster*, such an amount exceeded the time budget equation (indeed, social grooming time would have needed to *double*). We know that in Human Beings the deficit was made up by replacing social grooming with language; language being much used in primitive groups as it is with us in *gossip about* social relationships. Early *Homos* did not have formal language. With increasing brain size, time spent in social grooming that needs to vary with group size in order to maintain those groups had maxed out.

The ideal replacement in pre-language days was laughter. Human laughter is contagious and highly pleasurable. It turns out that that laughter produces a series of repetitive contractions of the diaphragm that is exhausting, and that that exhaustion results in endorphin release. As a group phenomenon, chorusing laughter, it is far more efficient than social grooming that only can involve a pair of individuals at a time. (Anecdotal reports suggest a similar function among contemporary *H. sapiens sapiens*.) As Dunbar (2016) posits, all of this made it possible to get *ergaster* on the road North without having to improve the time budget equation still further by positing the inventions of cooking and fire management.[14]

The third transition involves the appearance of archaic humans, *Homo heidelbergensis* around 600,000 ya with a brain size averaging 1,300 cm³, similar to our own. Environmental pressures (climate instability), absent during the 1,000,000+ of ergaster's long reign, drove the Evo-Devo of the new species. They, too, rapidly migrated North, reaching what is now Britain 100,000 years later. They held sway for about 200,000 years, in turn giving rise to a separate line, the Neanderthals,[15] around 300,000 ya. *They* were adapted to life in a colder, darker, Northern Europe. Further East, Heidelbergs gave rise to the Denisovans. This is all Prephenomenology. The Neanderthals had evolved larger eyes and a larger occipital cortex and visual system, customized specifically to process the low-light visual information present at higher latitudes, rather than the large frontal and temporal lobes of *H. sapiens* (AMHs), developed for increased social cognition and larger group size.

Even *with* laughter, the Heidelbergs with their big social brains would have come up about 40% short in their time budget equations. The only answer was cooking, which had a two-fold effect. It provided increased caloric intake with decreased food gathering time to meet these bigger brains' energy needs. But it also made cooking and eating into a more social activity; eating cooked, high caloric, easily digestible food is also known in primates to trigger endorphin release,[16] another factor that stabilizes larger social group size (unlike *ergasters*, the Heidelbergs, by calculation, had a social group size of 110–120). If we assume that the Heidelbergs were prelinguistic (that is, lacking grammatical speech) what other sources of endorphin release and group stabilization might there be? The answer might be group singing and percussion. We know that they possessed the mental and muscular apparatuses to control vocalization that would have been necessary for such singing. We also know (Dunbar, 2016) that present day gelada baboons live in social groups of 100–120 individuals, far larger than any of the other monkeys or apes. They sing. They have a series of melodic calls and counter-calls unlike any of these other primates. We also know, from studying ourselves, that music triggers endorphin release. We are still dealing here with a Prephenomenological hominin for whom the Phenomenological *Things Themselves*, to return to Husserl for a moment, were still quite different from what they are for us.

The fourth transition, still staying with Dunbar (2016), resulted in the appearance or AMHs (*H. sapiens*, not yet *H. sapiens sapiens*) equipped with 1,300 cm³ brains in Africa 200,000+/– ya. By 100,000 ya these modern humans had replaced the earlier hominin species in Africa, although not yet in Europe, Asia, and the Middle East (Bar-Yosef Mayer, Vandermeersch,

& Bar-Yosef, 2009) where Neanderthals, Denisovans, and some archaic humans continued to thrive. However, by 70,000 ya, in what is now known as the "Out of Africa event," they began crossing above and below the Red Sea into these areas. By 40,000 ya, they had filled Europe and gotten to Australia and, by 16,000 ya, they had, starting from Alaska, colonized all of the Americas! They did this on foot, lacking any sort of transport animal; it would seem that, along the way, these AMHs had evolved into a very different primate: us, *H. sapiens sapiens*.

These last three transitions raised two problems: how to fuel the ever-bigger brains requiring ever-bigger caloric intakes and how to socially bond the larger communities that these brains evolved to allow. Both entailed increasing time management problems that must have been socially and cognitively solved if hominins were to follow the path that would lead to us. *H. sapiens* and *H. sapiens sapiens* were up against the same time budget equations that had dogged hominins over the whole course of their 3,000,000 years of Evo-Devo. They now had 1,300 cm³ brains with large frontal and temporal cerebral lobes. These were necessary for navigating the larger social groups (now reaching Dunbar's number of 150 individuals), complex micro-societies, of which they were members. The answer had to be the development of formal language. Earlier theorists had posited that language had evolved/developed to facilitate group activities and to teach toolmaking and other crafts. An alternate theory is that language developed as a tool to enhance social bonding, a vastly more efficient one than social grooming. In keeping with this hypothesis, *H. sapiens sapiens* spend about 60% of their speech time gossiping about other individuals and relationships. Language became a tool for existing, for Being-in-World.

So, we have here a fifth transition that finally, after 6–8 million years, led to us, *H. sapiens sapiens*, the Wise Guys.[17] This did not involve a change in brain size. There is some uncertainty about when we want to date this transition as having occurred and what factors went into it.

Brain size, beginning with Taung and ending with us, is a useful rough index of the changes inherent in hominin Evo-Devo—but it is only that. The capacities of these larger brains, what they enabled individuals and, even more importantly, their social groups to do, also changed; changes that must have required more neurons, wired differently, to accomplish.

Prephenomenology

To briefly reprise the arguments on Phenomenology covered in Chapter 1, Husserl was concerned with Phenomena, the *things* in the world that we *experience*, defined by our Intersubjective Intentions, our *Intentionality*, toward them. A corollary to this hypothesis is that Phenomena differ for our various hominin ancestors: A large rock was a very different thing for *ergaster* (a crusher) that it was for AMH (the raw material from which to *manufacture* a cordiform hand ax or a spearhead).

Following Idhe (2012), "every experiencing has its reference or direction toward what is experienced, contrarily, every experienced phenomena refers to or reflects a mode of experiencing to which it is present" (p. 25). Husserl termed what is experienced a *noema* and *noesis* the mode of experiencing. This yields an equation expressing this correlation

noesis → noema

between what is experienced and the mode of experiencing. The equation is incomplete in that the experiencer, the subject, the I that is experiencing is left out. To complete it we have

(I) noesis → noema

(experiencer) experiencing → experienced

What is important to us here in Prephenomenology is that the equation involves a very different series of *I*s and very different kinds of experiencing as compared to each other and to us, *H. sapiens sapiens*.

I am positing that the three Evo-Devo trends (the change to upright posture, infant separation anxiety, and increasing brain size, Falk, 2016) and six phase transitions produced what can be best described ontologically as *Pre*phenomenology, by which I mean a process of hardware Evo-Devo that is biological (e.g., old-world monkeys to *Australopithecus* to hominins to *H. sapiens*) as opposed to technological (e.g., telegraph to telephone to pager to cell phone to smart phone). It is also a process that is Unconscious and that took place over millions of years rather than decades. Finally, as with Postphenomenology, it makes possible the creation and invention of more advanced (in this case, biological) software. The two questions we have to consider are how to make sense of the Evo-Devo of the changing brain that we have only the crudest sense of and what to make of the relation of Prephenomenology (the study of the Being of archaic hominins) to Phenomenology (the study of the Being of Human Beings).

What else can we say about Prephenomenology as compared to Phenomenology? In Heideggerian terms, we would have to be very doubtful about the possibility of *Throwness*, Being-in-Life with a conceptual understanding of Death. Since *Fallenness* represents a flight from Throwness, from a conceptualization of Death, it would also not be present. That leaves *Everydayness* as the state of Being present in hominins prior to the appearance of *H. sapiens sapiens*. They went about their lives (e.g., de Waal, 2019) in a caring but unreflective way. They knew of Death (obviously!) but their knowledge was very different than our own. For them, Death meant that someone became immobile and unresponsive, sometimes following injury, sometimes not, and their body began to smell and decay. Grief almost certainly accompanied this perception. They could observe that, after a time, this immobile, unresponsive body began to decompose and had to be disposed of in some way. There is evidence of possible burials in this period (particularly a Neanderthal cave pit in Spain), but it is contested.

We also know that the basic emotional states described by Panksepp (Panksepp & Biven, 2012)—SEEKING, FEAR, RAGE, LUST, CARE, PANIC/GRIEF, PLAY—were certainly present in primary form, possibly present in secondary form, but almost certainly not present in tertiary, cortical form. These governed behaviors and provided reasons for living. They offered gratification or failure. What was not present was any sort of awareness of or quest for *Meaning*, for the meaning of *Existence*. This would require higher levels of cognition and consciousness than were present in individuals up to and including AMHs. The neurobiology that made all this possible was something that I would call a *Prephenomenological Package*. It encompasses the Mirror Neuron System that was first elucidated in Macaque monkeys (Gallese et al., 1996) involving the Parietal Cortex, and the operations of the Right Preorbital Frontal Cortex powering Attachment (de Waal, 2019; Schore, 2009), also present in higher primates. Over the course of Evo-Devo that led to us, *H. sapiens sapiens*, these systems were coopted for higher cognitive and emotional purposes.

Dunbar (1992, 1993, 2016) has studied the trends and phase transitions in Paleoanthropology or, as we might now say, Prephenomenology. He suggests (1992) that there are two sorts of hypotheses advanced to explain why primates have evolved ever larger brains as compared to other mammals: the ecological and the social. The former has to do with factors like climate change and attendant trends like the environmental shift from jungle to savannah to winter discussed above, requiring increasingly creative adaptability, while the latter has to do with correlations between social group size and neocortical volume. Social group size was found to correlate with relative neocortical size, while ecological variables did not. This Social Brain hypothesis "provides us with a precise equation for predicting social group size from brain size" (Dunbar, 2016, p. 66). It favored a Social Intellect theory of primate and later hominin Evo-Devo. In it, the number of neocortical neurons present results in a theoretical limit on the number of social relationships an individual can simultaneously keep track of and the cohesive group size a primate species can maintain as a result. When a group breaches that number, it becomes brittle and begins to fragment. Dunbar determined that for *H. sapiens sapiens* (us again) that number is 150, eponymously christened Dunbar's Number. He found that the number held up across contemporary societies regardless of their complexity or primitivity and that it also held up historically and prehistorically through Neolithic times. It was the same for modern humans, and similar in hunter-gatherer and agrarian societies.

There is also a clinical feature of group size that we are not much accustomed to thinking about. It involves the psychopathology of object relations. Everyone is not necessarily capable, for reasons that we as clinicians know very well, of maintaining these social connections, and this may become a suitable subject for a therapeutic discourse. We now find ourselves living on a planet with 7 billion Human Beings connected in all kinds of seemingly different ways. Dunbar's number (150) becomes a measure of how many other Human Beings we can think ourselves as being individually connected to.

There are other ways that have been developed independently to understand and document these social connections that are so essential to an understanding of the Evo-Devo of Human Beings. The most important of these is Social Network Theory, in which the work of Christakis and Fowler (2009) and Barabási (2003, 2005a, 2005b) are prominent. I have discussed their work several times in the past (e.g., Leffert, 2013) but need to do so again, briefly, because it offers a bridge between the small group social bonding issues Dunbar (2016) is talking about in Prephenomenology and what we find ourselves dealing with Phenomenologically today.

We now live as members of multiple overlapping social groups of widely varying sizes. This situation allows some individuals to exist *in* society with very few social connections involving infrequent individual contacts—difficult but not impossible to do in less populous, less advanced cultures.

Where this observation fits in with our roles as therapists speaks to the différance between one-person and two-person psychologies, between the observer and the participant-observer. Conversation thus offers a powerful therapeutic tool to facilitate social learning in our patients, one that is often ignored or taken for granted. To put it very simply: *Therapeutic Conversation teaches Social Bonding.* The act of conversing in this way is itself a modality of Therapeutic Action. As therapists, we can mediate our isolated patients' increasing participation in social networks if we are able to conceptualize part of what we do in that way. I have found this observation to be even more obvious in this time of Plague. As 2020 wore on, anxiety and anger concerning the presidential elections and the Trump presidency pretty much fused with those of the pandemic and its management, or lack thereof. Conversely, the 74,000,000 Americans who voted for Trump experience themselves as more isolated by the results of this election they see as rigged and view the dangers of COVID as *vastly* overstated.

My patients seemed to fall into three groups[18] in the ways in which they make use of therapy and analysis during COVID. There was no particular correlation between these response types and diagnosis, intensity of transference, or frequency and duration of therapy. A small number of patients, deeply involved in the analysis of current life issues and their childhood roots, spent nearly all of their hours continuing to work on these issues, not mentioning the elections at all and the Plague only in passing.

There were a number of patients who seemed to need to spend nearly all of their time on the pandemic, their anxieties about the upcoming elections, and, later, the civic unrest that followed. More of my patients who lived alone fell in this group as did the few who were on the medical front lines.

We mostly explored these issues and the potential for existential collapse that they foretold. Whatever else they were dealing with, this was quite simply PTSD. I thought it best to meet these patients where they were and to meet them as a medical doctor as well as a Psychoanalyst and a Psychotherapist. This meant a Phenomenological Discourse about the situation we found ourselves in, reaching for present-day rather than genetic interpretations, talking, quite consciously, more about my own emotional reactions to what was happening in the world than I was usually wont to do. My plan here was to offer myself as a useable COVID-experiencing object that could be internalized. I talked with them about social isolation and mask-wearing not as good public health practices as they were spoken of in the media (and which of course they were) but as things that would reliably keep them safe. While uncertain about the therapeutic efficacy of doing so, I found that all of my patients' anxieties about contracting the disease (as of this writing, I believe one patient probably had COVID, one did have it, and no others have tested positive[19]) were greatly lessened, while anxiety about the societal situation remained significant but variable. This was something about which I could only share my feelings with them. I considered it therapeutic to do so, offering an example of affect regulation at a time of an actual trauma (the Plague and the election) we were all experiencing as destabilizing.

About half of my patients are working on both. They continue to work on core intrapsychic and interpersonal issues while also expressing anxiety about the then upcoming elections and the future of the country. Their experiences of and reaction to the Plague were the same as the other groups of patients, mostly reacting to the ways in which social isolation resulted in their having to curtail their lives. One patient, a bipolar man in his 30s who I have seen for two courses of therapy, one during adolescence and another begun recently, has struggled with internalized, self-directed anger. The anger, appropriately directed at his parents, could not remain there and, once internalized, became self-destructive. He hated himself for not being able to get on with his life. He began putting himself at increased risk, going to bars and restaurants and not social-distancing. I actively interpreted what he was choosing to do to himself and how it had more to do with what he wanted to do to the parents who had traumatized him in childhood and adolescence. As of this writing, it remains very much a work in progress.

I want to stress that my experience with my patients and myself is in no way representative of American society, or global society for that matter, in 2020. There are a number of reasons for this. Neither my particular patients nor I are financially stressed by the Pandemic beyond what we might usually experience. None of my patients have young, school-aged children that require care or home-schooling (anecdotally, the burdens faced by *these* parents during the Pandemic are extreme). Indeed, studies showing intense and pathological overuse of social media (e.g., Zhong, Huang, & Liu, 2021) as a result of depression and secondary trauma are beginning to appear (and will be considered below in terms of Postphenomenology). Again, my patients do not manifest this. In the best Phenomenological terms, we have been talking about the here-and-now effects of World on Self. Having done so, we can consider (it is unproveable) the extent to which we are also seeing the ameliorative effects of intensive psychotherapy and psychoanalysis on the effects of the pandemic. Let's now, however, return to Paleoanthropology and Prephenomenology.

Becoming Us—The Passing of Prephenomenology and the Advent of Phenomenology

How, exactly, did our Hominin ancestors (including AMH) become us, *H. sapiens sapiens*? The answer to this question remains somewhat murky with two lines of hypotheses. This is the *fifth* transition. We do know that our story begins in Africa (it *is* now our story and us that we're talking about). One hypothesis, based on recent research, finds AMHs appearing all over Africa very roughly 200,000 ± 50,000 years ago. They appeared to coexist with other hominin species.

As Mithen (1994) put it, things started to happen for AMH with the transition from the Middle (300,000–50,000 ya) to the Upper Paleolithic (50,000–12,000 ya).

> Changes in the archaeological record that may reflect the first appearance of *fully modern cognition* [emphasis added] appear after c. 50,000 BP [before the present] with the start of the Upper Paleolithic. Most notably, we see the introduction of bone, antler and ivory technologies, the creation of personal ornaments and art, a greater degree of form imposed onto stone tools, a more rapid turnover of artifact types, greater degrees of hunting specialization and the colonization of arid regions.
>
> (p. 32)

The whole of this is referred to as the "Upper Paleolithic Package." It is our first hypothesis concerning the Evo-Devo of us. Mellars (2005) offers a similar, more detailed account of these changes. He refers to it (11 years of research after Mithen) as an "explosion of symbolic behavior and expression," that it was accompanied by evidence (on bone or ivory) of symbolic notation systems, and that it is "inconceivable" without the presence of highly evolved language (signs, symbols, and syntax).

We really have no idea what made the package possible. We can say that there must have been a qualitative change in our cognitive abilities, but we don't know how this came about, and the 1,300 cm^3 brain we were running appears to have remained physically unchanged. Up to this point, we have explained change in terms of the time budget equation and increasing brain size. Perhaps, the explanation lies in the concept that we have used in contemporary times to explain functional changes in the brains of *H. sapiens sapiens*, that is, *Neuroplasticity* (Doidge, 2007, 2015). We know that our brains have developed capacities to do things that they were not originally wired to do. An example of this that we will get into in the next chapter is writing. (I will argue that writing is actually one of the beginnings of Postphenomenology.) Writing Developed (an example of Devo, not Evo-Devo) after our brains reached their current (final?) form. It then changed certain areas of the brain to perform it, and if incapacitated by, for example, stroke, other areas could take over. So, perhaps, the switch from Evo-Devo to pure Devo is what characterizes the changes of the Upper Paleolithic Package and Beyond.

Then something happened. The second hypothesis is that a relatively small number (anywhere from the hundreds to the thousands) of breeding pairs of *H. sapiens sapiens*, the Wise guys, if you will, appeared in Southern Africa roughly 70,000 years ago (the exact date is contested) and proceeded by migration[20] to colonize Eurasia. In the process, they encountered Neanderthals and Denisovans, with whom they interbred to a limited extent. They appeared simultaneously across *Europe* as evidenced in the archaeological record of 40–50,000 ya. There will be more to say about this in Chapter 4 when we talk about the Evo-Devo of consciousness.

To continue our speculations, what more, if anything, can we say now about the Evo-Devo of the neuropsychological hardware that accompanied the appearance of the Upper Paleolithic Package? First of all, it behooves us to admit that we are at something of a disadvantage trying to understand the neuropsychological Evo-Devo as compared to understanding the appearance of the *physical* evidence of the Upper Paleolithic Package. *That* research is solidly grounded in Paleoarchaeology: Skeletal remains and artifacts are collected, approximately dated, and described Phenomenologically as the things themselves. In other words, if a tool is more elegantly made in Europe 50,000 ya than one in Africa 100,000 ya, then that's simply what it is—we can't immediately say anything about the brain of the individual who made the elegant tool as compared to the earlier one. We can speculate, and that's what it is, conjecture, about the tastes, preferences, and sensorimotor capabilities of the toolmaker. What would drive the creation of an elegant tool? The two possibilities, not mutually exclusive, are that the tool is more efficient and that it is more aesthetically pleasing. (Mellars' (2005) conclusions about symbolism, expression, and language, although drawing on Dunbar's (1993), and Mithen's (1994) work on the appearance of "fully modern cognition" concern mental function, perhaps mental *software?*) What we want to do is to speculate, and it *is* speculation, about the Meaning of those changes and what they might say about those cognitive abilities of the Hominins who made them.

The first of our hypotheses about those abilities is that the coevolution of neocortical size, group size, and language (Dunbar, 2016) and the appearance of the Upper Paleolithic Package (Mellars, 2005) must have been accompanied by a *fundamental change in Consciousness*. We will defer a full exploration of that change as well as what came before it to Chapter 4. For any discussion of Prephenomenology, we do have to say something about the role and nature of Consciousness in these wielders of the Package. What we find in the archaeological record is evidence of reflective and self-reflective thought.[21] The evidence is three-fold: artifacts, cave art, and burial practices.

For example, I own an elegantly made cordiform flint hand ax (the basic tool of the stone age dating from about 60,000 ya) and a much cruder smaller one from around 40,000 ya. Both come from the Dordogne a department of Southwestern France rich in prehistoric remains and artifacts, dating back as much as 200,000 years (in my collection I have a hand ax from these early times that is little more than a flake of chert). I also own a much larger hand ax that requires both hands to wield it—*it* comes from North Africa, maybe 100,000 ago, and is a tool purposed for heavy work. Although crude, it shows evidence of several symmetrical broad facets and displays a primitive elegance. Unlike the chert flake ax that is a curiosity, I *like* this one. A critical piece of all archaeological study is *context*, how something recovered from the past is *situated*. It turns out that the cordiform ax and the large two-handed one were found among other artifacts and animal remains in what might be called general living situations. Now, the circumstances that led to an *intact* tool, as these three are, being abandoned are always cause for speculation. We simply don't know.

Let's consider the smaller, more modern, but cruder hand ax. It has an interesting context. It's about 40,000 years old (the technology to make better ones already existed for many thousands of years). First, such intact little axes are quite common while abandoned broken ones are never found. Second, multiple axes are found together, pounded in the ground to form circles. If we want to speculate about them, they can only have had a ceremonial function, and that can only mean a religious purpose. So, these Wise guys were at the least ritualistic in a religious sort of way.

Cave painting, beginning ca. 50,000 ya[22] also points to an extant religious function. They present fully realized animal paintings, negative images of human hands, and human stick figures (no fully realized images) of Human Beings. While some of these images are found in shallow caves that were used as living areas, others are located in much deeper, narrower caves, not living spaces, that had insufficient oxygen to support many humans for any length of time. There is no light in these depths, of course; archaeological evidence reveals that the artists brought simple lamps that burned animal fat with them so they could see to paint and draw. These deep caves show no evidence of any sort of habitation. The paintings were either made and abandoned, or rarely visited, we just don't know. They may well have been made and left for some supernatural purpose, again, we don't know for sure. It is easy to think of the handprints as artist signatures, the beautiful animal paintings as thanks or hopes for successful hunts, and the human stick figures as expressing some sort of prohibition against drawing humans with the same skill as drawing animals. Maybe to draw a living creature representatively was to kill it, to wish it dead, or to seek its death in a successful hunt—all things that wouldn't be done with humans. We know that Native Americans, confronted with photography in the 19th century, first believed that the images were life- or soul-stealing. The possibilities here are numerous, fascinating, and unknowable.

The treatment of the ill or the dead is a complex matter. Morbidity practices (Pettitt, 2010) that involve investigation, placement, dragging of the morbidly ill or the dead, sometimes accompanied by ritual cannibalism, are found in modern primates: chimpanzees and some apes. We are left with the question of how these (probable) morbidity practices among the *Australopiths* advanced to *mortuary* practices in Paleolithic hominins. While of great *archaeological* interest what *we* are interested in is figuring out what these different practices tell us about the hominins who performed them and what they thought about death, what happens after it, and when, Prephenomenologically, they started thinking about it.

Symbolic mortuary and caching (burial) practices appeared in Europe with the Upper Paleolithic Package around 50,000 ya.[23] Archaeologists posit that deliberate burials are sufficient evidence for the belief in the existence of an afterlife and that the inclusion of grave goods implies that the dead will need these things in that life. These practices sometimes included the application of ochre pigment to the body and burial with various objects, tools, weapons, and jewelry. These practices strongly suggest that the *H. sapiens sapiens* of the time were reflectively engaging the subject of death and that it mattered a lot to them. If these practices represent attempts to deal with the loss of loved ones, friends (or enemies), what Death is for someone, and what it is to undergo oneself, it is our increased cognitive power that frames such questions and makes them so urgent. (They remain so.) Observationally, the body decays and disintegrates (somewhat later, burials sometimes took place in the floors of living spaces as a means of keeping the lost ones with the family). The question we began to struggle with was what happened to the person when death occurred and the body became unresponsive and decayed. The roots of the mind-body problem that Descartes eventually formulated seem to lie in these probably Upper Paleolithic (or certainly Mesolithic) questions. We still don't have happy answers to these questions; our ancestors began with the belief in an afterlife, that is, some form of immortality, and, only quite recently, the acknowledgement by some of us that death of the body and death of the Self are one in the same. In Phenomenology, Kierkegaard took up the former (1849/1980) and Heidegger (1927/2010), a half-century later, engaged the latter. (Yalom (2009) offers an elegant subjective formulation of the problem.) In other words, roughly 50,000 ya, a naive Phenomenology entered Human Being *there*, that is, Dasein. It was driven by increasing cognitive ability and living in Europe, a much more complex environment than the African Savannahs.

There is of course an expansive literature on the origins of religion but, for our Paleoanthropological purposes, an understanding of the role of religion in the Evo-Devo of *H. sapiens sapiens*, we are interested in two broad issues. Early religious experience, which begins to be documentable (this does not mean it had no prior existence) in the Neolithic (Dunbar, 2016), is associated with sacred spaces; the first is shamanistic, involving some kind of a led experience while later (more advanced?) experience involves a place set aside for a shared *group* experience (back to Dunbar's number). Dunbar saw the appearance of religious experience as an element of human behavior that evolved to stabilize social group size. This is a process explanation of the appearance of religion (its invention, really) but there also exists an epistemological function that I believe existed side-by-side with it. This involved the umbrella issue of unknowability and Death—an issue that, to a somewhat lesser extent, still troubles us today.

Second, there was also another purpose. Fifty thousand years or so ago, we faced frightening life-threatening, or seemingly life-threatening, events that were unpredictable or incomprehensible. (We still face such experiences today; pandemics are just one example of them.) They ranged from relatively short-term, rapidly appearing events like sudden storms, forest fires, or eclipses to longer-term events like vanishing game and failed hunts, or changing climate.[24] We were probably capable of wielding the Representativeness or Availability Heuristics (Tversky & Kahneman, 1974/1982) but they were of no help here. The narrative memories of older members of the social group were sometimes of help but often weren't. Our response was to look for causality and, when that failed, to turn to the supernatural and then the development of ritual (either positive or negative) to invoke it or hold it in abeyance. Something including a combination of badness and evil also was sometimes imagined to be involved.[25] The proto-concept was that, if we could not predict or ward off such events, some higher order of individual, who was usually male and very much like us, could, and that pleasing or placating such creatures would or could solve the problem. These *social* rituals also entrusted power to religious leaders, who then struggled to maintain and expand it *for its own sake* (just as is often the case today).

The point is that these *H. sapiens sapiens*, these wielders of the Upper Paleolithic Package, *are* us. If you had the use of a time machine, went back to 50,000 BCE. France, found an infant whose parents had just been killed accidentally, brought the baby back to the present, and let it be adopted and raised by unknowing parents, the child would grow up to be just like us and *no one would ever know*. At this point, the modern Bio-Psycho-Social Self had become stable, *Pre*phenomenology has come to an end, and this Self could best be understood in Phenomenological terms.

There is still another phase transition, which I will number as the sixth[26] (Dunbar, 2016, ignoring the appearance of the Upper Paleolithic Package 50,000 ya calls it the fifth). It occurred roughly 12,000 ya at the beginning of the Holocene—the current geological epoch in which we live. *It* began following a millennial period or reglaciation, a "little ice age," termed the Younger Dryas. What happened to us at this time was that we began to build and settle in little villages in the Levant and the Fertile Crescent. It is not entirely clear whether, as Dunbar posits, village settlement preceded the invention of agriculture, requiring the latter to maintain them, or accompanied it. It is thought that the founding of villages was for purposes of protection against attack (human remains, through the Neolithic, demonstrate a stable rate of violent death due to warfare of 15%).

We do know that within 2,000 years walled cities such as Çatal Hüyük and Göbekli Tepe in what is now Turkey, and Jericho in modern Israel had appeared, boasting as many as 5,000 inhabitants and structured for defense. A Neolithic Package had appeared consisting of agriculture, settlements with rectangular rooms, polished stone tools and weapons, sewn and later woven clothing, and, in general, a refinement of the Paleolithic Package.

In the ascending hierarchy of social bonding practices (mutual grooming to shared laughter to gossip), Dunbar adds feasting accompanied by alcoholic beverages to hold larger groups together. There is archaeological evidence of the facilities and utensils with which to prepare such large group meals along with dedicated sites in which to conduct them. We see feasting in modern primitive societies taking place for similar purposes as well as in our contemporary "advanced" cultures (the food at such contemporary festivities is, alas, not what it once was). They serve cohesive social purposes as well as celebrating family transitions.

It is important to recognize that the settlement of villages and urbanization were not smooth processes (Woolf, 2020) as one sees when some invention is found to be so useful and necessary that it becomes permanently established. Villages and cities were constantly forming, collapsing, and reforming elsewhere or, sometimes, in the same place. There was a drive to form such groups that we will discuss shortly. It was not until the second round of urbanization, beginning in the Iron Age around 800 BCE, that these trends became permanent. The factor to be understood here involves Social Network Theory (Christakis & Fowler, 2009), something I have discussed a number of times (bear with me) and will briefly reprise here.

The Devo of Phenomenology

Whichever of these hypotheses about dates (50,000 or 12,000 years ago) is correct, we at some point became us and there was a shift from Evo-Devo to, for the present, Devo. An Indo-European world of villages appeared from roughly 9000–6000 BCE with the first Bronze Age cities appearing in the late fourth and early third millennia BCE. For poorly understood reasons, there occurred a generalized urban collapse in about the 12th century BCE (Cline, 2014), a kind of Dark Ages lasting about 400 years, and a rebirth of (this time) Iron Age cities around 800 BCE. Urbanization has persisted since then.[27]

We also went from a Prephenomenology to a Phenomenology of Explanation of Being and Existentialism (a search for Meaning as an abbreviated description). Phenomenology prioritizes Consciousness and its central focus on *Appearance* and *Intention*. In doing so, it abjures Metaphysics, offering a framework that is at once at odds with orthodox psychoanalysis theories that, in contrast, prioritize Metapsychology, assigning to them putative *Depth*. There is an immediate problem with these terms, at least with their usage since the Enlightenment. *Appearance* has been taken as implying superficiality and the contrasting presence of a superior *Depth*. Freud certainly founded psychoanalysis on such a premise that also equated depth with Meaning. Psychoanalysts and, to a lesser extent, Psychotherapists are implicitly and at times explicitly trained to meet Appearance with skepticism, albeit a benign skepticism. Again, the Existentialists (May, 1958; May, Angel, & Ellenberger, 1958; Yalom, 1980) and the Intersubjectivists (Stolorow, 2002, 2011; Stolorow, Orange, & Atwood, 2002), in their return to Phenomenology did away with the concepts of psychological depth and hidden meanings in favor of the Phenomenological concept that reality was always fully deployed and available for consideration. I added to this (Leffert, 2021) the formulation that Temporality or Historicity, concepts that were sketched but not explored by Heidegger (1975/1982, 1927/2010), were more ontologically sound than Depth.

Phenomenology, to recapitulate, takes up the objective study of subjective being, the Being of Human Beings. Being-in-World, Being *There*, Dasein. It has physical and temporal dimensions. It is the study of *Experience*, a study that must also consider the *Meaning* of the Experience *to the Subject*. Intersubjectivity provides objective stabilization of subjective experience except, and it is a *very big except*, that such stabilization can be incapacitated by the subject's psychopathology. This is a Phenomenological way of describing most of what we address as therapists: the treatment of systematic errors in the appraisal of Existence that led to Absurdity.

The roots of such errors often lie in metanarrative formation (Leffert, 2010), which ceases to be a problem in a pure Phenomenology (Husserl, 1913/1983). Jared is a 45-year-old philanthropist whose family wealth precluded any need to work and masked an overwhelming anxiety about failing at any career he might try. The eldest child of physically abusive and at times sexually overstimulating parents, he focused his Being-in-World on adhering to perhaps 25 or 30 axioms that he deemed the beneficial takeaways from a series of mostly childhood experiences. These had generated their own metanarratives, as, for example, in the face of conflict adhere to your original ideas no matter what, because they will be proven right (Jared was occasionally proven right and forgot the majority of times in which he wasn't). The metanarratives were marshalled in ongoing arguments with his parents even though they had been dead for a couple of decades. Later, they were marshalled in his analysis as reasons to avoid change. Separation from the ambivalently held parents became the central task of the analysis, one which a part of Jared strenuously opposed. This Resistance, a term that I rarely use because of its power implications (Leffert, 2013), did ultimately respond to my efforts to first interpret it and then recruit him into a partnership in which we could deal with it *together*.

But the Phenomenology of the first half of the 20th century could no longer work; our ever-expanding understanding of the Neurosciences had outdistanced its premise of an unanchored Consciousness. This did not, however, do away with Phenomenology: Husserl's Things Themselves had simply become ontologically more complex. One of the ways of describing this change was a need to *Naturalize Phenomenology*. Put a little differently, what is required is an interdisciplinary account of Phenomenology (and of Pre- and Postphenomenology as well, for that matter); one cannot consider a pure Phenomenology without also taking up the ontologies of neuroscience and the social sciences.

Naturalization brought with it a change in the strategies necessary to explain *Phenomena*. I believe, as this chapter and the preceding one should already testify to, that the task of naturalizing Phenomenology goes far beyond finding a place for Cognitive Science (e.g., Petitot, Varela, Pachoud, & Roy, 1999) within it and that human Evo-Devo must offer a part of the answer. What we have are new ways of understanding Mind and Brain, particularly the Social Brain: the Right Prefrontal Cortex, Cortical Midline Structures, and the Mirror Neuron System. These existed before we became us and were part of what I have termed a Prephenomenological Package. The Mirror Neuron System and the Prefrontal Cortex were coopted Phenomenally in *H. sapiens sapiens* as systems used in the appraisal of Intersubjective Appearance and Meaning.

We are interested in the role of the movement of information in Mind as the basis of Phenomenal reflection. This movement can be described in both cognitive and neurobiological terms. Nagel (1970) offers a kind of standard for the existence of a Phenomenal inquiry in the question: "What is it like to…?" The question can be Nagel's original one of "What is it like to be a bat?" (p. 394) or "What is it like to be me (or you)?" Or What is it like to imagine a red barn? One can then, with the aid of functional Magnetic Resonance Imaging (fMRI) see what area(s) of the brain light up when these questions are asked. We also make use of empathy and imagination to answer these questions, at times merging into Heuristics and Biases. To naturalize the movement of information in Mind, it involves the use of the Mirror Neuron System and the Right Orbito-Frontal Cortex. Nagel's question serves as a *collector of Phenomenological Data*. This is not as removed from what we do in the consulting room as you might at first think. We can, in fact, use it to collect data about a patient whenever we want, and, if we then fall back on a process of Intersubjective Validation, we can see what is amiss.[28]

In the process of naturalizing Phenomenology, we must confront the fact that much of it involves processes taking place outside of our awareness, that is, Unconscious Processes. At first glance, this would seem to fly in the face of what Phenomenology is all about; it does not. Husserl and Heidegger objected to the idea of a mind governed by processes barred from Consciousness by Repression. Their concepts of Consciousness and Unconsciousness were, in effect, pre-neuroscientific (as they were pre-naturalistic), and their critiques of a Phenomenological Unconscious were similarly flawed. If we want to understand the latter, we will have to discuss Social Network Theory (Christakis, 2019; Christakis & Fowler, 2009) which is the endpoint of the Evo-Devo of social bond formation, beginning with the *Australopiths*, that Dunbar (2016) has been talking about.

The human Self is a more-or-less-stable, disautonomous entity embedded in a slowly changing (Leffert, 2013) social matrix. The individuals who make up such a social network are termed *nodes*. The number of connections they have with each other varies; they can be bi-directional or unidirectional. Information and behavior spreads over these connections and is referred to as *contagion*.[29] A member of a network that is being looked at is referred to as an *ego* and nodes that are connected to and may influence egos are called *alters*. Chains of alters diminishingly influence an alter through three degrees of separation. Network behavior is always unconscious; the nodes are referred to as *zero intelligence units*.[30] Geographic distance per se does not seem to limit the degree of contagion; it is much reinforced by elements that we will see are Postphenomenological. These processes are describing a naturalizing Phenomenology. Social Networks exist in various sizes. Most of us know about 150 people (Dunbar's number, what else is new?), some of whom we see or communicate with frequently, others once or twice a year. However, we are also members of multiple larger networks (temporary, intermediate, or permanent) numbering in the thousands, millions, or even billions. 30,000 nodes attend a baseball game. They form a temporary network, part of the larger networks comprising all of the fans of the two teams. The nodes can spontaneously stand up and sit down, making up a "human wave" that advances clockwise (always clockwise, probably for the same reason clockwise *is* clockwise). A functioning Mirror Neuron System is required for a node to participate in the wave, to experience the standing and sitting back first in the alters, then in the Self. Although it has not been studied, we would expect that individuals on the autistic spectrum would not participate in waves and probably be incapable of other network practices as well.

Christakis and Fowler (2009) describe these very large Social Networks as Superorganisms, whose behaviors and contagions are often beyond the perceptions of individual nodes. Superorganisms in particular transmit contagion about moral action (Aunger, 2017), values, and tastes, some positive and some, unfortunately, highly negative. Nazi Germany and Pogroms are examples of the latter in large Superorganisms, lynching in smaller ones, probably ranging down to Dunbar's number. The recent terrorist attacks on the US Capitol are also an example, demonstrating how a mob can sometimes recruit itself. Christakis (2019) writes about the evolutionary origins of Superorganisms and their potential to do good. St. Augustine's definition of a people as "a multitude defined by the common objects of their love" is of particular relevance here. We possess an inherited capacity and desire (Evo) to form ourselves into groups small (150) and large (up to 10^9+) that can be shaped by leaders for good or ill (Devo). Much of these processes are Unconscious. Another way of looking at this is that these large social networks, behaving at times differently from the collection of nodes that make them up, influence who we are or become; they modify Selves temporarily or permanently; they change Appearance and Intention. In other words, they are Phenomenal structures, and understanding them serves to Naturalize Phenomenology.

As of this writing (January of 2021), the Superorganism that is America hangs in the balance. This is the culmination of a trend building over decades and finally activated by the power of a charismatic leader. There has been a violent separation of groups of nodes that will either lead to a cleavage into two Superorganisms (perhaps it already has) or else fall back into a single entity if our evolved social tendency to adhere into groups gains the upper hand. We are seeing this possibility in the presence of an expanding literature (Marche, 2022; Walter, 2022) on the possibility of civil wars occurring in the United [sic] States. By the time this book is published, we will all have a better answer as to which it will be.

To summarize, what am I trying to say about Phenomenology and its Naturalization here? First, *H. sapiens sapiens* are the only Phenomenal creatures, able to pass the test of asking the question, "What is it like to be a…?" Our ancestors and at least some higher mammals know (Noetic Consciousness) something *about* What it's like to be a… *but they are unable to ask the question*. They are unable to collect Phenomenal data, which involves Appearance and Intention, both of which in early 20th century Phenomenology were by definition Conscious, but we now know (a naturalizing constituent) also involve elements that are not part of a subject's awareness.

Here are some examples of very different sorts of Phenomenal data. What is it like to be a bat, who perceives the world ultrasonically? What is it like to be a Navaho Native American with 30 different words for rain? And what is it like to be an adult Human Being who has suffered extreme physical abuse as a child? Using Nagel's (1970) collector, Phenomenality does not differ from Subjectivity and provides a foundation for Intersubjectivity. Both very much serve to define *Experience*. Over the past few decades there has been a growing awareness of something else that is beyond Phenomenology that has come to be termed Postphenomenology (Idhe, 1995), and it is to this that we will now turn.

Notes

1 Following Dunbar (2016), I am using the term *hominin* to signify us (*H. sapiens sapiens*) and the various now-extinct archaic members of genus *Homo* dating back as much as 3,000,000 years. Whether the old-world monkeys of genus Pan or the extinct *Australopiths* should be included in the group remains much contested.

2 An atlatl javelin is a spear that is seated at the end of a throwing lever, the atlatl. Effectively increasing the length of the throwing arm, the atlatl allows the hunter or warrior to much increase the range and velocity of a spear throw.

3 In contrast to Prephenomenology, the terms hardware and software apply in their usual form to the technology of the mechanical devices whose invention has taken us into Postphenomenology as it is usually described (Idhe, 1990). Smart phones, for example, are composed of hardware that has been programmed with software in the usual manner; new editions of software can be installed that modify the way such devices function.

4 This developmentally paralleled a loss in neuroplasticity to a normal process of pruning in which about a quarter of the brain's neurons are lost in pre- or early adolescence, presumably because they were not in use. (Neurons are metabolically expensive to maintain if they serve no function.)

5 Recent work (as often happens) now suggests that these organisms indeed existed some millions of years earlier. While a problem for paleontologists, it doesn't affect our thinking about the appearance of Development, only the precise point in time that it appeared.

6 This short summary of the subject tells enough of the story for our purposes here. For a more complete account, see Leffert (2018), chapter three.

7 Around 2.5–3 mya ago the Evo-Devo line that led to us progressed from Australopithecus species to *Homo* species.

8 Given the adaptive results of this error, one has to wonder if some *as yet unknown process* is able to drive such doubling.

9 Time budget models are of great significance in understanding hominin Evo-Devo. The fact that these early species existed meant that they had to have ways of making ends meet, so to speak, which gives us a powerful tool for understanding their lives.

10 None of this precludes errors in grasping intentions, nor do such errors, if they are non-systemic, speak to failures in Intentionality.

11 If Intentionality (in monkeys, chimpanzees and orangs, and humans) is plotted against brain size, a straight line results. This *suggests* that neural volume is directly related to mentalizing competence, allowing us to hypothesize about Intentionality in our various hominin ancestors.

12 This is true (Dunbar, 2016, pp. 70–71) for Neolithic villages, Roman military units, Hunter-gatherers, Facebook friends, or modern US Army companies.

13 We know nothing about this drifting. If not continuous, did it take decades (impossible), centuries (unlikely), millennia (possibly), or was it more like a 100,000 y? Was it climate-driven? Migrations occurred in the context of a broad climate shift that produced wetter landscapes and large lakes in East Africa, the area of today's Kenya and the Sudan. This could have led initially to migrations north into newly habitable

territories. These lakes would then suddenly dry up, producing further migrations before they reformed, possibly creating a kind of people pump that drove some *ergaster* up and out of Africa altogether. Did it involve a coherent group of Bands or a sequential series of Band groups? We simply have no idea.

14 A handful of examples of scorched ground and bone suggesting opportunistic use rather than management of fire date as far back as 1,000,000 ya; *regular* evidence of cooking and fire management appeared around 400,000 ya. What began as casual cooking morphed into regular daily cooking. Again, it is important to think in terms of the evolved cognitive capacity that made this invention possible.

15 The Neanderthals became extinct without evolutionary issue, but we carry on average 2% of their DNA.

16 We know that we feel replete and warmly contented after a large meal of enjoyable food.

17 Neanderthals exist on a different evolutionary line appearing in northern latitudes (the Denisovans, a similar species, evolved further east and met a similar fate), rather than the tropics, evolving out of the *Heidelbergs* around 300,000 ya and becoming extinct around 30,000 ya. Although of great interest, perhaps even fascination, they are not relevant to the Phenomenological story we are telling.

18 I have one Trump supporter and COVID denier in my practice.

19 In retrospect, I believe I may well have contracted COVID on a plane coming back from Hawaii in late December of 2019. I had a moderate cough lasting for several weeks and malaise and fever for several days. By the time the virus was expected in February and March, my illness was over and there seemed little point in seeking a (at the time) virtually unobtainable COVID test. I cannot absolutely rule out the possibility that I unknowingly infected one patient that seemed to contract COVID in February. My wife did not develop the symptoms I did.

20 This spread of *H. sapiens sapiens* into Eurasia has been termed the "out of Africa event" (Dunbar, 2016). It is actually the third such event, preceded by that of the *ergasters* and then the Heidelbergs.

21 As we shall see in Chapter 4 (Tulving, 1985/2003, 2005), there are other neuroscientific terms for the capacity for such thought such as Auto-noetic Consciousness and narrative memory.

22 There are one or two examples of some kind of highly symbolic line drawings that date to 72,000 ya. These appear to be Neanderthal in origin, a separate line of Evo-Devo from the one that led to us. They offer tantalizing suggestions of different kinds of thought processes than the *H. sapiens sapiens*' cave paintings.

23 An exception involves remains found in Qafzeh Cave in Israel rubbed in ochre and buried with sea shells and deer antlers (Bar-Yosef Mayer, et al., 2009), suggesting "a level of symbolism currently associated with modern behavior" (p. 307). These remains only resembled those of *H. sapiens sapiens* and were thought to be contemporaries of European Neanderthals. This burial was dated to 92,000 ya and other markers of modern behavior have been found in African sites dating as far back as 200,000 ya. *This disparity of dates requires us to treat the time sequence, if not the Evo-Devo, of the appearance of these cognitive events as speculation.*

24 In northern climates, days shortened and the sun even disappeared in winter. There was no explanation to be had or reassurance that it would reappear—even if it had done so in past years. One of the functions of henges, particularly Stonehenge (ca. 6,000 ya), was to offer a simple astrological computer that would foretell the sun's return.

25 Polynesian cultures, for example, evolved elaborate systems of taboos as ways of expressing such evils and how to prevent them.

26 I would posit that we should consider the appearance of Postphenomenology as a seventh phase transition; we will take this up in the next chapter.

27 Taking the long view, it is not at all clear that our urbanized society as we now know it will continue indefinitely into the future; we now face such game-changing events as climate change and extreme social unrest. Human Beings have, at least since Neolithic times, assumed a degree of permanence of their countries, cities, civilizations, that was not always warranted.

28 Reliance on metaphysics here will *not* get us what we want.

29 Contagion is an interesting term given the context of the current COVID-19 Pandemic which it predates by a decade or so. While viral contagion is paramount, social contagion—beliefs about mask-wearing, etc.—is also a critical part of the pandemic.

30 This explains the tenacity and resistance to change of belief systems and political movements.

References

Ascaso, F. J., Lizana, J., & Cristóbal, J. A. (2009). Cataract surgery in ancient Egypt. *Journal of Cataract and Refractive Surgery, 35*, 607–608.

Aunger, R. (2017). Moral action as cheater suppression in human superorganisms. *Frontiers in Sociology, 2*, 1–19.

Barabási, A.-L. (2003). *Linked*. London, England: Plume Books.

Barabási, A.-L. (2005a). Network theory – The emergence of the creative enterprise. *Science, 308*, 639–641.

Barabási, A.-L. (2005b). The origin of bursts and heavy tails in human dynamics. *Nature, 435*, 207–211.

Baron-Cohen, S. (2000). Theory of mind and autism: A fifteen year review. In S. Baron-Cohen, H. Tager-Flusberg, & D. J. Cohen (Eds.), *Understanding other minds: Perspectives from developmental cognitive neuroscience* (2nd ed., pp. 3–20). Oxford, England: Oxford University Press.

Baron-Cohen, S., Leslie, A. M., & Frith, U. (1985). Does the autistic child have a 'theory of mind'? *Cognition, 21*, 37–46.

Baron-Cohen, S., Tager-Flusberg, H., & Cohen, D. J. (2000). *Understanding other minds: Perspectives from developmental cognitive science* (2nd ed.). Oxford, England: Oxford University Press.

Bar-Yosef Mayer, D. E., Vandermeersch, B., & Bar-Yosef, O. (2009). Shells and ochre in Middle Paleolithic Qafzeh Cave, Israel: Indications for modern behavior. *Journal of Human Evolution, 56*, 307–314.

Bowlby, J. (1973). *Separation: Anxiety and anger volume 2 of Attachment and loss*. New York, NY: Basic Books.

Bowlby, J. (1988). *A secure base: Parent-child attachment and healthy human development*. New York, NY: Basic Books.

Brentano, F. (1995). *Psychology from an empirical standpoint* (L. L. McCalister, trans.). London, England: Routledge. (Original work published in 1874).

Carey, N. (2012). *The epigenetics revolution: How modern biology is rewriting our understanding of genetics, disease, and inheritance*. New York, NY: Columbia University Press.

Carroll, S. B. (2005). *Endless forms most beautiful: The new science of Evo-Devo*. New York, NY: W.W. Norton & Co.

Christakis, N. A. (2019). *Blueprint: The evolutionary origins of a good society*. New York, NY: Little, Brown Spark.

Christakis, N. A., & Fowler, J. H. (2009). *Connected: The surprising power of our social networks and how they shape our lives*. New York, NY: Little, Brown and Company.

Cline, E. H. (2014). *1177 B.C.: The year civilization collapsed*. Princeton, NJ: Princeton University Press.

de Waal, F. (2019). *Mama's last hug: Animal emotions and what they tell us about ourselves*. New York, NY: W.W. Norton & Co.

Doidge, N. (2007). *The Brain that changes itself*. New York, NY: Viking.

Doidge, N. (2015). *Remarkable discoveries and recoveries from the frontiers of neuroplasticity*. New York, NY: Viking.

Dunbar, R. (1992). Neocortex size as a constraint on group size in primates. *Journal of Human Evolution, 22*, 469–493.

Dunbar, R. (1993). Coevolution of neocortex size, group size and language in humans. *Behavioral and Brain Sciences, 16*, 681–735.

Dunbar, R. (2016). *Human evolution: Our brains and behavior*. Oxford, England: Oxford University Press.

Erikson, E. (1963). *Childhood and society* (2nd ed.). New York, NY: W.W. Norton & Co. (Original work published in 1950).

Falk, D. (2011). *The fossil chronicles: How two controversial discoveries changed our view of human evolution*. Berkeley: University of California Press.

Falk, D. (2016). Evolution of brain and culture: The neurological and cognitive journey for *Australopithecus* to Albert Einstein. *Journal of Anthropological Sciences, 94*, 1–14.

Falk, D., Redmond, J. C. Jr, Guyer, J., Conroy, G. C., Recheis, W., & Weber, G. W., et al. (2000). Early hominid brain evolution: A new look at old endocasts. *Journal of Human Evolution, 38*, 695–717.

Freud, S. (1953). Three essays on the theory of sexuality. In J. Strachey (Ed.), *Standard edition* (Vol. VII, pp. 130–243). London, England: Hogarth Press. (Original work published in 1905).

Freud, S. (1957). Papers on metapsychology. In J. Strachey (Ed.), *Standard edition* (Vol. XIV, pp. 105–215). London, England: Hogarth Press. (Original work published in 1915).

Gallese, V., Fadiga, L., Fogassi, L., & Rizzolatti, G. (1996). Action recognition in the premotor cortex. *Brain, 119*, 593–609.

Gould, S. J. (1989). *Wonderful life: The Burgess Shale and the nature of history*. New York, NY: W.W. Norton & Co.

Heidegger, M. (1982). *The basic problems of phenomenology* (A. Hofstadter, trans. Rev. ed.). Bloomington: Indiana University Press. (Original work published in 1975).

Heidegger, M. (2010). *Being and time* (J. Stambaugh & D. J. Schmidt, trans.). Albany: State University of New York. (Original work published in 1927).

Hofer, M. A. (2014). The emerging synthesis of development and evolution: A new biology for psychoanalysis. *Neuropsychoanalysis, 16*, 3–22.

Husserl, E. (1983). *Ideas pertaining to a pure phenomenology and to a phenomenological philosophy: Book one: General introduction to a pure phenomenology* (F. Kersten, trans.). New York, NY: Springer. (Original work published in 1913).

Idhe, D. (1979). *Technics and Praxis, Boston studies in the philosophy of science 24*. Amsterdam, Netherlands: Springer.

Idhe, D. (1990). *Technology and the Lifeworld: From garden to Earth*. Bloomington: Indiana University Press.

Idhe, D. (1995). *Postphenomenology: Essays in the postmodern context*. Evanston, IL: Northwestern University Press.

Idhe, D. (2012). *Experimental phenomenology, second edition: Multistabilities*. Albany: SUNY Press.

Kierkegaard, S. (1980). *The sickness onto death* (H. V. Hong & E. H. Hong, trans.). Princeton, NJ: Princeton University Press. (Original work published in 1849).

Leffert, M. (2010). *Contemporary psychoanalytic foundations*. London, England: Routledge.

Leffert, M. (2013). *The therapeutic situation in the 21st century*. New York, NY: Routledge.

Leffert, M. (2016). *Phenomenology, uncertainty, and care in the therapeutic encounter*. New York, NY: Routledge.

Leffert, M. (2018). *Psychoanalysis and the birth of the self: A radical interdisciplinary approach*. London, England: Routledge.

Leffert, M. (2021). *The psychoanalysis of the absurd: Existentialism and phenomenology in contemporary psychoanalysis*. London, England: Routledge.

Main, M. (1991). Metacognitive knowledge, metacognitive monitoring, and singular (coherent) vs. multiple (incoherent) model of attachment. In C. M. Parkes, J. Stevenson-Hinde, & P. Marris (Eds.), *Attachment across the life cycle* (pp. 126–159). London, England: Routledge.

Marche, S. (2022). *The next civil war: Dispatches from the American future*. New York, NY: Avid Reader Press/Simon and Schuster.

May, R. (1958). The origins and significance of the existential movement in psychology. In R. May, E. Angel, & H. F. Ellenberger (Eds.), *Existence* (pp. 3–36). New York, NY: Simon & Schuster.

May, R., Angel, E., & Ellenberger, H. F. (Eds.). (1958). *Existence: New directions in psychiatry and psychology*. New York, NY: Simon & Schuster.

Mellars, P. (2005). The impossible coincidence. A single-species model for the origins of modern human behavior in Europe. *Evolutionary Anthropology, 14*, 12–27.

Mithen, S. (1994). From domain specific to generalized intelligence: A cognitive interpretation of the Middle/Upper Paleolithic transition. In C. Renfrew, & E. W. Zubrow (Eds.), *The ancient mind: Elements of cognitive archaeology* (pp. 29–39). Cambridge, England: Cambridge University Press.

Nagel, T. (1970). What is it like to be a bat? *Philosophical Review, 79*, 394–403.

Nieder, A., Wagener, L., & Rinnert, P. (2020). A neural correlate of sensory consciousness in a corvid bird. *Science, 369*, 1626–1629.

Panksepp, J., & Biven, L. (2012). *The archaeology of mind: Neuroevolutionary origins of human emotions*. New York, NY: W.W. Norton & Co.

Petitot, J., Varela, F. J., Pachoud, B., & Roy, J.-M. (Eds.). (1999). *Naturalizing phenomenology: Essays on contemporary phenomenology and cognitive science*. Stanford, CA: Stanford University Press.

Pettitt, P. (2010). *The Paleolithic origins of human burial*. London, England: Routledge.

Reardon, S. (2012). The humanity switch. *NewScientist, 214*, 10–11.

Schore, A. N. (1994). *Affect regulation and the origin of the self*. Hillside, NJ: Lawrence Erlbaum Associates.

Schore, A. N. (2002). Neuropsychoanalysis, attachment theory, and trauma research: Implications for self psychology. *Psychoanalytic Inquiry, 22*, 433–484.

Schore, A. N. (2009). Right-brain affect regulation: An essential mechanism of development, trauma, dissociation, and psychotherapy. In D. Fosha, D. J. Siegal, & M. F. Solomon (Eds.), *The healing power of emotion: Affective neuroscience, development, and clinical practice* (pp. 112–144). New York, NY: W.W. Norton & Co.

Stolorow, R. D. (2002). From drive to affectivity: Contextualizing psychological life. *Psychoanalytic Inquiry, 22*, 678–685.

Stolorow, R. D. (2011). *World, affectivity, trauma*. New York, NY: Routledge.

Stolorow, R. D., Orange, D., & Atwood, G. E. (2002). *Worlds of experience: Interweaving philosophical and clinical dimensions in psychoanalysis*. New York, NY: Basic Books.

Tulving, E. (2003). Memory and consciousness. In B. J. Baars, W. P. Banks, & J. B. Newman (Eds.), *Essential sources in the scientific study of consciousness* (pp. 575–591). Cambridge, MA: MIT Press. (Original work published in 1985).

Tulving, E. (2005). Episodic memory and autonoesis: Uniquely human? In H. S. Terrace, & J. Metcalfe (Eds.), *The missing link in cognition: Origins of self-reflective consciousness* (pp. 3–56). Oxford, England: Oxford University Press.

Tversky, A., & Kahneman, D. (1982). Judgment under uncertainty: Heuristics and biases. In D. Kahneman, P. Slovic, & A. Tversky (Eds.), *Judgment under uncertainty: Heuristics and biases* (pp. 3–20). Cambridge, England: Cambridge University Press. (Original work published in 1974).

von Senden, M. (1960). *Space and sight: The perception of space and shape in the congenitally blind before and after operation* (S. Schweppe, trans.). London, England: Methuen & Co. (Original work published in 1932).

Walter, B. (2022). *How civil wars start; and how to stop them*. New York, NY: Crown.

Woolf, G. (2020). *The life and death of ancient cities: A natural history*. Oxford, England: Oxford University Press.

Yalom, I. D. (1980). *Existential psychotherapy*. New York, NY: Basic Books.

Yalom, I. D. (2009). *Staring at the sun: Overcoming the terror of death*. New York, NY: Jossey-Bass.

Zhong, B., Huang, Y., & Liu, Q. (2021). Mental toll from the coronavirus: Social media usage reveals Wuhan residents' depression and secondary trauma in the COVID-19 outbreak. *Computers in Human Behavior, 114*, 1–10.

Chapter 3

Postphenomenology and Its Evo-Devo

Introduction

As Rosenberger and Verbeek (2015) put it at the very outset of their edited volume *Postphenomenological Investigations*

> Over the past decades, an expanding group of scholars has been developing a novel approach to the social and cultural roles of technology, building upon Don Idhe's phenomenological analyses of human-technology relations ... they have started to study technologies with a blend of empirical and philosophical research methods—ranging from the epistemic role of the Mars explorer vehicle to the role of technologies on education and from the impact of hands-free calling on driving behavior to the role of sonography in decisions about abortion.
>
> (p. 9)

The Postphenomenological Investigations conducted so far share two elements. First, they investigate technology not in its own right but "in terms of the *relations between human beings and technological artifacts*" (p. 9); they focus on the way that technologies shape relations between Human Beings and World. Postphenomenologists do not consider these artifacts as instrumental objects in their own right, but rather as mediators of Human experience and practice in the *Umwelt* and *Mitwelt*. "Second, they all *combine philosophical analysis with empirical investigation*" (p. 9). This discipline began to take root at the end of the last century (Idhe, 1979; Latour & Woolgar, 1986). All this tells us much of what we need to know about the *terroir* of Postphenomenology. It focuses on the relations humans have with their machines, relations that necessarily change Dasein. Let's unpack it a bit.

Postphenomenologists are, by definition, interdisciplinary philosopher-scientists.[1] (This, for us as Psychotherapists and Psychoanalysts, has led to a new wave of what are best-termed philosopher-scientist-psychologists.) Their work has much to do with the field of Science Studies (Latour, 1991/1993) in which, for example, Latour and associates followed research workers around in a biological lab at Scripps Institute in La Jolla, California (Latour & Woolgar, 1986)

DOI: 10.4324/9781003349556-4

as they went about research tasks that involved interacting with machines. Latour (1991/1993) came to Phenomenologically offering an ontology of existence that posited large, branched chain hybrids of the social and the scientific as the only way to describe reality. Both Latour and Idhe independently understood that you could not separate the machines, the way they were being employed, and the psychology of the investigators who employ them.

Postphenomenology is a late 20th-century discipline. The explosion of personal technology in the 21st century has only made it more compelling. Of particular interest to Postphenomenologists is the evolution of cell phones (Wellner, 2016) and their usage. They began in the late 20th century as just that, compact, portable little telephones that enabled people to stay connected to each other. They were initially social network enablers facilitating connections across degrees of separation as described by Christakis and Fowler (2009) and Barabási (2003). I have discussed Social Network Theory in the past (Leffert, 2013, 2017) without considering the technology involved; we will make up for that omission here. These cute little phones became so much more. There was an *Evolution* in these devices from Cell Phones to Smart Phones that enabled them to connect to the internet in parallel to the Development of their users to make them, in effect, expanders of the Self. We will consider all of this. The Evo-Devo of Postphenomenology in which the Evo is occurring in machines takes place at a vastly speeded up rate from that of biological Evo-Devo. As with the pure biology, the Evo of machines impacts the Devo of Selves as it feeds back to produce a Devo in the machines.

Idhe (1990) offers a very useful illustration of the distinction between Phenomenology and Postphenomenology. An example of a pure Phenomenology would be the statement

I see — World

that might appeal to Husserl (1913/1983) or Merleau-Ponty (1945/2012). A similar example of *Post*phenomenology that might appeal to Idhe would be the statement

I see — through an optical artifact — World

where such an artifact might be a telescope or a microscope or eyeglasses or a Cell Phone with visual enhancement software or a new, albeit primitive, digital retina (Chader, Weiland, & Humayun, 2009).[2]

I now find myself coming to a problem in what we are trying to consider here. It is contained in the use of the adjective *Post* in Postphenomenology. It can have several meanings. One is that of its coming after Phenomenology.[3] Another is a temporal meaning: that the discipline developed after Phenomenology developed—late 20th century versus mid-19th century. A third relates to what historical material is being considered, and here Idhe (1990) takes things back to the Early Modern Period (1500–1800). Finally, technology is taken to involve devices or machines of some kind (I will posit that it can also involve biology, or biological machines). Postphenomenology, as I want to understand it, limits itself neither to these date ranges (1500–present) nor to technology as so defined. For reasons that will shortly be clear, the only term that I can find that works is *artifact*, taken in the sense of *something created by Human Beings for a practical purpose* (Merriam-Webster's Dictionary, 2004). I have no wish to burden the reader with still more terminology, but I think we must use the term *mental* artifact (or some such) to refer to things we have created at least in part for mental, psychological, or cognitive purposes. Postphenomenology, then, looks at the way we Human Beings exist in World as the product of a Self that includes its neurobiology and the mental artifacts that this particular Self has taken up. *Mental artifacts produce an enhanced Dasein.* Since the millennium there have been fundamental changes in Dasein—the relation of Self to There. In discussing Postphenomenology I also want to extend things backward, that is to extend Postphenomenology further back in time than do most Postphenomenologists, to look at artifacts created as far back as the Neolithic Period—9000 BCE, give or take.

In Postphenomenology there are at least three kinds of mental artifacts. The first involves data storage—we could be talking here about a ledger, a notebook, or a thumb drive. The second involves devices that are used to lookup information—here we have encyclopedias, or the programs *Google* and *Wikipedia* on computers and cell phones. Lastly, we have communication devices—cuneiform tablets, letters and mailboxes, and texting/social media. These are devices that serve to maintain and enhance Social Networks.

Postphenomenology also offered a reaffirmation of Postmodernism. Dealing with the relations of Humans to technology, Foucault's (1980, 2000) concept of Power and its relationship to Knowledge and Derrida's (1978, 1972/1982) development of Deconstruction and textual analysis (readings, authors, subjects, marginalia) are particularly important. Power (Lukes, 2005) as a force that shapes the content of the biological-machine interface and the social constructivism (Hoffman, 1998) that it entails are also relevant here.

A Brief History of Postphenomenology

If we are going to consider when a Postphenomenal ontology with its own mental artifacts appeared as opposed to the appearance of the *discipline* of Postphenomenology as a means of studying it, we perhaps need to go back as far as 100,000 years. Regardless, we are talking about writing, we Human Beings' fundamental need to store information (Fischer, 2005). That stored information is then used to communicate with ourselves or others across time and space. The very early examples of using incised lines, notches, or dots as means of mnemonic storage, thought to be used as tallies or to keep a lunar calendar, seem to have been with us at least as long as we have been *H. sapiens sapiens*.[4] Such tallies have been seen in knotted fibers going back as far as such fibers have been preserved. Going forward, the Ishango bones from what is now Zaire, dating back 9,000 years, shows dozens of identical markings, incised over time, some of them corresponding to lunar cycles. These all serve as external memory storage. They are Postphenomenal in that they represent mental artifacts, machines if you will, that expand the capacity of Self to connect with World, particularly other Selves.[5] As social systems expanded, the need for these artifacts expanded as well.

These markings convey information about quantity. For markings to convey additional information about qualities and characteristics, pictures are called for. Cave art dating back tens of millennia convey information about animals that seems to relate to hunting and potentially religious experience. The combination of marks and picture-mnemonics led to the introduction of *pictography*. Idhe (2010) very broadly construes writing "as the practice of making signifying *inscriptions* that have some recognizable *meaning* to the reader of the inscriptions" (p. 129). Some of these inscriptions can be dated as far back as 20,000 BCE. If we were to confine ourselves to inscriptions of inscribed language, we would have to move forward from this point at least 15 millennia.

More complex societies, such as the Bronze Age cities[6] of the Fertile Crescent, needed to record more information. That led to the development of writing Proto-cuneiform lozenges of the pottery phase of the Neolithic Period that gave way to cuneiform tablets needed for accountancy purposes; these were held in storage as mnemonics or accompanied shipments of animals and commodities that vouched for the arrival of the same quantities that made up the original shipment. Religious inscriptions appeared soon after—ceremonial ceramic "nails" were quite common in the fertile crescent, with cuneiform inscriptions dedicating temples and palaces to particular gods. Hieroglyphics appeared in Egypt a few centuries later and were coopted for vast burial inscriptions as well as used for commercial purposes.

Early practitioners of this Postphenomenology produced written scripts that could then be seen in the complex mental and social life that they in turn made possible. They introduced a Postphenomenal dichotomy that would persist into the present between common and specialized use of mental artifacts. Information about quantity, quality, and characteristics in the Neolithic and Bronze Ages was used by everyone; accountancy and religious inscription were specialized practices used by specialists in the conduct of their particular societal roles. This early bifurcation in Postphenomenal artifacts has continued into the present. Books, letters, and, much later, Postphenomenal machines have had, on the one hand, personal and social functions, and specialized vocational functions on the other. Existentially, what both these functions have in common is the furtherance of personal Meaning and the avoidance of living a Fallen life based in Absurdity.

Mathematics and alphabets continued to develop from the Bronze and Iron Ages, moving on into the classical Greek and Roman periods. In the field of literary-religious epics, the Middle Bronze Age saw the appearance of the *Gilgamesh epic* and the Early Iron Age the *Odyssey*, both in written form.[7] Manuscripts were handwritten on clay, papyrus, and animal skins and were impossible to own, except for governments, religious organizations, their libraries, and the wealthiest of individuals. They provided the content for the chanting and reading taking place in social-religious convocations that fostered social group cohesiveness (Dunbar, 2016). The evolution of these media changed the development of brains in ways that fed back to the evolution of new generations of artifacts.

The next phase of that evolution was the invention of the movable type printing press and the printing of the eponymous Guttenberg Bible in the 1450s. The printing of these 170 odd vulgate bibles did not change anything with respect to the manuscript bibles preceding them for about a millennium-and-a-half. No, what the Guttenberg Bible was, what it *was*, was a proof of concept. Within a century, tens of thousands of books were appearing, so many that remainder sales were necessary. Even more important was NEWS. Printed broadsides made their way throughout the Early Modern Period (1500–1800). In 1517, Martin Luther wrote his 95 theses against the sale of indulgences by the catholic church and, as legend has it, nailed them to the door of the Wittenberg cathedral. Be that as it may, printed broadsides of the theses, carried on horseback, outdistanced news of the putative act. While few people could read in 1500 at the start of the Early Modern, most could by 1800, and Martin Luther published his German translation of the bible so anyone could read it. Handwritten news sheets, *avvisi*, appeared in Early Modern Europe with Venice, in 1565, publishing the *notizie scritte* on a regular monthly basis. It sold for the smallest Venetian coin: a *gazette*. Newspapers, printed with movable type printing presses on inexpensive paper, first appeared in Strasbourg (Europe) in 1605 and in Boston (North America) in 1690.

The next major evolutionary change involved the widespread use of the mail for social rather than just governmental[8] and commercial purposes. Personal letter writing dates from the Early Modern Period, increasing massively in the 19th century and beyond. Such correspondence made possible the geographic extension of Social Networks to include the kinds of infrequent network contacts described be. The opportunity to write to people at a distance (or to hire a letter writer or reader if one was illiterate) expanded the Self's practice and perception of the world they inhabited—an early Postphenomenal experience.

The first mechanical Postphenomenal device was the electric telegraph that appeared in the mid-19th century. As a *social* instrument, it conveyed bits of information (the familiar ten words or less), family news, usually bad family news, about death or illness. (It was adopted by the military in time of war for the purpose of rapid communication.) Telephones for personal use then appeared in the late 19th century, radio broadcasting and motion pictures in the early 20th century. They served very different Postphenomenal purposes. Early telephones provided an enhanced channel for social communication and an albeit expensive channel for such communication at extended geographic distances. I stress here the social rather than the informational purposes of such communication; it enhanced an individual's sense of being a part of their network. As an example, telephone conversations taking place in late November of 1963 often included information about how and where the speaker had found out about the assassination of John F. Kennedy (a "marker event" such as the Japanese attack on Pearl Harbor on December 7, 1941, or the destruction of the Twin Towers on *9/11*, September 11, 2001).

This brings us to the second sort of Postphenomenal device in that we all found out about these events via radio or television. These devices brought us news and entertainment, often in real time, and did so on an on-demand basis. Except for the latter feature, motion pictures and the appliance for viewing them (theaters) served a very similar function. Television, in effect a kind of functional cross between commercial radio and motion pictures, appeared in households mostly in the early 1950s. These devices interacted with the Self to stabilize, for good or ill, group norms[9] and beliefs in the nodes that made up superorganisms (Christakis & Fowler, 2009). They had profound effects on the rural population of the first half of the 20th century, drawing them into local and national Social Networks. The United States of the 1950s was a much more tightly organized Superorganism than it had been a century earlier, the result of multiple Postphenomenal events.

I have been speaking here in the past tense only because technology and Postphenomenology still had so much more to offer us or, arguably, to demand of us; no advance comes without a price. The last quarter of the 20th century and the first quarter of the 21st century saw these changes around the appearance of the smart phone and the personal computer. Many of these changes remained unimaginable, even as they began to take place; the Postphenomenal events that we will see in the remainder of the century are equally hard to imagine. Pagers in the 1960s and cell phones in the 1970s offered convenient, highly portable means of personal communication, allowing people to stay in touch with each other at long[10] or short distances. Personal computing appeared in the 1980s, functioning as a new appliance that performed tasks like writing, mathematics, and bookkeeping that were formerly done by hand or other machines. They also offered a platform for playing crudely represented games. These devices, at this point, did not change the Self; they simply offered a quantitative continuation of the Postphenomenal trends we have been talking about, only with shinier bells and whistles. What made the *qualitative* difference was the combined appearance of the Internet and Social Media in the mid-1990s. Computers became windows on the world and cell phones became smartphones, devices that combined cellular and mobile computing. Their features could be uniquely customized by the user; they *were* truly personal. Their use for two-way communications traffic ballooned from 1% of all such traffic in 1993, to 50% of such traffic in 2000, to 97% in 2007 (Hilbert & Lopez, 2011).

After their initial invention (e.g., cell phones in the 1970s) these devices evolved out of the interaction between Self and device. Whereas the biological Evo-Devo of hominins played out over spans of hundreds of thousands and, unusually, tens of thousands of years, human-artifact Evo-Devo takes place annually, or even more often. This Evo-Devo resulted from a qualitatively different sort of process. In the past one could, for example, have tried to develop a faster operating printing press or a more effective television antenna. Here, someone set out to invent or refine something because it was thought people would like the results better and buy more of them. Smartphones, however, were a different matter. When they were invented, it was with the idea in mind that they would become smaller, more streamlined, devices that added mobile computing. Nobody knew at the start, or planned for the fact, that people would so want to run little, customizable programs and data bases on them. These would come to be called *Apps*. What was, I think, unexpected was the way Smartphones exploded into an entirely new market for Social Media. This was truly Evo-Devo. The device would evolve, people would develop new uses and needs, and the device would evolve into something that did these things better. The BlackBerry was an early device, blown away by the iPhone and, later, the Galaxy. They deployed touch screens and, whereas the BlackBerry had tiny keys for typing, the iPhone and the Galaxy could convert their touch screens to keyboards. People discovered the phones, discovered that they wanted things from them that didn't exist, and smartphone developers offered them what they wanted. App development was thrown open to the world with anyone from large corporations to individual developers putting them out for people to select from; there are now nine million smartphone Apps available for the three *billion* smartphone users to choose from.

The first social media device was, arguably, the electric[11] telegraph, appearing in the 1840s in the United States. Mentioning it in the same breath as texting on a Smartphone shocks us with the sense of just how far we have come. Coming into service in the first decade of the new millennium, *texting* and Apps like Facebook and Twitter were taken up first by innovators, then by everyone else, and became ways in which individuals, *nodes*, could be in constant touch with their Social Networks. This applied to the Dunbar's number of individuals in our social groups or in the Superorganisms of which we are also a part. By the end of that decade, it was not an unusual sight to spot a group at a restaurant, each member sitting quietly and privately texting.

Postphenomenal Neuroscience and Its Evo-Devo

There are three Evo-Devo milestones relating to the Self that arose out of the 10,000-year span of human-artifact Evo-Devo. The first, the development of the capacity for formal language in *H. sapiens sapiens* as a part of the Upper Paleolithic Package 50,000 ya (Mellars, 2005; Mithen, 1994), was *possibly* the result of biological Evo-Devo that differentiated the wise guys from the Anatomically Modern Humans. Be that as it may, it was, for the present, the last such possibility. We know that early notations, seemingly used to keep track of things, appeared around 10,000 ya and, over the next 6,000 years, morphed into formal, grammatical writing (and reading) systems in the Fertile Crescent, probably beginning in the Bronze Age city of Uruk (home of Gilgamesh) ca. 3000 BCE. For our purposes, what's important here is that there could be no *anatomical* changes in the Brain to account for this appearance of writing. This means that existing Cortical structures, the Parietal Cortex in particular, were adapted to fulfill the new needs that Human Beings, living in ever-more-complex social, intellectual, and emotional situations, had developed. This adaptation was the result of both conscious and unconscious processes. A different but parallel line of development involved the invention and playing of musical instruments. The process in Development that makes these advances possible is Education. For this repurposing of cerebral hardware for functional literacy—reading and writing—Education is best accomplished if begun in Middle Childhood. This preserves particular groups of Cortical neurons that would otherwise have been subject to the normative pruning process that takes place in early adolescence (at least a quarter of cortical neurons are lost to pruning, probably in the service of increasing the energy efficiency of the brain). As we know, neuroplasticity (Doidge, 2007) demonstrates that literacy can be developed at a later date as can the playing of musical instruments, but they are less well accomplished.

The second milestone involves the Evo-Devo of Human Beings into *Cyborgs*. The term was coined by Clynes and Kline in 1960 to refer to a living being possessing organic and biomechatronic body parts. Arguably, Human Beings with artificial legs, hearing aids, glasses, or contact lenses are Cyborgs. The 20th and 21st centuries have seen us all emerge as Cyborgs. The term has come to signify human-technology mixtures. Such technology falls into two broad categories: restorative and enhancing mixtures. A different form of Cyborg is the human *biological* transplant recipient, the first examples of which were corneal transplant recipients at the beginning of the 20th century, kidney transplant recipients at mid-century, and heart transplant recipients by the 1980s. The first were experienced (as it were) as transparent and the rejection of the second, while medically disturbing, was a survivable event. Transplanted hearts were a different matter. As a vital organ, *their* rejection was life threatening; a Human Being's relationship with their transplanted heart is always on shaky ground and never transparent. Transplanted hearts are at our very centers, but they can only be known intellectually or from a scan or x-ray and we are left to experience them only in fantasy.

Let's return to the biological-machine Cyborg. Idhe (2019) refers to their development as the cyborg process, a "gradual accumulation of human-technology hybridization" (p. 34). Some Cyborgs occupy a central place in our fantasies. USAF Colonel Steve Austin, the protagonist of the popular 1970s television show (played by the actor Lee Majors, who developed his own fantasies about the role) *The Six Million Dollar Man*, was the quintessential Cyborg. Postphenomenologically, the term has come to be highly active in fantasy-formation (Idhe, 2019) as people came to relate more and more to the human-technology interface. These are embodiment fantasies that, if thought of psychoanalytically at all, have been erroneously swept up in the dustbin of pathological narcissism and omnipotence. They relate technology and power, but they really do require a lot more analytic thought about what we are and what we become. We will explore the Cyborg concept and its relation to that of Human Being in the sections that follow. I would argue here that the quintessential Cyborg as of 2021[12] is a Human Being with a Smartphone and there are now three billion of us. As of now, our organic-mechanical interface is sensory and neuromuscular. We use touch, the muscles of the hands, and speech to input information to the artifact and sight and hearing to get information out of it. It would seem likely that some sort of direct artifact-brain interface will be developed, probably sooner than we might expect. In fantasy, this interface already exists. The study of fantasy—individual, conscious and otherwise, group, and its expression in movies, digital games, science fiction[13]—is very much a part of the discipline of Postphenomenology. Fantasy can easily go awry but, all too often, we don't ask our patients about their technologies.

The third and most sophisticated Postphenomenological issue of human-artifact Evo-Devo involves changes in Self-representation growing out of the Internet and Social Media. Simply put, the latter allow us to place a working representation of ourselves (an *External* Working Model?) onto the former and to consciously relate to it or leave it there *unattended* for periods of time. Such a representation becomes a part of the Self, a very new *kind* of part. We experience and perceive, say, our Facebook page in much the same way as other parts of our Self-Representation; the page is, as well, very real. We would expect the Brain to store and process this information along with other aspects of Self-image and working models in its Cortical Midline Structures (Uddin, Iacoboni, Lange, & Keenan, 2007). We will look at these last two in some detail and note how the second leads to the third.

Cyborgs

Turkle (2008) offers this description at the beginning of her chapter "Always-on/Always-on-you"

> In the mid-1990s, a group of young researchers … carried computers and radio transmitters in their backpacks, keyboards in their pockets and digital displays embedded in their eyeglass frames. Always on the internet, they called themselves "cyborgs" … When their burdensome

technology cut into their skin, causing lesions and scar tissue, they were indifferent … They were learning to walk and talk like new creatures, learning to inhabit their own bodies all over again, and yet in a way they were fading away, bleeding out into the Net.

(p. 121)

These young researchers morphed, over the next few years, into MIT's "Wearable Computer Group." Turkle posits that they were beginning to define a new state of the Self that would, over the next decade or so, become a "Tethered Self" that has a life both on and off the internet. Now (2021), nearly all of us fall into this group, reaching out at will but also at the disposal of anyone who wishes to contact us.

Let me offer a brief memoir of my own experience as a different kind of Cyborg (Idhe, 2019) that takes us beyond the Smartphones of 2021. On my chest, about three fingerbreadths below my left clavicle, resides a firm rectangular bump about half the size of and twice as thick as a Hershey Bar. It has two electrical leads (I can feel them) that are threaded through an artery and touch the wall of each of my heart's ventricles. It has been there for eight years. It is called an Implantable Cardioverter Defibrillator (ICD). Unlike an artificial titanium/Teflon knee or hip, it is a hyper-technological device with its own onboard computer, connection to the internet, and internal power source. It was made by St. Jude Medical, cost Medicare in the low six figures, and functions like an EMT team. In our terms, it represents restorative technology. It comes with an identification card I carry with me and a book-sized device that sits in my office and handles the internet communications between the ICD and St. Jude. So why do I have it, what exactly does it do, and how do I experience and feel about it?

Some years ago, I developed atrial fibrillation (AF), a common cardiac arrhythmia that doesn't do much. There is a risk of blood clots forming in the heart, but this is managed with anticoagulants. It was decided in 2012 that I faced a risk of more serious *ventricular* arrhythmias that could stop my heart, and the ICD was implanted in a 15-minute surgical procedure performed under light anesthesia. Its task is two-fold: to pace my heart at 60 beats per minute to stabilize the AF and, in the face of a serious arrhythmia, to deliver an electric shock that would convert me back to a normal rhythm. (As I write this, at greater length than I imagined, I realize that, as a Cyborg, this ICD is much more important to me than I thought.) Writing about her own experience of a prosthetic leg, Sobchack (2004) argues that we strive to both embody such devices and to render them *transparent*. I believe it is much the same for Smartphones, where we forget (if we ever knew about) their technological features. (This is the ready-at-hand vs. present-at-hand dichotomy, but we'll get to that.) She does not, however, consider herself a Cyborg which she takes to mean being enhanced rather than restored, and does not lose sight of the limits of her biological flesh. She means by this, I think, to reject any

Postphenomenal fantasy, that the prosthesis bestows special powers on her. But that is not what makes her a Cyborg (in the same way that fantasy alone does not make one a Cyborg, only, perhaps, a Cyborg *in* fantasy); it is the human-artifact construction that does that.

I find that my ICD is *very much* present-at-hand, and, precisely because my life may depend on it, I am very much aware of it as a part of my Self. When the device was "installed," I was told that I probably wouldn't even feel the shock if it came. Things proceeded for a few months. The ICD paced away at 60 bpm, we each minded our own business, and I noticed nothing. I didn't really experience it as a part of me, as a part of my Self. Then, out of the blue, I felt like something had picked me up and thrown me against a wall. It took me a minute to figure out that I had been shocked. It was a whole-body experience. It was not pleasant.[14] In the next half-hour, this was repeated several times. I was placed on a medication for a time that controlled this new ventricular arrhythmia that was necessitating the shocks. A routine then began in which St. Jude would periodically send me reports about how my heart was doing, and I would see the arrhythmia specialist who implanted the ICD quarterly. He would place an electromagnetic lead on my chest that would then "interrogate" my (it *had* become "mine") ICD to see how it and I were doing. My ICD has a battery with a five-year life span, give or take, after which it will have to be replaced (it currently says it has enough of a charge to last another 2½ years).

The ICD has merged itself, as it were, into my Self-Representation. I find I can "see" it in my mind's eye on my chest, can feel it with my fingers and can feel where the leads leave the device. It doesn't look or feel any different than any other part of my body and, like my arm for example, it doesn't feel special or important but, also like my arm, I would be very frightened if I think about it being removed or ripped out. It, most definitely, is not transparent, I tend to be aware of it occasionally, and find that slightly soothing. I feel safer travelling because I have it *to care for me* in a strange country if I need it to. My point in recounting all this is that *this* is what it feels like *to me* to be this kind of Cyborg.

It is possible that, at some point in my future, my heart, even with its ICD, will no longer be up to its task and I could become a different kind of Cyborg: a heart transplant recipient. For such a recipient, transparency is impossible; from my current perspective, looking into the future, it generates fantasies of salvation.

Smartphones—The Quintessential Postphenomenal Tool

What is interesting about the Smartphone is that we use it to open an entirely new channel for connecting with World, acutely miss it if we misplace it or lose access to it, yet it does not feel like a part of ourselves. The part of the world it connects us with is Cyberspace. Is this lack of Selfness like the arm we just talked about or something more? I can imagine my Smartphone, which I have customized to meet my particular needs, but I do not imagine it as connected to me in any way and I don't experience pain or fear at the thought of losing it. I am, however, prepared to return home if I have left it behind, depending on distance, time, etc., because I have come to need it for my daily life.

In Postphenomenal terms, Cell Phones have become a part of our Everydayness (Wellner, 2016). In Heideggerian terms, they can be "handy," ready-at-hand (*Zuhandenheit*), but also present-at-hand (*Vorhandenheit*) to be studied for themselves, not just used as tools. The distinction is between picking up an *unregarded* hammer to hit a nail and picking up a hammer to *regard* it as a particular member of the class of hammers. When problem solving, Smartphones can become a part of Thrownness but can frequently become Fallen when they are used to surf the internet in place of thinking or doing something meaningful. Idhe (1995) contrasts tools such as hammers, whose context is the world in which things are what they are taken to be, with the Smartphone which takes us from the here-and-now, potentially across space and time to a virtual space where we can leave a part of ourselves. This ability to occupy and interact with others in virtual space affects us individually as well as societally and culturally. These effects are still very much in their infancy.

I find that, if I think about it, I experience my Smartphone as a channel if I use it to communicate with someone else or to obtain information, but, if I use it to do things, as an endpoint in and of itself. I recently received my COVID inoculations. I installed a small APP at the request of the hospital that vaccinated me. It texts me every day or two to ask me how I'm feeling and asks a few questions that I tap a response to. What's interesting is that I experience this as coming from the Smartphone itself, not the CDC communicating with me through the phone. It might be different if there were a *person* there, but there isn't.

A Smartphone,[15] broadly speaking, functions in four areas: social media and texting, work, information, and recreation and entertainment. It seems very likely that these experiences are not universal; individuals vary the use they make of Smartphones for personal and sociocultural reasons. As a source of information, the experience seems not much different from finding something in a book or encyclopedia, albeit with a much better index, now called a search engine (hence *Wikipedia*, a *Wiki* = fast encyclopedia, and Google, currently the ultimate search engine). As a source of entertainment, it blurs into more specialized artifacts, game consoles and 3D viewers; for music and cinema, it can power devices that enhance both of these experiences. As a tool for obtaining or retrieving information, it functions very much like a memory prosthesis, remembering research you've done or notes you've made. The conscious experience of these functions is so much of a tool at-hand in Everydayness and so much not a part of the Self. We don't feel like Cyborgs as we use these artifacts in these ways. The problem here lies in *Consciousness*. What we consciously experience about ourselves *may not be what we actually are.*

To anticipate what we will be saying about Consciousness and Unconsciousness in Chapter 4, in talking about the *experienced* Consciousness of the Self, we are talking about the Consciousness of the Left Cerebral Hemisphere (the "Left Brain" or LB). LB Consciousness does not experience its Smartphone as a part of itself or experience itself as a Cyborg when it uses the Smartphone in this way. This subjective experience is, however, not necessarily an *accurate* representation of what's going on in the Self.[16] If we consider *Right* Brain Consciousness, we have reason to think that the non-linear, non-serially logical RB (Leffert, 2010) is neither as discerning nor as particular as the Left. It is, however, far better at grasping constructs, patterns, and relationships. For it to have access (ready-at-hand, *Zuhandenheit, not* present-at-hand, *Vorhandenheit*)[17] to its Smartphone, I would posit, it is more likely for it to experience it as a functional part of itself as a Cyborg. The LB would remain unaware of its neighbor's function in this area.

Social Media and texting are a different matter. In both, our Smartphone functions as a portal that we have customized (read: constructed) to enhance our embedding in the Social World (*Mitwelt* [Heidegger, 1975/1982]). Social Media and Twitter (at 140 characters per tweet), currently the quintessential examples, facilitate our embedding in Social Networks ranging in size from a few individuals to Dunbar's Number (2016), to Superorganisms (Christakis, 2019) like Donald Trump's erstwhile Twitter account. One can experience a connection with content that one acts upon, "likes" and "forwards" for example, but also a sense of oneness with the group that can be enhancing or very dangerous. Social Media can offer great emotional support and/or great harm, given its capacities for good or ill. Zhong and Associates (Zhong, Huang, & Liu, 2021) looked at Social Media usage among Wuhan residents in response to the COVID epidemic and found that it both served as a marker for Pandemic anxiety and depression but also that the users felt emotional and peer support as a result. Excessive Social Media usage could sometimes be as much of a problem before the Pandemic as it was during it.

Texting is different. It becomes an ongoing communication that two people can use to carry on a relationship, supplementing or even replacing being physically with someone. One can only imagine how much more difficult COVID-imposed isolation would be without this artifact and the functions it both enhances and replaces. A reason that texting replaced voice in many instances is because it can be carried on in private (Wellner, 2016), even in a social setting. One can maintain the two-person communication in the presence of others, *unknown to them*, in classes, cars, or around diner tables. These communications can take place in circumstances in which voice communication would not have taken place. Where voice is possible, people below the age of 24 still *prefer* text. The Smartphone becomes a transparent portal (like our ears) with its transparency being an indicator that it makes us functional Cyborgs. There are great individual differences here. Some people text (a new verb) a few times a day about specific matters where others converse, sending and receiving dozens or even hundreds of texts in a day. Most are somewhere in between. The degree to which a Human Being with a Smartphone becomes a Cyborg also varies enormously with the variance being in part age-related. For those having difficulty with the shift, the Smartphone remains an ill-controlled and seemingly unpredictable foreign body that is approached tentatively with anxiety and some doubt. This is very much like how telephones were adopted at the turn of the 20th century. Today, Smartphones are embodied in two different ways. The only partially embodied usually older users grasp their Smartphones firmly in one hand and stab at the keyboard with (usually) the index finger of the other. The accomplished younger and fully embodied users hold the phone lightly with both hands and texts with both, proofreading the screen, not looking at the keyboard. They integrate emotive symbols and abbreviations (e.g., OMG=Oh MY God!,: <),.: < (), some of them having made their way into the *Oxford English Dictionary* (Oxford English Dictionary, 1989). Within 20 years it will no longer be worthwhile to even mention these things unless one is a social historian.

The fact that the study of this aspect of Postphenomenology is so recent is at best an excuse for why it figures so little in the thinking and writing of Psychoanalysts and Psychotherapists. The Pandemic has forced us to shift our work from our offices to the telephone or videoconferencing. Responses among therapists have been mixed—some surprised to find it useful, some confirmed in their criticisms of it—but most seem to treat it as a new discovery even though it has been around for 40 odd years (Leffert, 2003). It has not yet led to an interest in texting. It tends to be seen by most therapists—who are not Postphenomenal scientists—as a defense against emotional contact rather than the *means of facilitating it* that researchers in the field posit to be. I hope this will change over time. Let me offer two very different case vignettes that illustrate how texting, like any form of behavior, can serve healthy or psychopathological purposes.

June, a 30-year-old liberal arts graduate student in the third year of a productive analysis, goes through her workday (currently distant learning) in constant contact with two or three women friends (she has male friends as well but her contacts with them are more limited) and whatever man she might be in a relationship with. This could amount to 50 or a 100 long texts a day (at best an educated guess). Broadly speaking, she maintains her Social Network connections with her friends and explores her relationship with the current man in her life. Rather than constituting any sort of defense against intimacy, texting reinforces intimacy for her. She brings this texted discourse into her analysis, associating to long-standing paternal conflicts, in a way that treats texting as transparent. The material involves events and feelings in the same way as it would with any kind of personal contact with another Human Being.

Wade is a 28-year-old mechanical engineer is in twice-weekly psychotherapy mostly centered on relationship issues. He approached relationships with intense ambivalence. His lifelong social anxiety is particularly intense in dealing with women and could easily be traced to his seductive and emotionally smothering mother. He kept his distance from women until college; with the appearance of Smartphones, he was able to approach them but at a (to him) distance. He met women only on dating sites, not in person, even though there were ample opportunities to do so at the large university he attended. In this way he met Marie, a graduate student in English Literature. He did very much want to have a meaningful relationship with her, and he used texting with her to overcome his anxiety. Texting and COVID allowed him to titrate the in-person contact they had as a couple; what I realized, and he didn't, was that a relationship on this level would not survive the end of the Pandemic. I pointed this out to him and suggested that this was an opportunity to work with his anxiety that might not come again and that failing to do so might make it impossible to develop the relationship he so wanted. We were indeed able to shift the discourse, for the first time, from Marie to his mother. He began to actually enjoy the time he spent being with Marie, not just texting with her, and the anxiety faded.

Cyberspace

We have not yet talked about the Phenomenal Meaning of Smartphones as portals into Cyberspace. Cyberspace is the social arena (Hakken, 1999) that is being created and recreated by the development of Advanced Information Technology (AIT). This is mostly about the "Cyber" part. We also need to address the fact that it is a *Space*, an *inhabited* Space, a postmodern concept fleshed out (and I do not use the term lightly) by Bachelard (1958/1994). It is the nature of that habitation that we want to explore. The ontology of that Space is twofold. First, it is individually customized and furnished just like one would furnish one's home, a separate process from customizing a Smartphone or a personal computer. It is, like other personal spaces, one that others can enter and leave at will. Also, like other spaces, it continues to exist even when we are not present in it, as my house exists unchanged when I am away from it. The second is the wide world of Cyberspace that we can venture or journey into in different ways. In the new century, this has come to be called the *Multiverse* (Kim, 2021), a compound name that brings together *multi-*, the many different kinds of Cyberspace, and the suffix *-verse*, a reference to a metauniverse, a place beyond the physical universe that we inhabit in our bodies.

Cyberspace and the Multiverse are studied today by an interdisciplinary community of Anthropologists, Philosophers, and Social Scientists. They function as Ethnographers, a discipline that endeavors to study the social practices of particular groups. In this case, it is the group of individuals who choose to inhabit Cyberspace (Hakken, 1999). Ethnographers will study the Space but will also interview the members of this group about their practices and how they feel. They also observe their behaviors in Cyberspace;

ethnographic practices are not so dissimilar from those of Psychotherapists and Psychoanalysts who, unfortunately, tend to ignore Cyberspace.[18] We see patients suffering from social phobia and those who choose to live in social isolation, both exacerbated by the Pandemic. In the days before IT, these people lived truly desperate lives. I have written in the past about a patient I treated in the 1970s, a Viet Nam vet suffering from severe atypical PTSD. His suffering was not related to combat experience. Rather, he had been stationed on a minute communications base; the sole facility situated on an isolated island deep in the southwest Pacific. The base was otherwise staffed with what we would now call brilliant computer geeks which Tom definitely was not. He had somehow offended one of them, and he was isolated and shunned for most of the year he was there. Today we would call this *ghosting*, a form of bullying. As a result, he emotionally collapsed. This was only recognized at the end of his tour of duty; he was discharged on full disability and the Veterans Administration paid for him to see me. His primary symptom was crippling social anxiety. Tom lived alone in a Volkswagen camper, parking it in different camping spots for the night. He was comfortable with me and visiting his parents, who seemed to simply not grasp the extent of his disability. Contacts with other people for self-care, car maintenance, and grocery shopping were agony. Beyond support, I really was not, at the time, able to do very much for him. Writing about the case three decades later, I realized that, from a very different and contemporary therapeutic perspective, I would have entered more actively into his life, going with him to perform these tasks and modeling social behavior for him. I would have become for him a usable object that he could, hopefully, internalize as opposed to simply offering him a therapeutic and safe Space (Bachelard, 1958/1994) insulated from the World he experienced as so dangerous.

Today, Tom and others like him live mostly in a multidimensional Cyberspace of their own construction and a Metaverse they would travel or adventure in. It would offer them a tolerable way of Being-in-World, of becoming a different kind of Dasein. Psychotherapeutically, Cyberspace would also offer them a place in which a kind of play therapy could take place, one that might improve their functioning in the physical world. Now, I would have offered him the opportunity to enter constructed spaces that would have allowed him, with me at his side, to experience mild aggression and excitement that he could work his way out of; something that he had been denied in the original traumatic experience. We probably would have played some electronic games together, drawn perhaps from Epic or Take Two software. I have not yet read of therapy conducted in this way, but I would expect it to be used as a part of child psychotherapy.

Who you are in Cyberspace (Suler, 2002) is a complex matter. The Multiverse allows us to present ourselves in as many different ways as we would like. I, for example, maintain my identity as a Psychoanalyst,[19] in a number of places in Cyberspace. In other places, like Google search results

I am presented (by the search engine) as a Psychiatrist (I don't actually use this term, but it serves to illustrate that there is a lot going on about us in Cyberspace that we don't or can't control) practicing in Santa Barbara. Finally, I have also chosen to present myself as a sculptor with my own website. All three of these identities dwell in the Multiverse quite comfortably, whether I'm active in them or not. Suler observes that these identity decisions are not entirely Conscious choices; something entirely consistent with the Right Brain contributions to their construction. Our Unconscious wishes and fantasies can leak out, coloring the presentation of ourselves that we put out into Cyberspace. *In the multiverse we can be anyone we want to be.* In Social Network terms (Christakis & Fowler, 2009), we exist in the Multiverse as multiple egos whose connections to each other and to alters at various degrees of separation are in part unconscious. The Pandemic, which limits connectedness in the physical[20] world, has driven most of us to spend more of our time in the virtual worlds of the Multiverse.

Suler (2002) pursues this question. We can choose to be whomever we want (actually whomevers, since there can be many of us), ranging from an avatar that is only slightly different from us to one who is flamboyantly different. The username(s) we choose, the information we post about ourselves, and the persona we adopt are all about how we present ourselves in Cyberspace. In some online situations—professional groups and associations—we are expected to present ourselves as we really are, but in others we are not. These are complex identity issues that are well-suited to Postmodern deconstruction (Leffert, 2007a, 2007b). These identities can differ/defer (Derrida, 1972/1982) as a result of quite objective motives; what we need to present about ourselves for different purposes. They also contain elements of Uncertainty and display things about ourselves that are Unknowable to us. But some of us present ourselves in ways that are largely fantasy, of a narcissistic or a grandiose bent, creatures that should be a subject of analysis if the person is in therapy. Multiple avatars can reflect a fragmented Self that cannot integrate itself or a Self that differs with the part of the Multiverse it is inhabiting. In recent months, most of us have become aware that there is also a very dark area in the Multiverse where people can live out and actualize sadomasochistic fantasies and sexual perversions, can use to traffic women, and offer child pornography. We have recently come to know of groups like the Proud Boys, Militias, and QAnon that use the Multiverse for organizational purposes[21] and, again, to gratify narcissistic fantasies. This is a social problem and only secondarily an enforcement problem; the role of Psychotherapy in its management is doubtful but Kleinian theory can be a useful way of characterizing the primitive impulses that are more easily expressed at the distance and anonymity the Multiverse can provide.

Let's return to our role as Ethnographers. Contemporary Ethnography imposes two different ways of Being on us. The lesser of the two is trying as hard as we can to be Modernist scientists. We already know (Leffert,

2007a, 2010) that it is impossible to avoid failing at this. We cannot simply be observers, only participant-observers, an honorable Postmodern existence. This is the interreferential piece of ethnography. Derrida (1974/1997) for example, would have subjected the terminology of the Multiverse and its inhabitants to rigorous *deconstruction* in order to explore and reach a fuller and freer sense of their social meaning. Where do terms like *blog, post, text,* and *tweet* come from, and what happens when we deconstruct them? The choice of media with which to enter Cyberspace also reveals things about us. Are we linear verbalizers likely to choose verbal media like texting or visualizers creating avatars employing Web graphics? Social Network theorists (Latour, 1991/1993; Latour & Woolgar, 1986, for example), combine the two into large hybrids of social and scientific knowledge. Addressing and studying the Dark Internet is very much an object of Ethnography—we would expect such studies to appear in the literature over the next several years.

When we enter Cyberspace, we cannot avoid unknowingly influencing and being influenced by what we find. Another way of describing this is to say we are in a realm of interreferential Uncertainty. This should sound familiar, since it characterizes the position of Relational and Intersubjective therapists, implicitly integrating Postmodernism and Phenomenology. Is there anything that the Multiverse fails to provide us with? The Pandemic has driven us into a bimodal existence in which we tend to live physically in isolation in our homes (even if we venture out into pods or service jobs) and virtually in Cyberspace. On the other hand, people have been driven out of this bimodal ontology, seeking physical contact in the outside world even when it has been manifestly dangerous to do so. There is also a lopsidedness in the ways in which they reach out into World. Motion picture theatres have not been much lamented, and the industry has seamlessly moved to provide Cyberspace access to newly released movies at a price similar to what one would have to pay in a theatre. The agonizing loss has been restaurants and bars with many people moving defiantly to occupy these purposed spaces (Bachelard, 1958/1994); "secret," unadvertised bars were found, at the height of the pandemic, to be open and well-patronized late at night. We have been talking in this chapter about what Cyberspace supplies and how we dwell in it. Do we know any more about these trends and what Cyberspace does *not* supply? As it happens, we do. Let's return to Dunbar's (2016) work that we considered in the last chapter.

Dunbar (2016), as we have discussed, offers an account of Paleoanthropology ranging from the appearance of *Australopithecus africanus* in southern Africa 4–5 mya to that of *Homo sapiens sapiens* perhaps 50,000 ya. He found correlations between neocortex size, social group size and the development of vocalizations and language, demonstrating coevolution of these social and cognitive capabilities (Dunbar, 1992). As these groups evolved, becoming ever larger, new social behaviors became necessary to maintain them. Social behaviors lead to endorphin release, with the necessarily larger endorphin release mediated by the increasing duration of these activities or the development of new behaviors. Our hominin ancestors made do with increasing amounts of time spent in social grooming as brain size increased, later being supplemented and replaced by language, particularly gossip. When *H. sapiens* and *H. sapiens sapiens* appeared, language was supplemented by shared musical performances and then feasting and consuming alcoholic beverages which yielded the highest levels of endorphin release (they still do). It was these activities that were lost when we were forced to lock down in semi-isolation. We all missed them.[22] The results taxed social bonds, contributed to stress, anxiety, and depression, making restaurant dining and drinking (drinking in bars and karaoke added even more to the experience) much craved for and sought after. Young adults were the most likely to seek out these experiences, defying lockdowns and prohibitions to do so. The reasons for making it so hard to enforce social distancing in these situations do not just amount to bad behavior, lack of moral sense, or political orientation but, in a far more fundamental way, descend into the Evo-Devo of prehistory. This has not been written about.

The Psychology of Cyberspace and Its Inhabitants

Cyberpsychology is the subdiscipline of psychology that studies the behavior and feelings of Human Beings, of Cyborgs, in any of the areas of the Multiverse. We are talking here about the nature and behavior of the Self[23] and its interaction with other Selves in Cyberspace (Attrill-Smith, 2019). Contrary to what people sometimes believe, multiple self-presentations can be projected by the Self both offline and online into the physical and virtual worlds; these multiplicities are much easier to deploy in the latter. The Self believes, regardless of any variation of circumstance, that it presents some true or true-fantasy aspect of itself to itself and to others, even, perhaps particularly, when such aspects are playful.

Our Cyberselves engage in all kinds of online activities ranging from working from home (e.g., Telemedicine) to flirting, dating and online sex, to gambling (sometimes pathologically), banking and shopping, to the dark side of the Cyberworld: crime, religious seduction, to the maintenance of terrorist organizations and the planning of terrorist activities (the treasonous attack on the United States Government that occurred on January 6, 2021 could not have happened without the use of the internet[24]). Our involvement in these many activities can be either solitary or as members of a multitude of social groups. These groups can be stable social networks (Christakis & Fowler, 2009) and exist for the long-term (e.g., Facebook groups) or can be short-term and ad hoc.[25]

We manifest both voluntary and involuntary Selves in Cyberspace. We seek to create Cyberselves (or Avatars) that manifest our actual, ideal, or ought selves (Higgins, 1987). The voluntary ones contain what we choose to present about our Selves while the involuntary ones involve what we have to say about ourselves if we want to gain admittance to many parts of the Cyberworld (renewing a professional license or obtaining CEUs come immediately to mind). They involve internet addresses and passwords. There is another sort of Cyberself with which our relationships are much more complex. These are Cyberselves that are created by others or even by programs operating their own search engines and algorithms. These can be for good or ill. A ready example of such an other-created Self can be found by Googling yourself (other Cyberselves can connect with this Self). To see what would happen, I just (March 30, 2021) Googled my email address, mleffert@aol.com. Some usual things appeared, but I also found that ResearchGate had, on its own, created a little site for me listing all of my publications, citations, and places I publish. I have no reason to believe that a Human Being had any part in the process. This feels sort of nice, actually, and I wonder if other Cyberselves have seen it and, if so, what they think about it and me.

The Cyberworld provides a vast technological-psychological space for the living out of relationships that was undreamt of in pre-Internet days. It would have expanded Bachelard's (1958/1994) understandings of space and how we occupy it. As Suler (2016) observes, when we "go" online, when we boot up our computers or Smartphones and enter their networks, when we "do" something—read, send messages, "talk" to others, "text" work, entertain ourselves—we experience ourselves as doing it *someplace*, not sitting in front of our computers or with Smartphone or earbud pressed to our heads. It is "a particular place with palpable features and agendas" (p. 22). The Space on the other side of our device screens or earbuds contains something of our Psyches. It is a transitional space containing parts of Self and other. It is a space that has been *monetized*, but this is no different than the other spaces we inhabit (the dwelling places we live in with family or friends cost money to occupy, just as do many of the things we enter into in Cyberspace). The online and offline worlds have become so enmeshed with each other that the aspects of ourselves that occupy them cannot be fully separate. We have dealings with others online that we also relate to in the physical world yet, for some socially isolated individuals, there are *only* online relationships. The supposed dualism of Online and Offline thus breaks down.

What are the features of this new space? Suler (2016) proposes a Cyberspace architecture comprised of eight dimensions, each a facet or quality of the digital infrastructure that shapes our online experience. They derive as well from the way our minds work. The first of these is *Identity*, which of course has a central Offline psychological role as well. The Online dimension involves the tools that are provided in different areas of Cyberspace that allow us to express who we are. Our psychological Being is articulated in how we choose to use these tools (or are inhibited in using them) to express our identities. The ways in which we choose to construct our online identities are not necessarily conscious. Suler posits, incorrectly and in a Modernist vein, that there is either who we really are or who we choose to or need to make ourselves out to be online. Post-structurally, in a *Post*modern vein, we are, *in part*, whoever we say we are. In different online places we present these different parts of Self. One can also choose to use the internet and venture into Cyberspace trying to *be* no one, but we cannot avoid revealing something of who we are in even the way that our browsing history allows search engines to construct some approximation of us.

The next is the *social* dimension (Suler, 2016), the sum of the online relationships we construct or enter into. Christakis and Fowler's (2009) Social Network Theory offers the most comprehensive tool kit for describing the way we relate to others (other "egos" actually) online. What they don't consider is the role of *memes*, the unit of social contagion first described by Dawkins (1976/2016) or influencers who are particularly powerful meme spreaders (we will talk more of this in the Afterword).

We enter into relationships with other individuals, small groups, large groups, and, sometimes, when we choose to "follow" someone, groups that can number in the millions.[26] These social connections can be bidirectional or unidirectional. They can be chosen or created for us. Personal identity and the social configurations in which we place ourselves or are placed into are interreferential. These relationships by their very nature tend to encourage transference and countertransference reactions; both introduce possibilities for distortion.

Suler (2016) then posits an *interactive* dimension. It entails two things: what we actually *do* in Cyberspace and how *adept* we are at doing it. The former sometimes divides itself into work and play (I connect with friends, shop, and pursue information, but I also treat patients, work on my writing, and manage my finances). Gaming is a pursuit that particularly illustrates how skill levels at *playing* can differ from person to person. In general, the more highly interactive a particular Cyberspace environment is, the more complex, and the steeper the learning curve to master it. When devices or software do not operate as they should—because of "bugs" or hardware failure—we may be more likely to project a personality onto it. The more important the impaired task is, the more intense our need to "solve the problem" and our inability to put it aside.

The dimension of how we communicate in Cyberspace is bimodal. The first began as programming language—telling a computer to perform a series of operations—that Evo-Devo'd into texting, first to the machine and then as the way to communicate and be with others. The second, requiring evermore powerful hardware and elaborate software, is visual and auditory. (Game playing, on the Apple 2 for example, was textual in the early 1980s and progressed to visual in the PC 486 of the late 80s.) We now use these dimensions quite easily for recreational purposes and for communication— FaceTime, Skype, or Zoom.[27]

Time in Cyberspace is different from time in the physical world. It has a speed and rhythm that varies with the architecture of the part of the

Cyberworld one is inhabiting. Beyond that, the great dimensional divide in Cyberspace is whether Cyberevents play out synchronously or asynchronously. Are they back and forth or "post and wait"? I can look up a paper that was written 10, 20, or 50 years ago. Alternatively, I can be on a website and a bubble pops up with someone wanting to know if they can help me, or I can text back and forth for hours. These are all very different experiences.

What is the nature of Cyberspace reality? What is real in the Cyberworld? Here, again, Suler (2016) gets it just a bit wrong, offering a modernist account. By its very existence, anything, including whatever is in Cyberspace, has *some kind* of reality, even if it is of the Post-structural and not the Newtonian variety. What he is talking about is linear, positivist reality, and there are many things in both the physical and the Cyber worlds that don't meet this definition. What is perhaps more relevant is the question of Intentionality (Brentano, 1874/1995). In a particular online situation, is it the aim of its creator and participants to, as much as possible, reference the linear reality of the external world (looking up something on Wikipedia, for example), or is its aim to introduce elements of fantasy and imagination? In either, there is a subjective dimension that can involve conscious and outright lying by participants or the creator of an online situation (careful reading of descriptions of items at auction on eBay can reveal this). In fantasy online experience the Left Brain can know it's a game, but the Right Brain can treat the scenario as real, along with the visceral and autonomic responses to match.

Finally, there is the dimension of physicality. Early on, we did our computing sitting motionless, typing in front of our computers. As the hardware used to enter Cyberworlds Evo-Devo'd, movement, usually hand, sometimes body, became more a part of the online experience, particularly if it involved gameplaying. To describe someone in Cyberspace, we would need to take the measure of all these eight dimensions of Being. What is most obvious is that, as Psychoanalysts and Psychotherapists, we don't do this in any sort of comprehensive way, although the Pandemic has perhaps directed our attention more to the Multiverse.

The question we want to ask of someone (or ourselves) is, "who are you on the internet, who are you trying to be?" The more complete answer is that a Bio-Psycho-Social-Self is engaged in projecting multiple representations of itself into Cyberspace; doing so may be the reason they are in Cyberspace, or it can be an unavoidable byproduct of what happens as they go about their online business. Suler (2016) posits that psychopathology across the diagnostic spectrum is exaggerated in Cyberspace. This would seem to reflect superego pathology and the relative absence of mitigating social controls on the internet. Cyberspace can be a highly regressive environment. The members lists of the American Psychoanalytic Association can serve as useful illustrations. These appeared in the 1990s, making it possible for members to engage in conversations about theory, elections, and psychoanalytic politics. Over the ensuing few years, these interchanges frequently became raucous and at times disrespectful (I would be the first to acknowledge my own participation in some of these). In some ways, they were simply giving voice to the power dimension (Lukes, 2005) of American psychoanalytic life with its rampant problems, but, at times, they descended into overt narcissistic pathology. Many members (again, myself among them) voted with their feet and simply left these members lists. Slowly, *slowly*, these discourses became more self-regulating (with some severe regressions); in addition, the hosts began to eliminate some of the most egregious posts.

This was, I think, fairly representative of internet regulation and self-regulation but, in very recent years, truly dark and primitive elements have appeared, as the internet was used by militias, the Proud Boys, QAnon, and others. These made our psychoanalytic disagreements tame stuff indeed. As Psychotherapists we have not much studied this trend, since it is at some remove from the patients we see. To the extent that it references the equally dark trends that we find in current social issues, climate change, politics, and civic and international conflicts, they should be on our horizon; we and our patients are already living with them and where they will take us in the decades ahead is impossible to say. We can all too easily assume we are living and working in a stable social and climatic situation. Such assumptions are unwarranted; what we know about the behavior of complex systems (Leffert, 2008) is that, while they appear stable, once a tipping point is reached (an unpredictable event), rapid, sometimes catastrophic change can and does occur.[28] I find that, given the *slightest bit* of encouragement, most of my patients want to talk about these things.

In trying to understand the psychology of the internet we have to bear in mind that, over the past two decades, it has morphed from a fringe phenomenon into a central means of Being. Researchers have become very interested in the question, for lack of a better term, is the internet good or is it bad (Clark & Green, 2019)? Until recently, there has been an absence of definitive findings, probably reflecting attempts to compare behavior and experience across too broad aspects of the Multiverse. As therapists this only reflects the necessity of trying to understand (and we must do this) our patients' internet usage on an individual basis. As I have observed, the isolated patients I treated in pre-Internet days would have been greatly helped by these contacts and today, during the Pandemic, it has helped people to survive emotionally. It has allowed therapy to continue. This is true of everyone in my practice. I have two patients, a woman in her 80s and another in her 20s, who have relied on Alcoholics Anonymous for their sobriety.[29] Shortly after COVID lockdowns began in the spring of 2020, AA switched to a Zoom format, which my patients found sustaining, but less so than the in-person meetings. Other, single patients have moved their social and romantic lives over to texting, FaceTime, and Skype. AA had joined the web of online support communities (Coulson, 2019) thriving on the internet. In keeping with these developments and contemporary social trends, online inclusion of people with intellectual disabilities (ID) (Chadwick, Chapman, & Caton, 2019) has made possible "personal development, entertainment, making and maintaining relationships, learning, and employment" (p. 265). In other words, the things that are possible for all of us on the internet are possible for people with ID.

More recent studies (Clark & Green, 2019) have provided increasing information on internet effects. Time spent socializing on the internet with existing friends increases feelings of Subjective-Well-Being while socializing with strangers does not. The positive consequences of an online contact vary with the extent to which it serves a relational purpose. The stronger the emotional connections between people, the more positive the effects of communicating with them online. This is especially true for private communications. Socially anxious individuals particularly benefit from online supportive contacts; control of the interaction and their self-presentations—things not as possible in in-person contacts—seem to be important factors in making these contacts work.[30] The technology, the quality of voice and video transmissions and the competence of the individuals using the technology correlate with the social gains that can be derived from these communications.

Virtual Relationships

We have yet to speak about a kind of cyberspace relationship that has its own type of reality. These are avatar relationships, consciously entered into by playful (this is not to say they are not serious) selves. There are at least two sorts of such relationships. The first involve relationships in which selves create avatars and send them forth to adventure in game-worlds that have been created-for-profit by IT companies. Sometimes the selves know each other in the physical world and set out by prearranged plans to adventure together in the virtual world but sometimes the players are avatars that have only met in cyberspace and form exclusively virtual relationships. The second sort involves relationships formed in cyberspace for the purpose of *having* relationships. They are sometimes between avatars and sometimes between selves claiming to be their physical world selves.

One can meet people in the Metaverse with or without necessarily expecting that the relationship will lead to a relationship in the physical world. They can be relationships between people who are presenting themselves as they are or people who present themselves fictitiously. The latter can involve exploitation and dark purpose as, for example, ISIS members recruiting young woman through social media to convert to Islam and travel to Syria to marry, ostensibly, the man they have been corresponding with. Others involve financially exploitative scams.

Virtual relationships can also be entered into for romantic purposes without any expectation that they will move to the physical world. Selves create avatars or present their fantasied ideal selves: in either case the "ground rules" are known to both parties at the start. Sometimes these are relationships between people unable, for whatever reasons, to form relationships in the physical world, but sometimes they are not, can become addictive, and can suck the life out of physical-world relationships. After all, how can a physical-world relationship between people as they are, compete with a fantasied relationship between avatars who present idealized, grandiose selves, as who they want to be and who they want to be with.

Existentialism and Absurdity in Cyberspace

For all its functionality, Phenomenology (and by extension, Postphenomenology) does not do a particularly good job of dealing with Meaning or Absurdity (Leffert, 2021). I have struggled with the question of the utility of the two terms—Phenomenology and Existentialism—for some time, tried to combine them (Leffert, 2016), and, ultimately, had to accept a rather messy epistemology for their interreferential space.

An intersection of Meaning and Absurdity has recently occurred around the existence of art on the internet. The question of what constitutes art, a sub-inquiry of what has meaning, became post-structurally messy in the early 20th century and has continued to be ever since. Marcel Duchamp illustrates this (Tomkins, 1996) with his series of "readymades," art as found objects, beginning in 1913. In 1917, he presented a urinal, entitled "Fountain." He was asked the question, "Why is this art?" and famously responded, "Because I say it is." His point, and it was a Postmodern point, was that the act of *naming* something art *makes* it art. The art world agrees, with surveys of critics, curators, and gallery owners having named Fountain one of the most important art works of all time. Let's fast forward a century to the internet and the world of Blockchain (a way of locking and ultimately encrypting data so as to make it unchangeable) and Bitcoin (using Blockchain to create internet currency). These in turn led to the creation of Non-Fungible Tokens (NFTs) that can be used to label a piece of code on the internet (text or images, for example). The code can be reproduced, but not the NTF: It becomes something far more definitive than an artist's signature for labeling something as original. Using NFTs to label and sell (usually auction) things on the internet has taken root in 2021. Roose (2021a) wrote an article about NFTs and, as a test case, labeled the article with an NFT, creating a single original, and planned to auction it off. He found (Roose, 2021b) that it sold for $560,000! The question, "Is this image art?" could at best be answered as, "Possibly." Roose found that most bidders on NFTs were men who had made money in IT. He interviewed NFT token collectors and found that they bought what they considered early prominent tokens that, they posited, if the "medium" persisted, could eventually accrue tremendous value. So, I went on Google and searched for NFTs. I found pictures, drawings, images, for sale (or sold) flat out, as numbered issues like fine art prints, or through ongoing auctions. Prices varied from dollars to thousands (in cryptocurrency, of course) of dollars. As a sculptor, knowing at least something about art, I thought that independent of price, some of it was ridiculous while some of it was, I thought, art. (Others have reached similar conclusions.) What's interesting is how new and unstudied this all is. By the time this is read, NFTs will either be an established medium or they will have pretty much disappeared for *this* purpose.

NFTs illustrate how Meaning and Absurdity confront each other on the internet. Each reflects as well Heidegger's dichotomy (1975/1982) of Thrown and Fallen. Everydayness is a separate issue. Activities are available in Cyberspace that throw us into meaning as we explore, create, and maintain and enhance relationships. Cyberspace also offers increasing opportunities for fallen behavior. In addition to the Dark Web, there are obvious things like Porn addiction and games that are graphically murderous and violent but imbue the player with a transient sense of power and accomplishment. The latter often constitute desperate attempts to find Meaning in a life that is lacking in it and a society that creates populations of passive, failed people with no opportunities for success or Meaning.

Focus on these kinds of Fallen activities can also interfere with and damage family and couples relationships (Drouin & McDaniel, 2019). They similarly damage adolescents who choose violent games over schoolwork that they don't experience as preparing them for anything they can grasp as available to them in life. The pathway of high school leading to college leading to some kind of professional training seems Absurd to them, although we are seeing a trend of adults in their 20s–40s figuring this out and seeking out school or training in subjects that will be meaningful to them in furthering their lives.

In writing about Meaning and Absurdity in Cyberspace, I find patients I see coming unbidden into my mind and where they fall into this spectrum, some who use the internet Meaningfully and creatively, and some whose existing psychopathology is expressed in their browsing history. I would posit that, as therapists, we simply don't spend enough time looking at our patients' internet behaviors. I see Louise, a married woman professional in her 60s, with PTSD and fairly severe ADHD. Her symptoms have focused on a rebellion against adulthood and deep passive wishes to be taken care of, as she never was as a child. Problems focus on work and her procrastination in doing it. I was able to discover that, when not actually seeing clients, she spent much of her time in mindlessly surfing the internet. This does not involve compulsive shopping (as it does for some people) but simply *looking*, just as she had watched her crazy family as a child. It was Fallen behavior. Also a talented artist, her time spent in this way detracted from time spent on her art, a major source of Meaning in her life. She felt so guilty about her procrastination in her work that she would not allow herself to do anything else until she completed it. She did intersperse the browsing with, at the very last minute, researching information necessary for her work with clients. Louise's internet practices needed to be analyzed in terms of its multiple functions with her passivity making the work more difficult. Her story is similar to other patients seen over the decades prior to the advent of the internet. What had changed was the contemporary opening up of Cyberworlds that had to be analyzed directly if progress was to be made.

We are left with Heidegger's third way of Being—Everydayness or *Alltäglichkeit*.[31] In Phenomenology it often does not get enough attention. It too manifests itself in Internet practices around getting non-reflective kinds of work done. Much work done on the internet—in these times of COVID, working from home—is of the Everyday variety. Researching a psychopharmacology issue can serve as an illustration. Seeking out side effects that a particular medication might have or a contraindication to prescribing it with some other medication are Everyday sorts of work; they are important kinds of practices that bring with them no special sense of personal meaning. On the other hand, seeking out and researching for precisely the right medication and dosage to solve a particular problem that a patient is having can be both meaningful and gratifying. The psychoanalytic perspective on clinical work, working Psychoanalytically from an Existential rather than a theoretical perspective, offers opportunities to do Thrown rather than just Everyday work in Cyberspace. (Indeed, I suspect that working from a single, rigid theoretical perspective of whatever ilk can easily lead the therapist to a Fallen rather than a Thrown experience.)

Conclusions

As we look back on the breathtaking changes in technology that we have seen over the past century, we can, all too easily, see an ongoing process beyond comprehension or expectation that goes forward into the centuries. But that is not the whole story. In the last chapter, we spoke of the qualitative changes in Evo-Devo that paleoanthropologists (e.g., Mithen, 1994; Renfrew, 1994) had described as the Upper-Paleolithic (ca. 50,000 ya) and Neolithic (ca. 11,000 ya) packages. I would posit that what we have been talking about is the appearance of a *Postphenomenological package*. It is here, *now*.

What validates this hypothesis is the presence of a clearly defined *Postphenomenological toolkit*. For example, the toolkit includes a Smartphone. Smartphones may well evolve, probably *will* evolve, into devices with more direct connections to the brain, both in output and input. At some point, they will probably become implantable. The devices' functions, however, will remain the same, communication, information retrieval and storage, and entertainment, even though it becomes ever-more sophisticated.[32]

Our advance into the Postphenomenological world, like the Prephenomenological and Phenomenological advances that came before it, cannot be judged in any sort of unitary fashion. We have ways in which it expands our lives and ways in which it increases the Meaning that we derive from our Existence. On the other hand, Postphenomenological critics like Turkle (2017) posit that technology, in taking us into Cyberspace, takes us away from each other. The set piece of a family or a group of friends seated at a restaurant table each quietly and individually communicating with World on their devices comes to mind. There is no single answer, of course. Devices don't either increase or decrease Meaning and relatedness. *They can do either*; it is entirely up to the user and what they do with it. An article in the current issue of *The New Yorker* (Kenneally, 2021)[33] that appeared literally in today's mail entitled "Mind Machines: The murky ethics of brain implants" illustrates this.

Epilepsy, and particularly intractable epilepsy, has been, along with Migraine Headaches, a condition of note at least since the advent of recorded history (and probably in Prehistory as well). The first written records date from 2000 BCE. The seizures it produces are caused by abnormal electrical activity in the brain. They were initially thought of as supernatural-religious events, sometimes linked to prophecy, sometimes associated with evil or witchcraft. Treatment has always been of primary importance with the first of the anticonvulsants, phenobarbital, appearing in 1912. Surgical treatment of intractable epilepsy, the separation of the two hemispheres of the Cerebral Cortex by cutting the Cerebral Commissures began in the 1940s with some success and little functional problems. The study of these "split-brain" patients (Sperry, Gazzaniga, & Bogen, 1969) offered much information about human consciousness. Brain implants have been recently found to be of considerable benefit in treating patients' intractable epilepsy, but there are issues around how these Cyborgs dealt with their new hardware. They lead us specifically to the dark side of the Cyborg experience.

In 2010 (Kenneally, 2021), Rita Leggett, a 49-year-old woman suffering since birth with intractable epilepsy, underwent a neurosurgical procedure in which she received an experimental cerebral implant: a cross-shaped silicone implant studded with 16 electrodes. It was subcutaneously connected to a transmitter in size very similar to a cardiac pacemaker positioned subcutaneously on the chest. *It* would then transmit the information wirelessly to a processing unit she was to always keep with her. After the unit learned the electrical activity of her brain it could tell when a seizure was immanent: It would signal her with a red light and a beep. Rita did not like the beep, so she turned it off. For the first time in her life, she knew when a seizure was on the way and had about 15 minutes to get to a safe place and take medication for it. It was a shock to have a machine tell her what was about happen in her head. This was a success, but a more complex one than had been imagined.

> The goal had been simple: to improve her life by giving her more control over her condition. The effect had been to make Leggett feel like an entirely new person. She had never had a Self that she could trust before … she spoke of the device as if it were a partner. "We were calibrated together," she said. *"We became one."*
>
> (p. 39, italics added)

This is the most explicit example of a Postphenomenal experience you might want, but wait, let's talk about another patient. Hannah Galvin, a woman in her 30s who had her first grand-mal seizure at 16, came to hate her implant. She experienced her seizures as outside of herself, not happening to *her*, not a part of herself. (This might have been an indication for psychotherapy.) She resisted her diagnosis. "I'm gone and I'm back and that's that" (p. 42), she said, and asked friends who witnessed a seizure to make a joke of it. As the epilepsy advanced, she lost her ability to do math. Three years in, when she was still unable to effectively titrate her dose of anticonvulsants, she became suicidally depressed. At 22, she decided to have the implant. We might have thought she would, psychologically, be a poor candidate for the device; we would have been right. She hated it from the start. She felt there was someone inside her head that wasn't her. Hannah had found it hard enough to even admit that she *had* epilepsy and the device was now constantly haranguing her about it. She fell into a deep depression. Postphenomenally Rita and Hannah are very different Cyborgs (arguably, Hannah was never a Cyborg), and this was predictable even before the devices were implanted.

Now for the really problematic part: The devices were not a standard treatment for epilepsy; they were offered as part of a very small, "first in human" study undertaken by NeuroVista, an early-stage Seattle firm. Scientifically, the study had been a great success, both as a proof-of-concept and for the data it obtained. But, and it's a big but, in 2013, three years after Rita got her implant, *NeuroVista ran out of money*. The study was shut down and the devices had to be removed. For Rita it was, therapeutically *and* psychologically, a great loss. She was able to adapt to the loss of what was a part of herself. The device had *taught* her about her epilepsy so that she was able to recognize the signs of an approaching seizure, take action to prepare for it, and take an anticonvulsant. In contrast, Hannah was vastly relieved when her device was removed. Kenneally (2021) describes the circumstances in which implantable device studies in general and this study in particular rest on "murky" ethical grounds. Poorly screened, with at times an absence of psychological follow-up, most of us would view these studies as unethical *at best*, criminal at worst. In other studies of implantable devices, suicides have taken place among subjects. Kenneally has Hannah saying she approves of her being a participant in the study to obtain much needed data on implant acceptance. Perhaps this data is needed, but in Hannah's case it seems obvious that she was not a suitable candidate and was somewhat lucky to have escaped with her life.

Let's turn now from Machine to Biological Cyborgs and an *approved* procedure: orthotopic heart transplantation. Differences jump out at once. The gravity of the procedure and its necessarily lengthy follow-up reflect transplant teams' awareness (Kaba, Thompson, Burnard, Edwards, & Theodosopoulou, 2005; Triffaux et al., 2001) of the psychological issues attendant on the procedure. In addition, available hearts, and hearts for which there is an immunological match, are in short supply.[34] Patients in need of a transplant must also want one and, by the time they reach that point on transplant waiting lists, the treatment they need to sustain life until a heart becomes available is close to heroic.

The psychological effects of orthotopic heart transplantation have been extensively studied (e.g., Okwuosa, Pumphrey, Puthumana, Brown, & Cotts, 2014; Triffaux et al., 2001). Posttransplant patients manifest diagnosable levels of depression and anxiety at a rate greater than that found in the general population. The patients studied had been treated psychopharmacologically with a variety of agents, particularly SSRIs, and some were treated with weekly psychotherapy. Treatment was successful at rates similar to those seen in depressed patients drawn from the general population. There are no studies or case reports of transplant patients treated with psychodynamic psychotherapy. The reported treatment approaches offer us little understanding of what it's like to be such a patient.

Another approach is to talk to transplant recipients about what the experience *means* to them; they easily discuss the experience in both rational and fantasied terms. The experience is that of having another person's heart inside of them (Inspector, Kutz, & David, 2004; Kaba et al., 2005). Three quarters of recipients felt that the new heart had given them a new life. Guilt was sometimes present: They had "taken" a heart from someone whose life had been randomly cut short. There was very much a sense of being the recipient of a precious gift; henceforth, the recipient had become its custodian. The heart as an organ is deeply imbued with meaning, as it has been since prehistoric times. It is, for the Right Brain, the center of emotion. Reminiscent of *Totem and Taboo* (Freud, 1913/1953) is the fantasy that the new heart would bring with it some characteristics of the donor. A particular fantasy was that the heart would transmit aspects of the gender of the donor to the recipient if the latter was of a different gender. The point here is that this is a matter of Postphenomenology that is as worthy of analysis as are the machine-based Postphenomenal devices.

Much of what I have been trying to describe in this chapter is caught in the midst of rapid change and may well look different a few years hence. It is very much about the increasingly disparate ways in which we are embedded in World with demarcation between it and Self becoming ever more obscure and ontologically doubtful. Meanwhile, World, again with our participation, has extended itself, this time into Cyberspace. The two aspects of Self that need to be addressed in this context are Consciousness, the tool that we use to consider it, and Death, which inevitably shapes who we are as Human Beings. We will turn to them now over the next two chapters (Merriam-Webster's Dictionary, 2004).

Notes

1 In a very real sense, they most resemble the philosophers of the Classical Age of Greece and, to some extent Rome, in which *both* the physical world (natural science) and human existence were their prevue.

2 Eyeglasses were invented in 1290, the telescope in 1608, and the compound microscope in 1619. While the latter was *invented* in 1619 it remained a curiosity until the

1660s when it became an instrument of science, that is, an artifact. Digital retinas have come into use to provide limited vision over the past decade.

3 In the same way that Aristotle's *Metaphysics* is so named because it came after Physics in a second-century Roman edition of his combined works (Aristotle, 1998).

4 Similar markings have been found in artifacts that predate Anatomically Modern Humans, so this remains a very open question; could, for example, Postphenomenology predate Phenomenology?

5 I would posit that, in a sense, Postphenomenal Being involves artifacts that constitute Self and not Self, World and not World—they are transitional phenomena.

6 Uruk, for example, dating to the fourth-millennium BCE.

7 They must, originally, have been passed on orally as chants wielded by storytellers.

8 Governmental courier services date back to Pharaonic Egypt in 2400 BCE. Rome developed a courier system in the first-century CE to which a separate system of citizens' mail was later added.

9 People have so come to believe that normative families should be like "The Nelsons" or "Father Knows Best" and that their own families were abnormal or deficient. Information about the normative nature of dysfunctional family life was thus suppressed in Social Networks.

10 Two early personal experiences come to mind. In the 1990s, living in the Midwest and having travelled to New York City, I talked with my wife on my cell phone as I walked down Madison Avenue and, a few years later, we both talked to our sons while having dinner in Rome. These now somewhat commonplace events conveyed, at the time, a sense of breathtaking immediacy.

11 *Optical* telegraphs had already been in use in France for a half-century.

12 I am specifying the date because the nature of the artifact accompanying the biological component is rapidly evolving and will probably be unrecognizable in the not-too-distant future.

13 For example, in the 1982 movie *Firefox*, Air Force Major Mitchell Gant (played by Clint Eastwood) is hired by the CIA to steal an advanced Russian fighter plane (the Firefox). The Firefox is operated via thought control through the use of a helmet that interfaces the pilot's brain directly with the plane's computer.

14 Interestingly, I have a couple of times felt that I have been woken out of a sound sleep with a shock. However, my loyal ICD tells me that no shock was given; I had *dreamt* the shock, it had moved into fantasy. In contrast, I have never dreamt of using my Smartphone, but such dreams are, of course possible.

15 I am emphasizing Smartphones over computers and iPads because they are so much more ready-at-hand.

16 An example of this is the familiar mind-body problem in which mind and body have been thought to be separate and different (Descartes, 1641/1999) because they are *consciously* perceived as different.

17 We will consider in chapter 4 whether or not this is a general property of RB Consciousness.

18 This could change as Cyberspace becomes more fully realized as an object of analysis.

19 Growing numbers of Psychoanalysts have websites that are designed to reach out to potential patients. On them they mostly refer to themselves as Psychotherapists, validating a sense that they consider Psychoanalyst and Psychoanalysis off-putting antique terms.

20 It is a mistake to refer to this, as has often been done, as the "real" world and, by extension, the Multiverse as "unreal." The Multiverse and our various presences in it are just as real as is our presence in the physical world we physically inhabit—the dichotomy is between the physical world and the Multiverse.

21 It is very doubtful that the Capitol riots of January 6, 2021, could have taken place without this method of communication and the texting of then President Donald Trump.

22   Increased activity in the multiverse could make up for this to a limited degree, but it lacked the physical and sensory experiences.

23   As a reminder, the Self we are talking about is not some mental structure but rather a Bio-Psycho-Social Entity (Leffert, 2018).

24   To keep the at times confusing nomenclature of the online world straight, the *internet* refers to the physical structures that support the Multiverse in all its Cyber realities.

25   As I write this, I realize that, while informative to the Baby Boom generation in 2021, it will seem quaint at best, ridiculous at worst, to the Millennial generation and beyond.

26   Donald Trump had approximately 70 million followers on Twitter, a circumstance that accrued considerable power to him until his account was closed by the host.

27   In 1999, I moved across the country and planned to continue working with some patients at a distance (Leffert, 2003). After careful research I could find no suitable audiovisual platforms to use for teletherapy and simply used the telephone. As the technology caught up with me, I switched to the audiovisual platforms but, perhaps surprisingly, perhaps not, many patients just preferred the telephone.

28   In modern times, the collapse of the Soviet Union or the appearance of COVID serve as excellent examples of rapid, catastrophic change.

29   I have had considerable success over the years in treating patients suffering from substance abuse, but *only if they were concurrently involved in Alcoholics Anonymous*. Inpatient treatment seemed to have little effect either way although it may have offered an implicit contribution.

30   I read in the Newspapers of therapists offering therapy via texting, which seems to be an extension of this. I know of no studies here.

31   Again, I make a hard distinction between Everydayness and Fallenness that other Phenomenologists do not.

32   Quite analogous in fact to a flint knife becoming more functional and elegant in the Neolithic as part of the Neolithic package (ca. 11,000 ya), ultimately morphing into a bronze blade in the Bronze Age (ca. 5,000 ya), and then an iron blade in the Iron age (ca. 3,000 ya).

33   For our purposes, a magazine article can be more useful than an article appearing in a scientific journal. The reason is that it is written by a *journalist* who focuses on interviewing their subjects and gets us more of the human information we are interested in as clinicians.

34   It's hard to imagine that we are more than at most two or three decades away from being able to culture a needed organ from a patient's own stem cells.

References

Aristotle. (1998). *The metaphysics* (H. Lawson-Tancred, trans.). London, England: Penguin Books.

Attrill-Smith, A. (2019). The online self. In A. Attrill-Smith, C. Fullwood, M. Keep, & R. J. Russac (Eds.), *The Oxford handbook of cyberpsychology* (pp. 17–34). Oxford, England: Oxford University Press.

Bachelard, G. (1994). *The poetics of space* (M. Jolas, trans.). Boston, MA: Beacon Press. (Original work published in 1958).

Barabási, A.-L. (2003). *Linked*. London, England: Plume Books.

Brentano, F. (1995). *Psychology from an empirical standpoint* (L. L. McCalister, trans.). London, England: Routledge. (Original work published in 1874).

Chader, G. J., Weiland, J., & Humayun, M. S. (2009). Artificial vision: Needs, functioning, and testing of a retinal electronic prosthesis. *Progress in Brain Research, 175*, 317–332.

Chadwick, D. D., Chapman, M., & Caton, S. (2019). Digital inclusion for people with an intellectual disability. In A. Attrill-Smith, C. Fullwood, M. Keep, & R. J. Russac (Eds.), *The Oxford handbook of cyberpsychology* (pp. 261–284). Oxford, England: Oxford University Press.

Christakis, N. A. (2019). *Blueprint: The evolutionary origins of a good society*. New York, NY: Little, Brown Spark.

Christakis, N. A., & Fowler, J. H. (2009). *Connected: The surprising power of our social networks and how they shape our lives*. New York, NY: Little, Brown and Company.

Clark, J. L., & Green, M. C. (2019). The social consequences of online interaction. In A. Attrill-Smith, C. Fullwood, M. Keep, & R. J. Russac (Eds.), *The Oxford handbook of cyberpsychology* (pp. 216–237). Oxford, England: Oxford University Press.

Clynes, M. E., & Kline, N. S. (1960). Cyborgs in space. *Astronautics, 26–27*, 74–76.

Coulson, N. S. (2019). Online support communities. In A. Attrill-Smith, C. Fullwood, M. Keep, & R. J. Russac (Eds.), *The Oxford handbook of cyberpsychology* (pp. 241–260). Oxford, England: Oxford University Press.

Dawkins, R. (2016). *The selfish gene: 40th anniversary edition*. Oxford, England: Oxford University Press. (Original work published in 1976).

Derrida, J. (1978). *Writing and difference* (A. Bass, trans.). Chicago, IL: University of Chicago Press.

Derrida, J. (1982). *Margins of philosophy* (A. Bass, trans.). Chicago, IL: University of Chicago Press. (Original work published in 1972).

Derrida, J. (1997). *Of grammatology* (G. C. Spivak, trans.). Baltimore, MD: Johns Hopkins Press. (Original work published in 1974).

Descartes, R. (1999). *Meditations and other metaphysical writings* (D. M. Clarke, trans.). New York, NY: Penguin Books. (Original work published in 1641).

Doidge, N. (2007). *The brain that changes itself*. New York, NY: Viking.

Drouin, M., & McDaniel, B. T. (2019). Technology interference in couple and family relationships. In A. Attrill-Smith, C. Fullwood, M. Keep, & D. J. Kuss (Eds.), *The Oxford handbook of cyberpsychology* (pp. 115–132). Oxford, England: Oxford University Press.

Dunbar, R. (1992). Neocortex size as a constraint on group size in primates. *Journal of Human Evolution, 22*, 469–493.

Dunbar, R. (2016). *Human evolution: Our brains and behavior*. Oxford, England: Oxford University Press.

Fischer, S. R. (2005). *A history of writing*. Netherlands: Reaktion Books Ltd.

Foucault, M. (1980). *Power/Knowledge: Selected interviews & other writings 1972–1977* (C. Gordon, L. Marshall, J. Mepham & K. Soper, trans.). New York, NY: Pantheon Books.

Foucault, M. (2000). *Power* (R. Hurley & Others, trans.). New York, NY: The New Press.

Freud, S. (1953). Totem and taboo. In J. Strachey (Ed.), *Standard edition* (Vol. XIII, pp. 1–161). (Original work published in 1913).

Hakken, D. (1999). *Cyborgs@Cyberspace an ethnographer looks to the future*. London, England: Routledge.

Heidegger, M. (1982). *The basic problems of phenomenology* (A. Hofstadter, trans. Rev. ed.). Bloomington: Indiana University Press. (Original work published in 1975).

Higgins, E. T. (1987). Self-discrepancy: A theory relating self and affect. *Psychological Review, 94*, 319–340.

Hilbert, M., & Lopez, L. (2011). The world's technological capacity to store, communicate, and compute information, *Science, 332*, 60.

Hoffman, I. Z. (1998). *Ritual and spontaneity in the psychoanalytic process*. Hillsdale, MI: The Analytic Press.

Husserl, E. (1983). *Ideas pertaining to a pure phenomenology and to a phenomenological philosophy: Book one: General introduction to a pure phenomenology* (F. Kersten, trans.). New York, NY: Springer. (Original work published in 1913).

Idhe, D. (1979). *Technics and Praxis, Boston studies in the philosophy of science 24.* Amsterdam, Netherlands: Springer.

Idhe, D. (1990). *Technology and the lifeworld: From garden to Earth.* Bloomington: Indiana University Press.

Idhe, D. (1995). *Postphenomenology: Essays in the postmodern context.* Evanston, IL: Northwestern University Press.

Idhe, D. (2010). *Heidegger's technologies: Postphenomenological perspectives.* New York, NY: Fordham University Press.

Idhe, D. (2019). *Medical technics.* Minneapolis: University of Minnesota Press.

Inspector, Y., Kutz, I., & David, D. (2004). Another person's heart: Magical and rational thinking in the psychological adaptation to heart transplantation. *Israel Journal of Psychiatry and Relational Science, 41,* 161–173.

Kaba, E., Thompson, D. R., Burnard, P., Edwards, D., & Theodosopoulou, E. (2005). Somebody else's heart inside me: A descriptive study of psychological problems after a heart transplantation. *Issues in Mental Health Nursing, 26,* 611–625.

Kenneally, C. (2021, April 26 & May 3, 2021). Mind machines: The murky ethics of brain implants. *The New Yorker, 97,* 38–43.

Kim, S. G. (2020). Metaverse: Digital earth, the word of rising things. *Hwaseong: Plan B Design.*

Latour, B. (1993). *We have never been modern* (C. Porter, trans.). Cambridge, MA: Harvard University Press. (Original work published in 1991).

Latour, B., & Woolgar, S. (1986). *Laboratory life the construction of scientific facts.* Princeton, NJ: Princeton University Press.

Leffert, M. (2003). Analysis and psychotherapy by telephone: Twenty years of clinical experience. *Journal of the American Psychoanalytic Association, 51,* 101–130.

Leffert, M. (2007a). A contemporary integration of modern and postmodern trends in psychoanalysis. *Journal of the American Psychoanalytic Association, 55,* 177–197.

Leffert, M. (2007b). Postmodernism and its impact on psychoanalysis. *Bulletin of the Menninger Clinic, 71,* 15–34.

Leffert, M. (2008). Complexity and postmodernism in contemporary theory of psychoanalytic change. *Journal of the American Academy of Psychoanalysis and Dynamic Psychiatry, 36,* 517–542.

Leffert, M. (2010). *Contemporary psychoanalytic foundations.* London, England: Routledge.

Leffert, M. (2013). *The therapeutic situation in the 21st century.* New York, NY: Routledge.

Leffert, M. (2016). *Phenomenology, uncertainty, and care in the therapeutic encounter.* New York, NY: Routledge.

Leffert, M. (2017). *Positive psychoanalysis: Aesthetics, desire, and subjective well-being.* New York, NY: Routledge.

Leffert, M. (2018). *Psychoanalysis and the birth of the self: A radical interdisciplinary approach.* London, England: Routledge.

Leffert, M. (2021). *The psychoanalysis of the absurd: Existentialism and phenomenology in contemporary psychoanalysis.* London, England: Routledge.

Lukes, S. (2005). *Power a radical view* (2nd ed.). New York, NY: Palgrave Macmillan.

Mellars, P. (2005). The impossible coincidence: A single-species model for the origins of modern human behavior in Europe. *Evolutionary Anthropology, 14,* 12–27.

Merleau-Ponty, M. (2012). *Phenomenology of perception* (D. A. Landes, trans.). London, England: Routledge. (Original work published in 1945).

Merriam-Webster's Dictionary. (2004). *Merriam-Webster's Collegiate Dictionary* (11th ed.). Springfield, MA: Merriam-Webster Inc.

Mithen, S. (1994). From domain specific to generalized intelligence: A cognitive interpretation of the Middle/Upper Paleolithic transition. In C. Renfrew, & E. W. Zubrow (Eds.), *The ancient mind: Elements of cognitive archaeology* (pp. 29–39). Cambridge, England: Cambridge University Press.

Okwuosa, I., Pumphrey, D., Puthumana, J., Brown, R.-M., & Cotts, W. (2014). Impact of identification and treatment of depression in heart transplant patients. *Cardiovascular Psychiatry and Neurology, 2014*, 747293.

The Oxford English Dictionary. (1989). *The Oxford English Dictionary* (2nd ed.). Oxford, England: Clarendon Press.

Renfrew, C. (1994). Towards a cognitive archaeology. In C. Renfrew, & E. W. Zubrow (Eds.), *The ancient mind: Elements of cognitive archaeology* (pp. 3–12). Cambridge, England: Cambridge University Press.

Roose, K. (2021a, March 25, 2021). Buy this column on the Blockchain! *The New York Times*, pp. B1, B6,

Roose, K. (2021b, March 27, 2021). A picture of my words is worth $560,000 in the NFT market. *The New York Times*, p. B7,

Rosenberger, R., & Verbeek, P.-P. (2015). A field guide to Postphenomenology. In R. Rosenberger, & P.-P. Verbeek (Eds.), *Postphenomenological investigations: Essays on human technology relations* (pp. 9–41). Lanham, MD: Lexington Books.

Sobchack, V. (2004). *Carnal thoughts: Embodiment and moving image culture.* Berkeley: University of California Press.

Sperry, R. W., Gazzaniga, M. S., & Bogen, J. E. (1969). The neocortical commissures: Syndromes of hemisphere disconnection. In P. J. Vinken, & G. W. Bruyn (Eds.), *Handbook of clinical neurology* (Vol. *4*, pp. 273–290). Amsterdam, Netherlands: North Holland Publishing Company.

Suler, J. R. (2002). Identity management in Cyberspace. *Journal of Applied Psychoanalytic Studies, 4*, 455–459.

Suler, J. R. (2016). *Psychology of the digital age: Humans become electric.* Cambridge, England: Cambridge University Press.

Tomkins, C. (1996). *Duchamp: A biography.* New York, NY: Henry Holt & Co.

Triffaux, J.-M., Wauthy, J., Albert, A., Bertrand, J., Limet, R., & Demoulin, J.-C., et al. (2001). Psychological distress of surgical patients after orthotopic heart transplantation. *Transplant International, 14*, 391–395.

Turkle, S. (2008). Always-on/Always-on-you: The tethered self. In J. E. Katz (Ed.), *Handbook of mobile communication studies* (pp. 121–138). Boston, MA: MIT Press.

Turkle, S. (2017). *Alone together: Why we expect more from technology and less from each other.* New York, NY: Basic Books.

Uddin, L. Q., Iacoboni, M., Lange, C., & Keenan, J. P. (2007). The self and social cognition: The role of cortical midline structures and mirror neurons. *Trends in Cognitive Sciences, 11*, 153–157.

Wellner, G. P. (2016). *A post phenomenological inquiry of cell phones: Genealogies, meanings, and becoming.* Lanham, MD: Lexington Books.

Zhong, B., Huang, Y., & Liu, Q. (2021). Mental toll from the coronavirus: Social media usage reveals Wuhan residents' depression and secondary trauma in the Covid-19 outbreak. *Computers in Human Behavior, 114*, 1–10.

Chapter 4

Consciousness and Unconsciousness

A Fresh Appraisal

Introduction

Consciousness (or at least certain aspects of it) is a fundamental, perhaps the fundamental, aspect of the Being of Human Beings. Over the past decade (Leffert, 2010, 2018), I have attempted to deal with the interreferential subjects of Consciousness and Unconsciousness a number of times. While the latter has been of great interest to Psychoanalysts (e.g., Freud, 1900/1953, 1915/1957) since the start of the 20th century, the former, sometimes termed the "hard problem," has been much taken up by philosophers going back millennia. Phenomenology (e.g., Husserl, 1913/1983, 2005) grew up around Consciousness, meaning to exclude consideration of any [Freudian] Unconscious as a basis for a consideration of Being. A third discipline, Neuroscience (e.g., Sperry, 1969; Sperry, Gazzaniga, & Bogen, 1969), had taken up the subject in mid-century and has played a major role in our recent thinking about it. The anatomical brain has, rightly or wrongly, become a stakeholder in the quest for consciousness. Psychoanalysis and Philosophy have both been moved to co-opt it, looking to Neuroscience to answer old questions and resolve attendant conundrums. None of these efforts have been singularly successful, nor I will posit here, should we expect them to be so.

Neuroscience in particular has attempted to offer a structural analysis of Consciousness, attempting to identify the functional Neuroanatomy behind the process. This, in turn, has only served to emphasize the mind-body dichotomy (Descartes, 1641/1999) involving the experience of Consciousness and the anatomical structures where it putatively resides. Psychoanalysis has mostly (clinically if, perhaps, no longer metapsychologically) continued to cleave to a *system* Unconscious to which thoughts and feelings unacceptable to the ego (I would, returning to Freud prior to 1923, prefer the term *Self*) are banished via repression and returned to Consciousness via interpretation. Hoppe (1977) has gone so far as to suggest

---

* It froze up on me. All Freud references are Standard Edition, the capital is correct. The reference dates are also correct.

DOI: 10.4324/9781003349556-5

repression's anatomical location, *the corpus callosum*, the commissures connecting the two cerebral hemispheres.

Another example of the kind of trouble a student or researcher (philosopher, psychoanalyst, *or* neuroscientist) can get into involves trying to add properties to it. In the IT (Information Technology) world, this is referred to as *feature creep*. Attention and Consciousness are intimately related. Different respected investigators (Dehaene, Changeux, Naccache, Sackur, & Sergent, 2006; Koch & Tsuchiya, 2007) have relied on functional neuroanatomy to distinguish these processes and reached different conclusions. After focusing on the subject myself a number of times, I have been forced to conclude that anatomical location or locations does not add very much to our understanding of or discourse on the subject. We are left to conclude that, for better or worse, Consciousness is a *Primitive*, a concept that cannot be defined in terms of previously defined concepts. Tarski (1946) explains the role of primitives:

> When we set out to construct a given discipline, we distinguish, first of all, a certain small group of expressions of this discipline that seem to us to be immediately understandable; the expressions in this group we call PRIMITIVE TERMS or UNDEFINED TERMS, and we employ them without explaining their meanings. At the same time we adopt the principle: not to employ any of the other expressions of the discipline under consideration, unless its meaning has first been determined with the help of primitive terms and of such expressions of the discipline whose meanings have been explained previously. The sentence which determines the meaning of a term in this way is called a DEFINITION ...
>
> (p. 118)

We have set out to construct a discipline he says, the discipline is *Consciousness Studies*. In setting out to define a primitive, what we often do is rely on intuition, something that gets us into trouble with Consciousness. *Intuition* tells us that the mind and the body are two quite separate things, the difference between willing my arm to go up and my arm actually going up (Descartes, 1641/1999), for example. I can *feel* that difference. Intuition also tells us that Mind has a location, that it is in our heads behind our eyes (they are also located in our heads) through which it looks out on the world.[1] (Interestingly, hearing and sound are not so located via intuition and are very much "out there" in the world. What we can say about this primitive is that it has certain properties (e.g., it is a mental state) and factors that govern its presence (e.g., being preconscious). Koch (Koch & Tsuchiya, 2007), like many other authors, in the past lamented the absence of a definition of Consciousness arguing that "this unfortunate state of affairs will remain until the mechanistic basis of these phenomena has been enunciated thoroughly at the neuronal and molecular levels" (p. 16). This position is not dissimilar from the ones I have taken in the past but have since come to reconsider from a Phenomenological/Existential point of view. This reconsideration involves Subjectivity as a central element of Consciousness and the relevance of Brain and Self as a matter of naturalizing Phenomenology (Petitot, Varela, Pachoud, & Roy, 1999). The mechanistic basis that Koch describes does not, I would now posit, offer much in the way of an increased understanding of Consciousness.

I plan to first offer a brief reprise of where I got to in the past (Leffert, 2010, 2018) exploring the neurobiology of Consciousness and then move on to taking it up as a Primitive. Searching the Neuroanatomy to find Consciousness has great appeal to all three disciplines—Psychoanalysis, Philosophy and Neuroscience—but it is, to date, not at all clear that the results, however interesting, will ever help us solve the Hard Problem. It becomes a problem, all too easily experienced, of confusing interest with utility.

Where We Have Gotten to—A Brief History

In 2010, I did not attempt to offer a definition of Consciousness but proposed instead to look at what such a definition needed to include, as well as the interesting ways that others had failed at it. While the anatomical components of the Self—brain and body—and its connections to World are necessary for the existence of Mind, there is no evidence that they are *sufficient* to provide an account either of Consciousness or Mind. Contemporary circles of neuroscientists and neurophilosophers (e.g., Edelman, 1989; Kandel, 2006; Koch & Greenfield, 2007; Solms, 2021) have nevertheless attempted to do just that. Others (e.g., Churchland, 2002) have offered more sophisticated arguments that, ultimately, have proved equally unsuccessful. I am not going to offer a reprise of my critiques (Leffert, 2010, 2018) of their positions here because they don't add to our understanding of Consciousness.

There are similar issues involving the linked concepts of a discrete, psychological System Unconscious and the defense mechanism of Repression that serves as its doorkeeper. They have been taught for over a century in training programs in Psychoanalysis and dynamic Psychology, Psychiatry, and Social Work. Like most psychoanalytic concepts prior to the end of the 20th century, *they were taught without supporting evidence* and largely continue to be taught in this manner. In other words, they are treated as if they are primitives, taken for granted, as if they were part of the "small group of expressions of this discipline that seem to us to be immediately understandable" (Tarski, 1946, p. 118). But they are not. We can all too easily confuse evidence with the Representativeness Heuristic (Kahneman, Slovic, & Tversky, 1982), which tells us, in effect, "I recognize this, I've seen it before, *so it's true*," with most of this process taking place outside of awareness. This has become so multigenerationally ingrained into our thinking that it is nearly impossible to convince most clinicians that it even *might* not be true.[2] If viewed from a perspective of irreducible personal subjectivity, this may not necessarily be such a problem. We observe clinically that patients (and ourselves!) remember some things and do not remember others. As the work (or life) proceeds, we remember things we have not remembered before and sometimes forget things. Researchers in the field of memory have a lot to say about this (e.g., Schacter, 1996, 2001) without reference to a Dynamic Unconscious. If, however, clinicians choose to categorize their readings and observations about memory as defining a system Unconscious, is it even more heretical to suggest that this isn't a problem, not really, and that they can do the same clinical work with the same results as those of us who do not accept this identity category, an Unconscious (Leffert, 2010; Willingham & Preuss, 1995), or the related one of Repression? This is really an argument about epistemological standing that recapitulates arguments dating back to the mid-20th century. They concern the debates over Psychology versus Metapsychology (Gill, 1976; Gill & Holtzman, 1976). They posited that psychoanalysis comprised two theories rather than one (Leffert, 2010). The first is a clinical theory relating to psychoanalytic ways of working with patients. It is grounded on clinical work and how it produces Therapeutic Action. It is a *Clinical* Theory. The second is a *Theory Theory*, a Metapsychology. It is beyond the clinical or the psychological. Things like Ego-Psychology and a System Unconscious fall into this identity category.[3] They are hypothetical and arbitrary; they lack supporting clinical evidence. A number of schools of psychoanalytic thought—Self Psychology, the Relational and the Intersubjective, the Postmodern, the Existential-Phenomenological—have set off from this point. I have also argued on a number of occasions (Leffert, 2021) that there is often a distinction between what an analyst thinks they are doing with a patient, what they tell others they are doing, and what they are actually doing (a potentially Unknowable); how they conceptualize what is going on in the Therapeutic Situation and what *is* going on. Our discipline is simply not a physical science and, as we have come to know, cutting-edge science, physical or otherwise, is also very much about uncertainty.

The critique I have offered in the past is of the existence of a System Unconscious dynamically organized along psychoanalytic lines, *not* of the existence of unconscious mental processes. Indeed, there are far more of *these* than there are conscious ones. Some of the contents of some of these processes do become conscious under different circumstances, and some of them are capable of remaining so. This is a Phenomenological representation of unconsciousness and says all we are really capable of saying about it.

Let's look at three different sorts of Neuroscience studies, a study that seeks to determine if a subject *is* Conscious (Owen, 2017; Owen et al., 2006), studies of split brains (Sperry, 1969; Sperry et al., 1969), and studies of different kinds of consciousness and memory (Tulving, 1985/2003; Tulving, Kapur, Craik, Moscovitch, & Houle, 1994) to see just what they can tell us about Consciousness.

In 1997 (Groopman, 2007; Owen et al., 2006), a 26-year-old school teacher named Kate Bainbridge fell into a coma after a strange illness and was hospitalized at Addenbrooke's Hospital at the University of Cambridge. In one of the coincidences that sometimes occur in Science Studies (Latour, 1991/1993; Latour & Woolgar, 1986), Adrian Owen, a neurologist doing research in positron emission tomography (PET scanning) moved into a lab next door to Kate's ward. He heard about her case and began to study her with a series of sophisticated experiments. PET scans reveal areas of increased metabolic activity and blood flow in the brain; they reveal if an area of the brain is cognitively active. Owen found that if he showed Kate pictures of her family, her brain showed the same activity as that of a normally conscious person and different from when she was shown pictures of random people. Since he couldn't be sure that he had captured her glance, he substituted headphones, recordings, and noise; he obtained the same results.

Owen (Owen et al., 2006) was uncertain whether the speech had been understood as opposed to simply recognized. To determine this, he asked the patient to perform two tasks: to imagine a game of tennis (a motor task) and to take them on a tour of her home room by room (a memory task). Again, the results were the same as with a normally conscious person. In an accompanying editorial "Is She Conscious?" Naccache (2006) attempted to deal with the conundrum that Owen presented; he had little success. The problem is that here is a Human Being in whom all the mental activity and associated neuroanatomical equipment that one normally associates with Consciousness is present and active, and yet, the person is *not* Conscious. So this would suggest that Consciousness is something else. Or we might instead label this sort of reasoning and the sophisticated experimentation that goes with it, the *neuroanatomical fallacy of Consciousness Studies*. Let's try something else.

Beginning in 1940 (Van Wagenen & Herren, 1940), in the days when anti-convulsant therapy was limited to Dilantin and phenobarbital, neuro-surgeons began to treat intractable epilepsy with Commiserectomies, the surgical division of the Cerebral Commissures that prevented the spread of waves of pathological electrical activity across the brain. They had considerable success. The procedure was further developed by Bogen and Vogel (1962). The Commissures were comprised of roughly 200 million axons joining the Cerebral Hemispheres. The procedure seemed to produce two "brains," a left brain (LB) and a right brain (RB), that were extensively studied (Galin, 1974; Sperry, 1969; Sperry et al., 1969; Wolford, Miller, & Gazzaniga, 2004). Sperry, who received a Nobel Prize for his work, went on with his associates to make movies of the behavior of the split-brain subjects he studied. What was most striking about these patients, who had had surgical procedures that had *profoundly* interrupted the way their brains communicated, was how they and their functioning were virtually indistinguishable from that of individuals with normal, that is non-divided, brains. Sperry saw them as having two separate minds, each unaware, that is, unconscious, of the other that, in normal individuals, make up a single blended mind.

Sperry and colleagues (Sperry et al., 1969) developed research protocols based on strategies to interview and test each brain hemisphere in isolation from the other. Significant information was already available to them. Language and speech developed in the LB and, in Commisurectomy patients, the LB is in control. The RB is not able to express itself verbally or in writing, but it can recognize and communicate the *sign* properties of words (if shown the printed name of an object, it can pick that object out of a box). Sensory and motor functions still decussate (cross-over) to the opposite hemisphere. When the RB is shown an image it cannot communicate about it, and the LB, if then asked about it, will usually confabulate but shows evidence of the image through activities of the autonomic nervous system. Their first film shows a young woman who, using a tachistoscope,[4] is shown a series of geometrical images in her left visual field (RB). When a nude pinup is mixed in with them she blushes and giggles. When she is asked what she saw her left brain (LB) confabulates and says a "white light." Then she giggles again and says to the examiner, "That's some machine you have there!"

A different subject is asked to arrange a group of blocks into a particular design. The Left hand (the RB, with its superior spatial vision) easily accomplishes this task. When asked to use the right hand (LB), the response is slow and error-filled. Then, all of a sudden, the left hand snakes out and grabs the correct block!

Some authors (Bogen, 2000; Hoppe, 1977) describe commisurectomized patients as dreaming only a little about day-to-day matters and lacking latent content. I would posit that these are LB dreams; there *are*, presumably, RB dreams that the patients don't have access to and the RB cannot tell us about them. The LB can learn about and deal with the split (Sperry et al., 1969): If a split-brain subject is asked to pick up an object with their left hand (RB), the LB can learn to take control by saying, for example "cube." The RB then uses this word-sign to pick up the designated object, by-passing the function of the commisure. We can, I think, posit that the LB represents the Psychoanalytic conscious/preconscious in normal individuals and the RB does pretty much what some of us assign to a System Unconscious.

What does this tell us about Consciousness? We know that the cerebral hemispheres are conscious in different ways, about different things, and operate very differently. They develop very differently as well, with the RB developing first as the seat of parallel cognition, emotional knowing, and psychosomatic integration and the LB the seat of serial logic, narrative, and self-reflection. Describing the Consciousness of the two hemispheres does not really tell us much about Consciousness itself, beyond the fact that it manifests itself differently in each.

Tulving (1985/2003), in a now classic paper, posits a relationship between different sorts of Consciousness and different sorts of Memory. Tulving aims to "relate memory to consciousness in terms of data obtained through clinical observation and laboratory experiment" (p. 579). He defines three kinds of memory—Procedural Memory, Semantic Memory, Episodic Memory—for each of which the experience of Consciousness is different. Procedural Memory is memory of how things are done; cognitively, perceptually, and motorically. Semantic Memory is memory of the symbolically representational knowledge that organisms possess. Episodic Memory is the memory of personal experience presented in narrative form. Tulving further concluded that Procedural Memory *entails* Semantic Memory as a specialized subcategory and that the latter entails Episodic Memory. These memory functions are *nested*, one within the other.

Each of these memory systems, the Procedural, the Semantic, and the Episodic, is characterized by a different kind of consciousness: anoetic (non-knowing), noetic (knowing), and auto-noetic (self-knowing), respectively. Non-knowing Consciousness is limited to perceiving, representing, and responding to the external and internal present—it does not reference non-present aspects of World or Self. Knowing Consciousness provides awareness of things present in World and those not present that are remembered and flexibly acting on these knowledges. Self-knowing Consciousness, a specialized subset of the knowing that we are most interested in, involves the remembering of personally experienced *events*. *It* involves self-reflection, an awareness of time, the construction of future events and, most important of all, an awareness of our own eventual deaths and the deaths of those we love.[5] One can locate the encoding and retrieval of these different kinds of Memory and Consciousness as taking place in different anatomical parts of the brain (Tulving et al., 1994), but doing so is not really of much help in understanding Consciousness. They also leave unanswered the question of where we find these functions in hominins, primates, and animals other than ourselves. It is important to note that, in spite of all this information about consciousness, Tulving (1985/2003) believes that "understanding consciousness, its *emergence* from the brain and its role in human intelligence and in human affairs can only come, *if it ever does come*, at *the end of a very long scientific journey*" (p. 588, italics added). The point here is that Tulving's conclusions are very similar to my own; that such Consciousness Studies, however interesting, do not really tell us anything more about what it is. The concept of Consciousness *emerging* from the Brain (I would say the Bio-Psycho-Social Self[6]) is of use, however, and points in the direction that understanding the behavior of complex systems, of which the Self is one, can teach us something about Consciousness.

The argument that has been made in the past by other authors including myself that *true Consciousness is Autonoetic Consciousness* and that only ourselves, some of our ancestors and perhaps a very few animals and birds are thus Conscious is one I can no longer sustain. Consciousness is Consciousness, and Tulving is describing different kinds of Consciousness; all three are Conscious. I would posit as well that many (how many I can't say) Human Beings do not manifest much Autonoetic Consciousness and that, in Heidegger's terms, they are not thrown; they are limited to the everyday and the fallen forms of Being.

Complexity and Consciousness

I have previously written (Leffert, 2008, 2010) about Complexity as a property of the Self that impacts the way Therapeutic Action and Change take place in Psychotherapy and Psychoanalysis. Complexity does also help us to understand more about Consciousness as a property of the Self; it is, after all, the Self and not the Brain that is Conscious.

While a comprehensive discussion of Complexity (e.g., Marion, 1999; Mitchell, 2009) is beyond the scope of this chapter, we can discuss a number of its aspects that bear on the nature of Consciousness. Complex systems are large, often very large. They change over time. *Their behavior is unpredictable from its antecedents or from that of its component parts.* This includes the propensity of Complex systems to manifest massive, sudden change when tipping points are unpredictably reached. Adjectives like indeterminacy, unpredictability, unknowability, and nonlinearity are frequently used to describe the behavior of Complex Systems. Such systems, like the Self, are so large, have such numerous components, and are constantly changing to a degree such that it is impossible to fully categorize, classify, or audit them. Attempts to categorize Consciousness in terms of the activity of some part of the Brain thus cannot succeed; searching for Consciousness in the Brain becomes something of a Grail quest with repeated failed claims of success.

The "sand pile game" illustrates complex behavior. Imagine a flat surface. Grains of sand are released from the same source and fall individually at the same rate and on the same spot. (The game can be modeled via a computer simulation (Bak, 1996; Bak, Tang, & Weisenfeld, 1987).) A sand pile builds up and, periodically, avalanches occur. None of this, the size and shape of the pile, when and where the avalanches occur, their shape, and the changing shape of the pile is predictable. In particular, they are not predictable from the behavior of each falling grain of sand.

The Self is a much larger example of such a Complex System. Its component cells know nothing about the behavior of the system and have only local knowledge of what's going on in their immediate vicinity (in Christakis and Fowler's (2009) terms, they make up a superorganism). These *localities* can and do sometimes behave in linear ways. (Shining a red light in one's eye reliably returns the perception of the color red—so long as one is not colorblind, however.) The hallmark, perhaps, of such a system as a whole is that its behavior is not equal to or predictable from the sum of the behaviors of its component parts and may constitute something entirely new. (The nature of the parts of the system do, however, shape and, at times, constrain the range, if not the timing of such behaviors.) Complex Systems thus manifest *emergent* properties.

One of those emergent properties of the Complex System called the Self is Consciousness. Conscious, reflective, thought can be linear and predictable (thinking about a task or course of action) or nonlinear and unpredictable (brainstorming or allowing oneself to associate freely). These two patterns suggest locally the activities of the left and right cerebral cortexes. If we are talking about Consciousness as an emergent property of the Complex System *H. sapiens sapiens*, we have to consider the place or presence of it in other, similar systems—vertebrates, mammals, birds, primates, and hominins.

Animal Consciousness?

Over the last few decades, there has been a fundamental shift in how we view Consciousness in animals. The prior view maintained that Human Beings were uniquely Conscious and, with the exception of Chimpanzees and African Grey Parrots, the only organisms capable of symbolic logic. Anoetic Consciousness/Procedural Memory was to be found in more or less all vertebrates, while Noetic Consciousness/Semantic Memory was to be found in Mammals (Tulving, 1985/2003). This has changed and, with it, the issue has been reformulated: We are both interested in how animals might be Conscious and in the *Evo-Devo* of Consciousness (Feinberg & Mallatt, 2016). Recent thought (Ogas & Gaddam, 2022) considers Consciousness in one-celled organisms. Paleoneuroscience involves a consideration of Consciousness in our hominin ancestors (Dunbar, 2016; Terrace & Metcalfe, 2005) and more thinking about animal Consciousness. This work moves beyond Tulving's classification of Consciousness and Memory. Thus we have primary or sensory Consciousness and Nagel's (1970) now-classic formulation that Consciousness involves being able to formulate the question *What is it like to be a …?*

Feinberg and Mallatt (2016) posit that the earliest forms of Consciousness, found in all vertebrates, first appeared in the so-called Cambrian explosion[7] (Gould, 1989), ca. 500 million ya. They involve mapped *exteroceptive consciousness*, distant, affect-free perceptions of the world having to do with neural representations that involve the lower midbrain. Evolution continued to *sentience*, literally "capable of feeling," encompassing large, memory-enhanced systems that include emotion and involve the cerebrum. These are the beginnings of the systems comprehensively described by Panksepp (Panksepp & Biven, 2012). They appeared in mammals around 60 million ya. This is a move from *sensory consciousness to subjective experience*. It also involves *interoceptive consciousness*, consciousness of bodily sensation. Nociception, the experience of negative sensations or pain, was probably the first of these to appear.[8] For Feinberg and Mallatt, the basic question remains the mind body problem, the "hard problem": How does a neurobiological Brain produce subjective experience? They posit that the way to solve the hard problem is to approach it simultaneously from three directions: the *philosophical*, the *neurobiological*, and the *neuroevolutionary*. I would suggest instead, following Latour (1991/1993), that we are dealing with a developing, very large, branched chain hybrid constructed of multiple elements drawn from these three sources in which, following complexity theory, the whole is different from and greater than the sum of its parts. But does this (Feinberg & Mallatt, 2016; Latour, 1991/1993) tell us anymore about the subjective consciousness we experience? I retain my doubts. I think we can perhaps say that Consciousness *is* sentience.

If we look at neural structure in very broad terms we can look at the evolutionary appearance of the experience of pain perception and regulation in the Cerebrum as opposed to the presence of perceptions of painful stimuli, nociception, in the midbrain. Feinberg and Mallatt (2016) survey the work of a great many authors that show these apparatuses to be present in reptiles, birds, and mammals. With them comes the appearance of operant conditioning and longer *experiences* of pain as contrasted with classical conditioning and avoidant behavior. (An animal *choosing* to continue in a painful situation for the purpose of achieving some *desired* goal.) They fit the behavioral criteria for affective consciousness. These are the same structures associated with affective consciousness and regulation in us, that is human beings. This is a very different kind of Consciousness than, for example, my ability to remember the first day of my psychiatric residency—but it *is*, however, Consciousness.

We cannot consider affective consciousness without describing the work of Jaak Panksepp (Panksepp & Biven, 2012). He posited seven primary affective states (SEEKING, FEAR, RAGE, LUST, CARE, PANIC, and PLAYfulness)[9] demonstrated through cross-vertebral studies and characterized as "initially unconditioned, 'objectless' neuroevolutionary, affect-laden response tendencies arising from [phylogenetically] very ancient lower regions of the brain, whereas all human cognitions are thoroughly conditioned by life experience and language processes located within higher neocortical brain regions" (Panksepp, 2009, p. 2). The latter involve what Panksepp posited as secondary and tertiary affective states. How these higher functions are distributed among mammals and birds has become a subject of some uncertainty and debate.[10]

I am going to suggest that there exists a particular kind of Consciousness—*Self*-Consciousness—present in some, for lack of a better term, of the higher vertebrates, and that Self-Consciousness presents, in different species, with a hierarchical series of evolving properties. These properties unfolded across mammalian and avian Evo-Devo, studied by zoologists, ethologists, paleontologists, anthropologists, and paleoanthropologists—an Evo-Devo of Consciousness. These properties can be documented or inferred as being present in hominin Evo-Devo (Dunbar, 2016).

If Consciousness is a Primitive, it does not mean that it is the same in all animals. Conscious, subjective *experience* exists in all vertebrates but differs from species to species. In his eponymous paper, Nagel (1970) chose the question: What is it like to be a bat? Bats have notoriously poor vision but they make up for it with a kind of sonar. They vocalize a series of hypersonic squeaks projecting a uniform field onto the world regardless of direction. The sounds bounce off of the objects that *we* see and enable bats to perceive our visual world auditorily. With the exception of the whales, porpoises, and dolphins, perception in the other vertebrates and us is passive-receptive; we can have no idea of what this active perception feels like (the closest we can come is shining a flashlight in a darkened room) and can have no *experiential* sense of what it's like to be a bat. We can, however, with uncertain accuracy, intuit it. This fits with our Theory of Mind (ToM) (Baron-Cohen, 2000; Baron-Cohen, Tager-Flusberg, & Cohen, 2000).

More recently, Tulving (2005) has argued that only Human Beings possess autonoetic Consciousness, that is the capacity for episodic or narrative memory and the ability to engage in mental time travel into the past and future. It involves the remembering of events in their subjective time—*chronesthesia*. The Self, the remembering Self, is present in autonoetic Consciousness where it is not in the other memory systems. Tulving avoids the question of just when in human Evo-Devo (Dunbar, 2016) these capacities appeared. His is a more nuanced position than it might at first glance appear. It allows, for instance, for the fact that some other vertebrates can have semantic memory for undated facts that happened in the past and can know something of Death (and, as we shall see, manifest some capacity for mourning) both essential features of Existential/Phenomenological Consciousness. Tulving narrows his arguments to the properties of one kind of Consciousness (autonoetic) and one kind of memory (episodic).

Many authors, challenging Tulving (2005), have recently (e.g., Clayton, Bussey, & Dickinson, 2003; Schwartz, 2005) looked at the question of whether other vertebrates and primates manifest episodic memory. They have studied scrub jays, chimpanzees, and a lowland gorilla. Results showed that they all could tie a "when" to a particular memory such as the placement of an item of food (when and where it was hidden or cached, etc.). However, episodic or narrative (the old term) memory tells a story, a story of the events surrounding some object or feeling that occurred in the past and the ability to imagine such a thing taking place in the future. This is not what these researchers demonstrate. What they show is the ability of certain animals to "date-stamp," if you will, semantic memory. An argument can be made that the absence of speech is what makes this impossible to prove, but an equally plausible (perhaps more plausible) argument is that language and its capacity are necessary building blocks for episodic memory.

Can the presence of emotion tell us anything about consciousness in animals? Panksepp (Panksepp, 2008; Panksepp & Biven, 2012), as we saw, identified seven primary affective states documented in studies across vertebrates and arising in the lower regions of the Brain. He posited the existence of secondary and tertiary emotional states with the latter in particular arising out of complex neocortical interactions incorporating activity at all levels of the Brain (I would argue that 'all levels of the Self' is a more accurate and encompassing way of putting it). I would argue that there are a number of capacities—empathy, self-awareness, grief, consolation, an awareness of Death—which, when taken together, form a complex that offers evidence of autonoesis. In addition to being found in *H. sapiens sapiens*, that is, in *us*, they are found in Chimpanzees, Gorillas, Elephants, and Dolphins. (Elephants, BTW, have four times the central nervous system neurons that we possess.) They manifest the subjectivity of Consciousness (Koch & Greenfield, 2007) while at the same time being externally observable and identifiable. We experience them subjectively in ourselves and observe them in other Human Beings and in these animals. For example, these animals console each other in response to emotional or physical pain. They manifest self-awareness by passing the mirror test (this is suggestive, Tulving aside, of Autonoetic Consciousness). In the mirror test, the subject is anesthetized and a mark is placed on their forehead. In a positive result, when provided with a mirror, the subject sees and immediately touches the mark on their head. (Humans pass the mirror test at about age 18 months, when the Left Brain[11] is myelinized and comes online.) As King (2014) observes the tertiary emotion grief:

> Should [bonded] animals no longer be able to spend time together—the death of one partner being one possible reason—the animal who loves will suffer in some visible way. She may refuse to eat, lose weight, become ill, act out, grow listless, or exhibit body language that conveys sadness or depression.
>
> (p. 9)

King stresses that grief does not require or point to a *cognitive knowledge* of Death. Grief is powered by absence and perhaps, perhaps, an awareness that the absence of a loved partner is permanent.

Then there are the observations of birds like African Gray Parrots and New Zealand Keas who seek out and emotionally relate to each other and to us. An African Gray is found sitting on a backyard fence in a Tokyo suburb. He is taken to a veterinary hospital to be looked after where he announces his owner's name and address and is returned home. Keas, termed the world's smartest birds, communicate with each other by vocalizations and can empathically sense emotions in humans. What can be concluded from these observations is less certain.

If we look at mammals, birds, and reptiles (Bekoff, 2007; King, 2014), formerly thought to possess only what Tulving (1985/2003, 2005) termed noetic consciousness, a more complex picture has emerged. Tulving's sharp demarcations of separate kinds of Consciousness do not hold up in real world conditions; an individual's Consciousness at any one time involves interreferential, shifting elements of all three of the forms of Consciousness—anoetic, noetic, and autonoetic—that he posits.

For Panksepp (2008), the central question is, "How does neural activity create affective experience?" (p. 47). Affective experience lies in the foundations of subjective Consciousness. Consciousness combines affective *states* generated in the lower brain with cognition that arises out of its interaction with information that is, in effect, harvested from perception.

There is no reason to doubt that such a process occurs in other animals. Affects in isolation are primary, pre-propositional states that are hard to define or ascribe to *experience*. The cognitive component can only come from simultaneous noetic Consciousness that combines Semantic Memory with real time perception. The neural evidence for affects exists in the observation that profound affects can be generated by Localized Electrical Stimulations of Specific Neural Systems (LESSNS). The effects of stimulating specific subcortical brain regions are homologous across the Class Mammalia (this includes us). This is highly suggestive that other mammals experience the same primary process emotional states we do; these states demonstrate their presence in animals in much the same way as they do in us; animals, unlike some of us, are simply unable to talk about them.

If we ask just who (or what) experiences these feelings or the thoughts that may be appended to them, the answer is the Bio-Psycho-Social Self that exists as an ever-more-complex entity in increasingly evolved and developed mammals. This property of Selfness is inseparable from Consciousness.

So Where Do We Go from Here?

What is important for us is that Consciousness, a primitive, is a mental phenomenon and a dimension of experience that is subjective. Contrary to Koch (2019), we saw that elucidating its mechanistic basis, however interesting, even compelling, does not further our inquiry into this subjective process. At its extreme point, we know that large amounts of brain tissue can be lost without impairing Consciousness, while

> Beginning subcortically and plunging into the brain stem is a tangly, snarly collection of neurons called the reticular formation (RF), which seems to collect information "downstream" from the brain stem and the peripheral and autonomic nervous systems and connects bilaterally "upstream" with the nucleus reticularis of the thalamus (NRT) and the intralaminar nuclei (ILN) of the thalamus. From there, connections branch out all over the brain.
>
> (Leffert, 2010, p. 168)

Somewhere in this group of structures, I believed in 2010, we would find the biological origins of Consciousness, or Koch's "mechanistic basis" of the phenomenon. We knew that bilateral lesions of even a few cubic millimeters, the size of a couple of grains of rice, could produce irreversible coma. I felt at the time that, by avoiding the seductions of the mind-body problem, I could say more definitive things about what exactly Consciousness is. A careful reading of what I had to say (Leffert, 2010, 2018) suggests that I was seduced instead by functional neuroanatomy. Although it is certainly fascinating to use fMRIs and PET scans to observe what areas of the brain light up in response to verbal or auditory direction of cognitive activity (e.g., Owen et al., 2006), this process, while suggestive of the *presence* of Consciousness does not tell us much about what it *is*. I am left with the conclusion that the neuroanatomy, always an interest of mine, does not tell us all that much about Consciousness, not really.

I want to be clear, however, that I am not abandoning *physicalism* as it relates to the understanding of consciousness. Physicalism simply states that something, in this case Consciousness, exists in the physical world and has physical properties that can be studied. We have tried to study Consciousness empirically and have found these attempts mostly unsatisfying. This does not mean that it cannot be empirically studied, only that we do not yet have the tools for such study but most likely will at some point in the future. It is tempting to confuse measuring the electrical activity occurring in the brain when one is conscious or conscious of particular things with actually measuring Consciousness. The problem lies in trying to understand Consciousness physically as some kind of sum of the electrical activity of the neurons in the brain; this is what neuroscientists have attempted and failed at. Such research has been of critical importance; who doesn't want to understand how neurons work and interact with each other? Key neuroscience research took place during the second half of the 20th century and the first decade of the 21st century that effectively tackled this Neuroscience. The payoff in understanding of these studies largely tapered off thereafter. Although researchers continued to understand more about how things worked in the Brain, this did not offer additional help with the "Hard Problems" such as Consciousness and Human Being and Consciousness and Mammal Being. This resulted in a number of authors (e.g., Koch, 2019) shifting their focus from the micro to the macro, from Neuroscience to Neurophilosophy.

This limitation on what we can understand from today's Neuroscience is not an attack on physicalism. It only means that we *currently* lack the physical tools to reveal anything interesting *about* Consciousness, not that those tools cannot exist or that we won't have them some day.[12] This failure had led to equating Consciousness with Metaphysics; a degradation of the term's ontology, if you will, and a continuation of Descartes' (1641/1999) formulation of a mind-body dichotomy with Mind being the location of Consciousness. He, in effect, posited Brain and Mind are ontologically different and incapable of being integrated. Spinoza (1676/2011), and, into the present, Damasio (2003) posited that Mind and Body offer differing views, in the vein of quantum theory, parallel attributes, of the same thing. If we take a close look at this, we find that it doesn't tell us much about what Consciousness is and what properties it has. For example if we use the contemporary 60-channel Electro-Encephalogram to record the electrical activity of the Brain we find that particular patterns are present when an individual is Conscious as compared to when an individual is not. These patterns do not either define or describe Consciousness. They represent only, as Koch (2019) describes, Neural Correlates of Consciousness (NCC)—present when someone is Conscious, otherwise absent.

In addition to NCC, there are two other elements (Tononi, Boly, Massimini, & Koch, 2016) that we have to consider if we are talking about the functional neuroanatomy of Consciousness. One is the Physical Substrate of Consciousness (PSC) and the other is Integrated Information Theory of Consciousness (ITT). ITT is the new big thing in Consciousness research. Integrated Information is denoted by Φ, this signifies information that is specified by a system that cannot be reduced to information specified by its parts. Such an experience "is unitary, meaning that it is composed of a set of phenomenal distinctions, bound together in various ways, that is irreducible to non-interdependent subsets" (p. 452). Tononi (2017) conclude that, in IIT, "a physical system has subjective experience to the extent that it is capable of integrating information" (p. 288). Φ is also the measure of a system's complexity: the information that is present in a system that is greater than the total of the information present in each of its parts. "*A system is conscious to the extent that its whole generates more information than its parts*" (Seth, 2021, p. 61). It is both *informative* and *integrative*. At the end of the day, Consciousness is, simply, integrated information. Concealed in the neuroscience, then, is a powerful Phenomenological premise.

Tononi (2017) posits a somewhat (but not entirely) different argument than I have been making, that the two main problems posed by consciousness can be profitably approached from a neuroscience perspective. The first is to determine just what features of the brain determine the presence of consciousness. Most authors acknowledge that consciousness has to do with a conversation between certain thalamic nuclei and the hemispheres of the cerebral cortex. The second is what specific features of the brain determine how consciousness is experienced. This problem also speaks to my suspicions that consciousness is different in different individuals. What, for example, makes specific areas of the cerebral cortex contribute different things to conscious experience?

IIT is currently a hot, and hotly contested, theory of Consciousness. As Seth (2021) observes, its extraordinary claims require extraordinary evidence to substantiate, evidence that cannot be obtained.

We can tell through observation and the use of various instruments (an EEG, for example) whether someone *is* Conscious, but to know anything more *about* their Consciousness—the Consciousness *of*—in the moment or historically, we must rely on subjective reports of their human experience. Consciousness of is of particular importance when it is of *feelings*. This is a much-contested point within psychoanalysis: Can feelings exist if they are not conscious? Freud (1915/1957) at the very start said "no." Many of us (and I include myself in the past here) like to imagine that someone can have a feeling, like anger, say, and not be aware of it while appearing to an observer to be angry. We also can see our role, through the interpretation of defenses, as enabling a patient to experience their anger. This is not the same thing as saying the anger existed *Un*consciously.

Norm, a physician in his late 40s, came to see me, suffering from loneliness and isolation. I observed in passing that circumstances would arise in which some feeling would seem obvious but in which he felt nothing. When I mentioned this, Norm told me that friends or family would say the same thing: They thought he must be feeling something in circumstances in which he felt nothing. This involved both negative and positive feelings. He was simply not conscious of the feelings and interpretation did not make him so. He only became defensive. Norm was not stupid and could easily observe situations similar to ones he had been in that led to other people having and demonstrating feelings. I would like to tell you that, as Norm's analysis progressed, he began to experience such feelings. Alas, such did not prove to be the case. He learned, instead of becoming Conscious of feelings, *to infer their presence* in himself and to then act on them appropriately. In theory, Norm should have come to experience the feelings, *to become* Conscious of them; in practice the physical and emotional traumas he had been subjected to in childhood had been so great that they remained sealed off, not Unconscious. We had, instead, created an adaptive work-around.

Toward a Philosophy of Consciousness

We face another, epistemological problem in trying to apprehend Consciousness. We cannot experience Consciousness separately from being conscious of or about *something*; Consciousness is wedded to Intentionality (Brentano, 1874/1995). If we shift from experience to functional Magnetic Resonance Imaging and PET scans to see what the *Brain* is doing, we find that the parietal cerebral cortex is always involved in Consciousness but when we offer someone different things to become conscious of, or look at what they are conscious of, different areas of the Brain light up. So the subjective experience of Consciousness is unitary but the functional neuroanatomy tells us of pluralities; the parietal cortex lights up, but something else lights up too. Scientists have no way to deal with this kind of conflicting multiplicity of data beyond throwing one or the other of them out and losing it in the process.

Philosophy, however, has a great deal to offer. Different schools of Continental philosophy have offered ways of dealing with multiplicities. In particular, we have Heidegger's (Heidegger, 1927/2010; McManus, 2012) different concepts of Being, *Zuhandenheit* and *Vorhandenheit*. Looked at from the context of the arguments I am making here, they involve differing sorts of mental activity, differing sorts of cognition, or, even more foundationally, different sorts of Consciousness. Zuhandenheit signifies readiness-to-hand or, more colloquially, "handiness." Heidegger's famous example of Zuhandenheit is a *hammer*. We pick it up and use it to hammer something without thinking about it or, in Heidegger's terms, without *theorizing* about it. In this frame of reference we only notice it if something goes wrong with it as we use it; the handle breaks and the head flies off, for example.

In such cases, we apprehend an *unreadiness-to-hand*. Zuhandenheit also involves a particular form of Dasein's Being, everydayness (*Alltäglichkeit*). This fits closely with Noetic Consciousness and the non-reflective knowledge of hammers and hammering.

Vorhandenheit in contrast signifies "presence-to-hand" in which the hammer is perceived rather than picked up to use. It connotes that attitude of a scientist or an observer, an interest in the Class of hammers. It is meant to tie a number of concepts together (McManus, 2012); *decontextualized properties*, for example, as opposed to *situational characteristics*. Present-at-hand dominates intellectual and philosophical thought; it is Reflectively Conscious and involves the knowing of Self in World. It is a discipline of *ontology*. Vorhandenheit is developed; it is preceded by Zuhandenheit. It appears as a part of Development in childhood and then as an aspect of education in childhood and adulthood.

Heidegger relates Vorhandenheit to science and, in doing so, incorporates *practice* into its meaning of *examination*. These are contained in what he proposes to be the "theoretical attitude." So we now have a number of ways of consciously approaching a hammer. First is that it is at-hand (Zuhandenheit). We have to hammer something and we non-reflectively see it on our work bench, we pick it up, and, well, we hammer with it. When we are done, we put it down and get on with what we are doing. The next involves a trip to the hardware store where we find several different hammers present-at-hand (Vorhandenheit). We passively inspect them and choose one to buy. But there is also a practice element to Vorhandenheit. We have, say, a particular kind of nail that we anticipate having to repeatedly hammer into some sort of construction we plan to do. We might then practice or experiment. We take up the nail and try hitting it with a number of different hammers. This looks superficially like at-handedness, but it is not. Here we are reflectively conscious of the hammers and the hammering, performing a kind of science. We are studying the hammering and its finished product, not simply hammering in a series of nails and moving on. Science involves the "replacement of one kind of *concerned involvement* with another" (McManus, 2012, p. 66, italics added). Heidegger (1927/2010) insists that these involve *different kinds* of Being, where we understand Being to be subjectively about us as embodied in the concept of Dasein. We also need to recall that *Consciousness is a property of Dasein*.

Heidegger, then, is exploring the Being of Consciousness, that it is Dasein who is Conscious. It is of singular importance that in *da-Sein*, being there, the *there*, contrary to what Gertrude Stein might assert, is not a physical location but the mental location of the Self's Being, what it is conscious of.

Solms (2021), in keeping with Heidegger, posits two sorts of Being, an objective and, for example, a subjectively perspectival. As he begins his book, *The Hidden Spring*, he notes that the earth objectively revolves around the sun and spins around its own axis. But a *sunrise* subjectively requires a perspective and a viewer who experiences it in their own way in order to exist. This is, of course, simply a description of Dasein.

Zuhandenheit in isolation also addresses a particular problem in Consciousness Studies: Is Consciousness present in the animals, birds, and insects that make use of tools? Such tool use is rudimentary—a stick, sometimes slightly shaped, to pluck small prey like insects out of holes, rocks to break up shellfish, or dropping the latter from height to crack them open. All of these are noetic, everyday, and Zuhanden, not Vorhanden. These tool-users are entirely caught in the moment of taking up what is ready-at-hand.

The Preconscious Revisited

I have repeatedly (Leffert, 2010) offered a critique of Freud's (1915/1957) formulation of a dynamic Unconscious separated from Consciousness by a putative repression barrier. This is not to say that the majority of a vast array of mental processes don't take place outside of Consciousness (Leffert, 2010; Willingham & Preuss, 1995) and cannot become conscious. *Some* of these do input to functions that are Conscious (e.g., information from the retina that enters the visual cortex through radiations of the Optic Nerve) or first reach intermediary functions. Another example involves the use of a tachistoscope (McKeever, 1986), an experimental device that flashes images of words or pictures across the visual fields so rapidly that a subject is never conscious of them. The subject, however, then acts or responds as if they saw the word or picture. What we are observing here is that the image is too quick for the Left Brain to see it. But the Right Brain with a 2–3 ms processing time "sees" the image just fine and sends *information* about it to the Left Brain across the cerebral commissures *outside of awareness*.[13]

This critique of a dynamic Unconscious does not mean that Freud was wrong about a Preconscious containing thoughts and feelings that move in and out of Consciousness. Subjectively, there is a fallacy in our experience of Consciousness as a constant experience of Self and World. This experience grows out of the Left Brain's synthetic functions. Indeed, if we focus on being conscious and what we are conscious of (when we are self-reflectively, autonoetically Conscious, we have to be conscious *of* something) we find, not an integrated awareness of being but rather a series of episodes that we have, unbeknownst to ourselves, seamlessly stitched together. Associations are examples of such episodes.

The Preconscious contains what is available to Consciousness: It receives upstream inputs from perception and the lower brain and downstream inputs from memory and cognition coming from higher cortical centers. Going back to the example of the hammer, when we are simply hammering we are functioning with *Zuhandenheit* and are noetically conscious.

Another downstream input to the Preconscious has to do with how we function in the face of Uncertainty (Leffert, 2016). It demonstrates just how much of what we are actually conscious of is the result of the synthetic functions of Left Brain Consciousness. Nisbett and Wilson (1977) in one of the most frequently cited papers in psychology, "Human Inference: Strategies and

Shortcomings of Social Judgment" (expanded into a later book [Nisbett & Ross, 1980]), set out to prove empirically that mental processes such as preferences, biases, and choices were inaccessible to and not a part of Consciousness. They set out to study introspective awareness of higher order cognitive processes. When they asked their subjects why they made certain choices or why they had particular preferences, they readily offered answers or explanations. When, however, the investigators asked follow-on questions to explore the reasons behind the preferences and explanations, Nisbett and Wilson soon found that that they did not have the slightest idea why they made these particular choices. In other words, the decision-making process that their subjects thought resided in Consciousness did not, and what was entering Preconsciousness downstream from the rest of the Mind-Body was not a valid answer to why the particular choices were made or preferences exercised.

If we move on to consider the whole process of decision-making under uncertainty (Kahneman et al., 1982; Kahneman & Tversky, 1979/2000), we find ourselves reaching similar conclusions. As we saw in Chapter 1, much of our decision-making undertaken under conditions of Uncertainty involves the use of cognitive shortcuts termed heuristics. They fall into several broad categories; the two most frequently encountered are the Representativeness and the Availability Heuristics. In the case of the former, a subject "decides"[14] that an event resembles and is a member of a class of events; it does not address the validity of the existence of the putative class.[15] Similarly, in the Availability Heuristic, an event occurs on the heels of a series of other events, similar to each other, and the subject "decides" on the basis of its *availability* that the event is also a member of *this* putative class. Kahneman and his colleagues were talking about how we make decisions compared with how we think we make decisions. The point here, however, is that their work *also* describes what we are able to be conscious of: The particular Heuristics we have developed over the course of our lives help to determine both what we can be conscious of and what we at least tend not to be conscious of.

We are left with two further Kahneman concepts—Bias and noise (Kahneman et al., 1982; Kahneman, Sibony, & Sunstein, 2021). These were developed out of their striving to understand how decisions are made in circumstances that lack certainty. They also shape what we are capable of being conscious *of*. We all demonstrate a degree of Bias even if we don't acknowledge it or, more likely, aren't able to even be aware of its presence. (This is particularly true in our so-divisive early 21st-century America.) Again, we are deviating from Kahneman and Tversky's decision-making paradigm (Kahneman & Tversky, 1979/2000) to describe the way in which the thinking of individuals differs leading to a conclusion that Consciousness is different, feels different, and has a different content in different people. The Postmodern arguments (Leffert, 2007) for irreducible subjectivity, interreferentiality, unique onetime experience of thoughts, ideas, and feelings, and uncertainty all apply here as well. It is my hypothesis that being conscious in my head, even conscious of the same thing, is different in my head than it is in yours. These differences have been implicitly observed and implicitly[16] *treated* by Psychoanalysts and Psychotherapists but have not been the subject of empirical inquiry prior to the appearance of the decision-making literature we have been studying. Bias entails *systematic error*. For our purposes, it colors the way that we think about things. Bias arises out of individual development and, as Erikson (1950/1963) observed, the societies that shape it. Looked at from a different perspective (Panksepp & Biven, 2012), it can appear in secondary and tertiary affects. An example of bias can be found in the way we experience someone dressed in a suit as opposed to the same person appearing ungroomed and in ragged clothing. The shaping of thought that occurs can be adaptive or limiting or both. Psychological bias can be confirmed "either by observing that a factor that should not affect a judgment does have a statistical effect on it, or that a factor that should affect judgement does not" (Kahneman et al., 2021, p. 162).

Noise (Kahneman et al., 2021) is a different matter. It is a manifestation of *non*-systematic error. We see it when we find individuals who, evaluating the exact same situation (insurance underwriters is Kahneman's example), reach different conclusions. If we again apply Kahneman's work on decision-making to Consciousness we find substantiation for the diversity we have been talking about. Whereas noise may produce unwanted variation in decision-making, it produces different problems when we see it in Consciousness. A good example of both in the fall of 2021 is COVID vaccination. The *decision* to get a vaccination is heir to the impact of all the factors—heuristics, biases, noise—that we have been considering. When we look at peoples' *thinking* about getting vaccinated, what they are Conscious of, we find very problematic noise. (There is also *systematic* error arising in conflicting sociocultural values.) This is not going to devolve into a discussion of why vaccination is a good thing and why don't some people just see that. The point is that peoples' thinking about it is so different, with a bit more people thinking it's a good thing compared to those who think it's not and the former group *believing* it's a matter of science. What is most striking is how each group is simply unable to comprehend how the other group thinks as it does. The choice involves the properties of the egos (individuals, social network *nodes*) of two different Social Networks (Christakis, 2019, 2020; Christakis & Fowler, 2009) that are understood to be different but go by a variety of poorly differentiated names. The conscious incomprehension of the noise can be seen, for example, in school board meetings where the audience breaks into fist fights on some subject. This is not a question of science (although it is in part a question of the social experience of science that the two groups have): An inquiry along the lines proposed by Nisbett and Wilson (1977) shows that science the *discipline* rapidly falls away from the discussion.

Noise and Bias have great relevance to therapeutic concepts of process, psychopathology, therapeutic action and interpretation. Both involve the patient's (and sometimes the analyst's) hearing something other than what is said or experiencing something other than what happened in a session. Bias involves systematic error: The most common forms of systematic error in psychotherapy and analysis are transference, countertransference and their interaction. As a result, sometimes the verbal content of the patient's and therapist's communications is incorrectly heard; sometimes the *words* are heard correctly but the affect accompanying them is distorted or misperceived and, in the process, alters their meaning. Such distorting bias can also be a factor in therapeutic action. Its identification, interpretation, and working through by therapist and patient acting together results in the patient's increasing freedom [from bias] in thought and action that is the goal of the psychodynamic therapies.

Noise, a variability in judgment, can operate both positively and negatively to affect Consciousness. It can allow us to try different things, make different choices, and to discover what we prefer. It also may make it hard to get a fix on what we think about something, leading to non-systematic error. It is a factor in the therapeutic situation in which patient and therapist are always trying to draw conclusions about something. Therapists and analysts, in my experience gleaned from numerous "scientific" meetings and case presentations, do not consider the possibility that they might be wrong anywhere often enough. An awareness of the limits imposed by Uncertainty is a safeguard here. Kahneman and colleagues (2021) describe this dilemma as wanted diversity versus unwanted variability.

I have taken the position that Consciousness, the hard problem, is psychological, that it is supported by, among other things, the neurological hardware of the Bio-Psycho-Social Self. This is very different from a Quantum Theory approach that would posit that they were simply different aspects of the same thing. Broken neurological hardware is another source of noise in the system Consciousness. What I am referring to here is evidenced by conditions such as Schizophrenia and severe, refractory, endogenous Mood Disorders. We know here that the hardware is not functioning properly, that this is a kind of noise that has a high degree of variability, and that it impacts how a person is conscious and what they are conscious of.[17]

For our purposes, the conclusions to be drawn from these many diverse observations are the same; mental activity that is experienced as and thought to be a part of Consciousness turns out not to be. Nor is it capable, upon reflection, of becoming Conscious on its own—that is to say, that it is also not Preconscious. Consciousness is, by its very nature *subjectively* experienced and defined. But these *seemingly* conscious things, the explanations for our choices, are not. They are false explanations. What we are seeing instead are the mind's synthetic functions; Consciousness likes nothing so much as a good story and can make one up to suit. It is highly imperfect as are its possessors. What *is* possible in the psychoanalytic therapies[18] is for the therapist, informed by the decision-making literature, to audit their patient's use of heuristics and manifestations of bias and to *explicitly* make them aware of these processes and possible alternatives to them. Patient and therapist can then explore the former's history and developmental psychopathology in order to understand what brought these practices into being.

Sharon, a middle-aged married woman, has spent much of her adult life in therapy or analysis. Her independent wealth allowed her to not face the massive neurotic inhibitions that had made it impossible for her to practice her profession and allowed her to instead rationalize an apparent pseudo-decision not to do so. It took years of work for a history of childhood physical (slapping, punching) and sexual (family nudity) abuse to emerge through her defenses. This history had eluded her previous therapy and analysis. What was most obvious about Sharon was how narrow her life was, how it was constrained by anxiety, and how convinced she was that she would fail at whatever she tried to do. A combination of confrontation and encouragement eventually allowed her to take on new activities that she found to be both enjoyable and meaningful.

As our work proceeded, I began to notice that Sharon would repeatedly tell me stories about childhood and past adult experiences where she had faced some problem. Each story came with a morale that she would triumphantly repeat to me as a reason for doing, or, more often, not doing something in the present. She so took the not-doing for granted that she rarely mentioned it and it took me some years to figure out that it was going on. As I pursued my interdisciplinary studies (e.g., Leffert, 2016), I realized that I was seeing the Representativeness Heuristic in action. Sharon found that many situations or events fell into representative classes that entailed automatic responses. Because the morales, if not the reasons for them, were in Sharon's awareness, I was able to point out to her what she was doing whenever the Heuristic appeared. She didn't like it. She didn't like it because it forced her, a person who insisted she was in control of nearly everything, to acknowledge that she was not in control of a fair amount of what she did. The work on Representativeness and making it conscious, significantly opened up Sharon's world for her and permitted her to experiment with uncontrolled ways of being.

Consciousness, Absurdity, and Meaning

Folk Psychology, the Rationalist Philosophy of the 17th century, The Enlightenment of the 18th century, and, later, Intentionality and Phenomenology in the 20th century all positioned Consciousness at the pinnacle of Human Reason, of our mental function. Specifically, conscious inquiry was imagined to lead naturally to the discovery of personal meaning by an individual as it pertained to themselves as well as to society. As we have discussed, there is ample reason to mount an epistemological critique of this position. The critique draws on observations collected from a number of areas: Neuropsychology, Postmodernism, Existentialism, and Heuristics, Biases, and Noise. These disciplines have all told us that Consciousness can be a rich, but also deeply flawed way of being. Its flaws impact its effectiveness as a tool with which to explore and develop the highest of functions, a search for personal meaning.

We are left, then, with a conclusion that takes us back to philosophy and to Existentialism (Camus, 1942/1989, 1942/1991, 1948/1991; Leffert, 2021) in particular: *Consciousness is Absurd.*

Absurdity at its most basic is a discrepancy between Self and World. Everything we have been saying about the various pitfalls to which Consciousness is prone leads to such discrepancies. The world we are talking about is the combination of Heidegger's *Umwelt* and *Mitwelt* that is, of necessity, subjectively perceived and processed. As I have observed (Leffert, 2021), the discrepancies manifest themselves in the two most significant variables of Human Being, of Dasein, Meaning and Desire. They manifest themselves in Absurdity, an absurdity of the individual as well as an absurdity of the Social Network in which they reside. Arguably, in a time of COVID, climate change, and pseudo-populism, we are living now in a time of global absurdity. This absurdity in turn can produce a sense of meaninglessness and a failure of desire. As Stoltzfus (2003) puts it,

> The absurd describes the state of mind of individuals who are conscious of a discrepancy between desire and reality: the desire for freedom, happiness and immortality, and the knowledge that life imposes limits on desire even as death announces finitude.

(p. 1)

We are dealing here with issues that are fully deployed in Consciousness and, if we are therapists who are informed by Existentialist ideas, require our particular attention. Therapists who focus on what is *Un*conscious tend to either give these issues short shrift or see them as symptoms that will clear by themselves in the face of the usual psychoanalytic therapies. In my experience, this seldom happens.

Unfortunately, it seems that no one has had much luck coming up with any sort of objective, that is "scientific," definition of Consciousness. The same is true of my efforts here. Nagel (1970) sees Consciousness as impossible to objectively define yet present in ourselves and many other creatures, here on earth and elsewhere in the universe.[19] Nagel captures these debates with a question that has found favor with many authors, 'What is it like to be a bat?" which captures the sense of an essence of consciousness. Such properties, in some schools of philosophy, are called *qualia*. Seth (2021) picks up on this, bringing us back to the Phenomenology of Consciousness: "For an organism to be conscious, it has to have some kind of phenomenology for itself" (p. 12). This phenomenology is different from the functional and behavioral properties of the conscious Self. Unfortunately, attempts to form an evolutionary theory of Consciousness tend to draw heavily on these properties (as my own efforts to form an Evo-Devo theory of Consciousness in this volume have relied on). Consciousness has been confused with intelligence, manifestations of behavior, tool-making, and language. Seth simplifies the problem by defining Consciousness as "any kind of subjective experience whatsoever" (p. 14). The result of the question "why there is something like …" is the acknowledgement of the observation that some organisms are subjects of experience. This is a phenomenological observation. Another question, one we have so far been unable to answer, is: How does Conscious experience relate to the physical machinery of the Bio-Psycho-Social Self? The property of experience *does* have a physical basis (this is simply a restatement of physicalism). Still another question is whether we need to answer this one to understand Consciousness the aspect of Being or is it just a related inquiry?

According to Seth (2021), the *real* problem of Consciousness Studies is to "*explain, predict,* and *control* the phenomenological properties of conscious experience" (p. 22). The real problem, a phenomenological problem, exists aside from the putative *hard* problem, the search for the NCC (Koch, 2004), which is, I would now posit, of limited interest. It treats the existence of Consciousness as a given, what in fact *makes* us Human Beings. We must distinguish Consciousness (awareness) from Wakefulness (arousal). (Was Kate Conscious but not Wakeful?) We ascertain the presence of Consciousness in ourselves through a collection of subjective assessments, but we ascertain it in others through a series of objective procedures not that different from those employed by Owen (2017) when he asked the question "Is she conscious?" of Kate who was in some kind of altered state. The discontinuity between these two ways of knowing—involving different epistemological practices—is dysphoric.

We cannot be conscious without being conscious *of* something, and what we are conscious of are either *perceptions*, sensory inputs arising in sensory organs of some kind, or *thoughts*, arising in the neuronal activity of the cerebral cortex and the thalamic nuclei. Both are "on" in Consciousness all of the time with one or the other being the major focus of "conscious of." Conscious of is another way of thinking about "how things seem." Seth goes on to talk about what he calls the "Beholder's Share." We have already talked about von Senden's (1932/1960) studies of vision in people surgically treated for congenital cataracts. Those treated by the time of early adolescence developed normal vision, while those treated later saw only highly dysphoric waves of color. So when we look at a cup and *perceive* a cup, what we are seeing is the Beholder's Share, the top down part. This is what we are Conscious of, not the waves of color; it is the perceptual part of consciousness. In the same way, Consciousness is also shaped by the presence of language, and so-called "wild children" (Dennis, 1951) who grew up in isolation or with animals began with a non-verbal Consciousness.

These views of Consciousness yield a very different understanding of it than Tulving's (1985/2003) layered approach, one much more in keeping with Panksepp's (2012) hypothesis that includes primary affective Consciousness, non-verbal Consciousness, in mammals. So, aside from the presence of verbal reporting, is what I know about an animal's Consciousness, say my dog Henry's Consciousness, all that different from what I know of my friend

Lin's Consciousness? I don't have an answer to this question beyond beginning to wonder if the *knowing* itself is all that different.

I am left to draw together what we have been saying about Consciousness, ours and others. The many authors I have cited in this chapter and previous ones all make reference to the "hard problem," deem references to the PSC an essential part of their arguments, and sometimes conclude that they have drawn some definitive conclusions about it. We do know that experience, that is, Consciousness, arises from a physical basis, an emergent property (Leffert, 2010), but we don't know much about how or why that should be. Instead, as Seth (2021) describes it:

> Accept that consciousness exists, and then ask how the various phenomenological properties of consciousness—which is to say how conscious experiences are structured, what form they take—relate to properties of brains, brains that are embodied in bodies and embedded in worlds ... The challenge is to build increasingly sturdy explanatory bridges between mechanism and phenomenology.
>
> (pp. 271–272)

We are looking again to explain, predict, and control, seeking to reconcile the physical with the phenomenal. This is a restatement of the problem of grasping the integrated whole of the Bio-Psycho-Social Self, a whole that is greater than the sum of its parts. We can be Conscious of this Self and direct ourselves to be particularly Conscious of each of its components. I can, for example, direct myself to be Conscious of my physical brain and body, of my having thoughts, or of the world in which I live.

It is the Phenomenology of the Self and its inseparability from the Phenomenology of Consciousness upon which we must keep our focus if we are to understand what it means to be Conscious and to be Conscious of. If we treat Nagel's (1970) test—What is it like to be a ...—as a Phenomenological exercise, we can answer that question for mammals and some birds possessing a cerebral cortex but we can also offer a degree of intuition about it for more primitive creatures.

If we are to think in terms not only of our being Conscious but of what makes our Consciousness different from that of other mammals a different kind of answer emerges. Our Consciousness includes language. It also includes Simulation and Mental Time Travel; we can remember our Selves at various points in the past but also project our Selves into the future. The capacity to do these things does not require that they be error free and the fact that Henry can't do these things does not mean that he is not Conscious. The Phenomenological aspect of our Consciousness' that sets us particularly apart is our knowing about our own Deaths. I must be careful about how I phrase this because there is widespread disagreement about what Death entails: Does physical death of the body, for example, entail death of, for lack of a better term, the Soul? Our answers about this are no better than our answers about Consciousness; indeed, they manifest some of the same problems. If Consciousness is Absurd then the ultimate Absurdity is the Consciousness of Death. Let's turn to this now.

Notes

1 This line of observation (which seems obvious now) was absent in ancient civilizations (Koch, 2019); the ancient Egyptians and Greeks believed that it was the *heart* (not the brain, which was devalued) that was the center of reason and emotion. It is not at all clear how they reached this conclusion, possibly because the anatomy of the heart (tubes, connections, blood, etc.) looked promising while the brain (essentially pink glop) did not. Still, today, in contemporary folk psychology, the brain is the center of reason while the heart remains the center of emotion.

2 Arguably, the Representativeness Heuristic, while useful in some contexts, is a potent, non-evidential force that contributes to the way we hang onto theory-once-learned. When we are exposed to a new theory, the Availability Heuristic (Kahneman, et al., 1982) comes into play and we tend to subsequently, for a time, recognize it in our clinical work.

3 Identity Category is a term of Postmodern critique. It posits, successfully, I believe (Leffert, 2010), that classification of a phenomenon forecloses further search for its meaning.

4 A device that flashes images at some point in a visual field, too rapidly to be grasped consciously.

5 We remember the events of our lives but, if we read a book or a newspaper, watch events on television, or listen on radio, we can remember the stories of these events as well.

6 We tend to speak of the Brain as a kind of shorthand that pretends to a separateness from the rest of the Self that we know (Leffert, 2018) does not exist.

7 During this span of a 100 million years, give or take, representatives of all the phyla of the animal kingdom appear in the fossil record.

8 Beginning as physical sensations, these evolved in our hominin ancestors to *psychological sensations*.

9 Think of this as a contemporary, neuropsychological re-working of Freud's drive theory with its two drives—libido and aggression.

10 This all becomes rather complex. I would, for example, tentatively posit that the psychological defenses, as we know them, are tertiary affects.

11 This is entirely consistent with the fact that subjective, self-aware Consciousness is a Left Brain phenomenon (Leffert, 2010).

12 This would be analogous to understanding infectious disease after the advent of the compound microscope in the 17th century as a tool of science.

13 Again, although interesting, the neuroanatomy per se is less important than the mental processes.

14 *Decision* implies a conscious, evaluative process that in fact has not taken place.

15 As May (1958) observed, this particular oversite has plagued much of psychoanalytic thinking and theory building.

16 Neither patient nor therapist is aware of the fact that this is one of the processes the therapeutic couple is engaged in.

17 We know, for example that perceptions are blunted in severe depressions and distorted in hallucinatory psychoses. (Temporal lobe tumors and epilepsy are notorious for olfactory hallucinations.)

18 This can also be done by Cognitive Behavioral Therapists (CBT) and Dialectical Behavioral Therapists (DBT) and, indeed, has a significant implicit role in them.

19 There is even a debate (Pagel, 2017) about whether the Internet is conscious.

References

Bak, P. (1996). *How nature works*. Oxford, England: Oxford University Press.

Bak, P., Tang, C., & Weisenfeld, K. (1987). Self-organized criticality: An explanation of l/f noise. *Physical Review Letters, 59*, 381–384.

Baron-Cohen, S. (2000). Theory of mind and autism: A fifteen year review. In S. Baron-Cohen, H. Tager-Flusberg, & D. J. Cohen (Eds.), *Understanding other minds: Perspectives from developmental cognitive neuroscience* (2nd ed., pp. 3–20). Oxford, England: Oxford University Press.

Baron-Cohen, S., Tager-Flusberg, H., & Cohen, D. J. (2000). *Understanding other minds: Perspectives from developmental cognitive science* (2nd ed.). Oxford, England: Oxford University Press.

Bekoff, M. (2007). *The emotional lives of animals: A leading scientist explores animal joy, sorrow and empathy—And why they matter*. Novato, CA: New World Library.

Bogen, J. E. (2000). Split-brain basics: Relevance for the concept of one's other mind. *Journal of the American Academy of Psychoanalysis and Dynamic Psychiatry, 28*, 341–369.

Bogen, J. E., & Vogel, P. J. (1962). Cerebral commissurotomy in man: Preliminary case report. *Bulletin of the Los Angeles Neurological Society, 27*, 169–172.

Brentano, F. (1995). *Psychology from an empirical standpoint* (L. L. McCalister, trans.). London, England: Routledge. (Original work published in 1874).

Camus, A. (1989). *The stranger* (M. Ward, trans.). New York, NY: Vintage Books. (Original work published in 1942).

Camus, A. (1991). The myth of Sisyphus (J. O'Brien, trans.). In *The myth of Sisyphus and other essays* (pp. 3–138). New York, NY: Vintage Books. (Original work published in 1942).

Camus, A. (1991). *The plague* (S. Gilbert, trans.). New York, NY: Vintage Books. (Original work published in 1948).

Christakis, N. A. (2019). *Blueprint: The evolutionary origins of a good society*. New York, NY: Little, Brown Spark.

Christakis, N. A. (2020). *Apollo's arrow: The profound and enduring impact of Coronavirus on the way we live*. New York, NY: Little, Brown and Company.

Christakis, N. A., & Fowler, J. H. (2009). *Connected: The surprising power of our social networks and how they shape our lives*. New York, NY: Little, Brown and Company.

Churchland, P. M. (2002). *Brain-wise studies in neurophilosophy*. Cambridge, MA: MIT Press.

Clayton, N. S., Bussey, T. J., & Dickinson, A. (2003). Can animals recall the past and plan for the future? *Nature Reviews Neuroscience, 4*, 685–691.

Damasio, A. (2003). *Looking for Spinoza*. Orlando, FL: Harcourt Inc.

Dehaene, S., Changeux, J. P., Naccache, L., Sackur, J., & Sergent, C. (2006). Conscious, preconscious, and subliminal processing: A testable taxonomy. *Trends in Cognitive Sciences, 10*, 204–211.

Dennis, W. (1951). A further analysis of reports of wild children. *Child Development, 22*, 153–158.

Descartes, R. (1999). *Meditations and other metaphysical writings* (D. M. Clarke, trans.). New York, NY: Penguin Books. (Original work published in 1641).

Dunbar, R. (2016). *Human evolution: Our brains and behavior*. Oxford, England: Oxford University Press.

Edelman, G. M. (1989). *The remembered present a biological theory of consciousness*. New York, NY: Basic Books.

Erikson, E. (1963). *Childhood and society* (2nd ed.). New York, NY: W.W. Norton & Co. (Original work published in 1950).

Feinberg, T. E., & Mallatt, J. M. (2016). *The ancient origins of consciousness: How the brain created experience*. Cambridge, MA: MIT Press.

Freud, S. (1953). The interpretation of dreams. In J. Strachey (Ed.), *Standard edition* (Vols. IV & V). London, England: Hogarth Press. (Original work published in 1900).

Freud, S. (1957). The unconscious. In J. Strachey (Ed.), *Standard edition* (Vol. XIV, pp. 166–215). London, England: Hogarth Press. (Original work published in 1915).

Galin, D. (1974). Implications for psychiatry of left and right cerebral specialization: A neurophysiological context for unconscious processes. *Archives of General Psychiatry, 31*, 572–583.

Gill, M. M. (1976). Metapsychology is not psychology. In M. M. Gill, & P. S. Holtzman (Eds.), *Psychology verses metapsychology: Essays in honor of George S. Klein* (pp. 71–105). New York, NY: International Universities Press.

Gill, M. M., & Holtzman, P. S. (Eds.). (1976). *Psychology verses metapsychology: Essays in honor of George S. Klein*. New York, NY: International Universities Press.

Gould, S. J. (1989). *Wonderful life: The Burgess Shale and the nature of history*. New York, NY: W.W. Norton & Co.

Groopman, J. (2007, October 15). Silent minds what scanning techniques are revealing about vegetative patients. *The New Yorker, 83*, 38–43.

Heidegger, M. (2010). *Being and time* (J. Stambaugh & D. J. Schmidt, trans.). Albany: State University of New York. (Original work published in 1927).

Hoppe, K. D. (1977). Split brains and psychoanalysis. *Psychoanalytic Quarterly, 46*, 220–244.

Husserl, E. (1983). *Ideas pertaining to a pure phenomenology and to a phenomenological philosophy: Book one: General introduction to a pure phenomenology* (F. Kersten, trans.). New York, NY: Springer. (Original work published in 1913).

Husserl, E. (2005). *Phantasy, image consciousness, and memory (1898–1925)* (J. B. Brough, trans.). Dordrecht, Netherlands: Springer.

Kahneman, D., Sibony, O., & Sunstein, C. R. (2021). *Noise: A flaw in human judgement*. New York, NY: Little, Brown Spark.

Kahneman, D., Slovic, P., & Tversky, A. (Eds.). (1982). *Judgement under uncertainty: Heuristics and biases*. Cambridge, England: Cambridge University Press.

Kahneman, D., & Tversky, A. (2000). Prospect theory: An analysis of decisions under risk. In D. Kahneman, & A. Tversky (Eds.), *Choices, values, and frames* (pp. 17–43). Cambridge, England: Cambridge University Press. (Original work published in 1979).

Kandel, E. R. (2006). *In search of memory*. New York, NY: W.W. Norton & Co.

King, B. J. (2014). *How animals grieve*. Chicago, IL: University of Chicago Press.

Koch, C. (2004). *The quest for consciousness a neurobiological approach*. Englewood, CO: Roberts and Company Publishers.

Koch, C. (2019). *The feeling of life itself: Why consciousness is widespread but can't be computed*. Cambridge, MA: MIT Press.

Koch, C., & Greenfield, S. A. (2007). How does consciousness happen? *Scientific American, October*, 76–83.

Koch, C., & Tsuchiya, N. (2007). Attention and consciousness: Two distinct brain processes. *Trends in Cognitive Sciences, 11*, 16–22.

Latour, B. (1993). *We have never been modern* (C. Porter, trans.). Cambridge, MA: Harvard University Press. (Original work published in 1991).

Latour, B., & Woolgar, S. (1986). *Laboratory life the construction of scientific facts*. Princeton, NJ: Princeton University Press.

Leffert, M. (2007). A contemporary integration of modern and postmodern trends in psychoanalysis. *Journal of the American Psychoanalytic Association, 55*, 177–197.

Leffert, M. (2008). Complexity and postmodernism in contemporary theory of psychoanalytic change. *Journal of the American Academy of Psychoanalysis and Dynamic Psychiatry, 36,* 517–542.

Leffert, M. (2010). *Contemporary psychoanalytic foundations.* London, England: Routledge.

Leffert, M. (2016). *Phenomenology, uncertainty, and care in the therapeutic encounter.* New York, NY: Routledge.

Leffert, M. (2018). *Psychoanalysis and the birth of the self: A radical interdisciplinary approach.* London, England: Routledge.

Leffert, M. (2021). *The psychoanalysis of the absurd: Existentialism and phenomenology in contemporary psychoanalysis.* London, England: Routledge.

Marion, R. (1999). *The edge of organization Chaos and complexity theories of formal social systems.* Thousand Oaks, CA: Sage Publications.

May, R. (1958). The origins and significance of the existential movement in psychology. In R. May, E. Angel, & H. F. Ellenberger (Eds.), *Existence* (pp. 3–36). New York, NY: Simon & Schuster.

McKeever, W. (1986). Tachistoscopic methods in neuropsychology. In H. J. Hannay (Ed.), *Experimental techniques in human neuropsychology* (pp. 167–211). Oxford, England: Oxford University Press.

McManus, D. (2012). *Heidegger and the measure of truth.* Oxford, England: Oxford University Press.

Mitchell, M. (2009). *Complexity: A guided tour.* Oxford, England: Oxford University Press.

Naccache, L. (2006). Is she conscious? *Science, 313*(5792), 1395–1396.

Nagel, T. (1970). What is it like to be a bat? *Philosophical Review, 83,* 435–450.

Nisbett, R. E., & Ross, L. (1980). *Human inference: Strategies and shortcomings of social judgement.* Englewood Cliffs, NJ: Prentice-Hall.

Nisbett, R. E., & Wilson, T. (1977). Telling more than we can know: Verbal reports on mental processes. *Psychological Review, 84,* 231–259.

Ogas, O., & Gaddam, S. (2022). *Journey of the mind: How thinking emerged from chaos.* New York, NY: W. W. Norton & Co.

Owen, A. M. (2017). *Into the grey zone: A neuroscientist explores the border between life and death.* New York, NY: Scribner.

Owen, A. M., Coleman, M. R., Boly, M., Davis, M. H., Laureys, S., & Pickard, J. D. (2006). Detecting awareness in the vegetative state. *Science, 313*(5792), 1402.

Pagel, J. F. (2017). Internet dreaming—Is the web conscious? In J. Gackenbach, & J. Bown (Eds.), *Boundaries of self and reality online: Implications of digitally constructed realities* (pp. 279–295). New York, NY: Academic Press.

Panksepp, J. (2008). The affective brain and core consciousness: How does neural activity generate emotional feelings. In M. Lewis, J. M. Haviland-Jones, & L. F. Barrett (Eds.), *Handbook of emotions* (3rd ed., pp. 47–67). New York, NY: Guilford Press.

Panksepp, J. (2009). Brain emotional systems and qualities of mental life: From animal models of affect to implications for psychotherapeutics. In D. Fosha, D. J. Siegal, & M. F. Solomon (Eds.), *The healing power of emotion: Affective neuroscience, development, and clinical practice* (pp. 1–26). New York, NY: W.W. Norton & Co.

Panksepp, J., & Biven, L. (2012). *The archaeology of mind: Neuroevolutionary origins of human emotions.* New York, NY: W.W. Norton & Co.

Petitot, J., Varela, F. J., Pachoud, B., & Roy, J.-M. (Eds.). (1999). *Naturalizing phenomenology: Essays on contemporary phenomenology and cognitive science.* Stanford, CA: Stanford University Press.

Schacter, D. L. (1996). *Searching for memory.* New York, NY: Basic Books.

Schacter, D. L. (2001). *The seven sins of memory*. Boston, MA: Houghton Mifflin Company.

Schwartz, B. L. (2005). Do nonhuman primates have episodic memory? In H. S. Terrace, & J. Metcalfe (Eds.), *The missing link in cognition: Origins of self-reflective consciousness* (pp. 225–241). Oxford, England: Oxford University Press.

Seth, A. (2021). *Being you: A new science of consciousness*. London, England: Faber & Faber.

Solms, M. (2021). *The hidden spring: A journey to the source of consciousness*. New York, NY: W. W. Norton & Company.

Sperry, R. W. (1969). A modified concept of consciousness. *Psychological Review, 76*, 532–536.

Sperry, R. W., Gazzaniga, M. S., & Bogen, J. E. (1969). The neocortical commissures: Syndromes of hemisphere disconnection. In P. J. Vinken, & G. W. Bruyn (Eds.), *Handbook of clinical neurology* (Vol. 4, pp. 273–290). Amsterdam, Netherlands: North Holland Publishing Company.

Spinoza, B. (2011). *Ethics: Treatise on the emendation of the intellect and selected letters* (S. Shirley, trans.). Indianapolis, IN: Hackett Publishing Company. (Original work published in 1676).

Stoltzfus, B. (2003). Camus and Hemingway: The solidarity of rebellion. *The International Fiction Review, 30*(1/2), pp. 42–48.

Tarski, A. (1946). *Introduction to logic and the methodology of the deductive sciences*. Oxford, England: Oxford University Press.

Terrace, H. S., & Metcalfe, J. (Eds.). (2005). *The missing link in cognition: Origins of self-reflective consciousness*. Oxford, England: Oxford University Press.

Tononi, G. (2017). The information integration theory of consciousness. In M. Velmans, & S. Schneider (Eds.), *The Blackwell companion to consciousness* (pp. 287–299). Malden, MA: Blackwell Publishing.

Tononi, G., Boly, M., Massimini, M., & Koch, C. (2016). Integrated information theory: From consciousness to its physical substrate. *Nature Reviews Neuroscience, 17*, 450–461.

Tulving, E. (2003). Memory and consciousness. In B. J. Baars, W. P. Banks, & J. B. Newman (Eds.), *Essential sources in the scientific study of consciousness* (pp. 575–591). Cambridge, MA: MIT Press. (Original work published in 1985).

Tulving, E. (2005). Episodic memory and autonoesis: Uniquely human? In H. S. Terrace, & J. Metcalfe (Eds.), *The missing link in cognition: Origins of self-reflective consciousness* (pp. 3–56). Oxford, England: Oxford University Press.

Tulving, E., Kapur, S., Craik, F. I. M., Moscovitch, M., & Houle, S. (1994). Hemispheric encoding/retrieval asymmetry in episodic memory: Positron emission tomography findings. *Proceedings of the National Academy of Science, 91*, 2016–2020.

Van Wagenen, W. P., & Herren, R. Y. (1940). Surgical division of commissural pathways in the Corpus Callosum: Relation to spread of an epileptic attack. *Archives of Neurology and Psychiatry, 44*(4), 740–759.

von Senden, M. (1960). *Space and sight: The perception of space and shape in the congenitally blind before and after operation* (S. Schweppe, trans.). London, England: Methuen & Co. (Original work published in 1932).

Willingham, D. B., & Preuss, L. (1995). The death of implicit memory. *Psyche, 2* (15).

Wolford, G., Miller, M. B., & Gazzaniga, M. S. (2004). Split decisions. In M. S. Gazzaniga (Ed.), *The cognitive neurosciences III* (pp. 1189–1209). Cambridge, MA: MIT Press.

Chapter 5

Death and Death Anxiety

A Further Search for Meaning

An Appointment in Samarra

It seems that a merchant in Baghdad sent a servant to the marketplace to buy food for the day. The servant returned shortly, white with terror. He had encountered Death in the marketplace and Death seemed to threaten him. The servant borrowed the merchant's horse to flee to Samarra to hide from Death. The merchant went to the market that afternoon to buy provisions for his own supper and he too met Death. He asked him why he had threatened his servant. Death replied, "I didn't threaten him. It's just that I was surprised to encounter him at the marketplace because I have an appointment with him this evening, in Samarra.

—*Ancient Mesopotamian folk tale*

Introduction

Death. To paraphrase Heidegger, Death is the Impossibility of Possibility. It is an Absurdity, but then, it is also a prerequisite of Meaning. Even today, Death is much more poorly understood than we, as "scientists," imagine it to be. As philosophers, to understand Death subjectively, we must delve deeply into Folk Psychology, the Meaning we, as diverse individuals of diverse backgrounds, attach to it. There is general contemporary agreement that the physical body dies and decays (turns to dust as the Old Testament tells us). The death of a putative non-corporeal Self, a Soul if you will, is a very different matter. Despite what we might conclude as scientists and philosophers, it seems that roughly 80% of people believe in life after death and some sort of heaven. God is also involved in some fashion. (This also means, by the way, that 80% of people come down on Descartes' side of the Mind-Body problem[1] as opposed to Spinoza's, a very different position from that held be contemporary neuroscientists and philosophers.) This belief serves as a kind of patent medicine, a tonic used to ameliorate Death *Anxiety*.

Death Anxiety is as old as Consciousness. Its roots lie deep in prehistory, touching some of our hominin ancestors. Even vertebrates that do not possess Autonoetic Consciousness have at least an inkling of it. Some authors (e.g., Ogas & Gaddam, 2022) extend it back to single-celled Pre-Cambrian

DOI: 10.4324/9781003349556-6

organisms. Proto-Religion followed by Religion proper represent *H. sapiens sapiens'* first attempts to deal with Death and Death Anxiety, the great unknowables. Religion produced a series of worship services, power hierarchies, and mortuary practices that have continued into the present. Mortuary practices began (Pettitt, 2010) as an attempt to negotiate the passages from life to death and from death to an imagined afterlife. These concerns made our prehistoric ancestors into proto-Existentialists, already struggling with the same concerns taken up in contemporary times by Kierkegaard and Camus. One would imagine that the belief in an afterlife would neutralize Death Anxiety. It turns out, however, that this tonic is only sometimes effective and, even then, only at the very end of life. Physical death remains a very different matter from psychological death with an intact capacity to instill anxiety in us.

Yalom (2009) cites Epicurus as formulating three ontological statements that can serve as a treatment for Death Anxiety: the Mortality of the Soul, the Ultimate Nothingness of Death, and the Argument of Symmetry. We will delve into these later.

If we, as we should, want to integrate the Evo-Devo of the neurobiology of the Self with its philosophical underpinnings, we need to turn to Existentialism (Leffert, 2021) and its consideration of Meaning and Death. The index function that both the neurobiology and the philosophy describe is the awareness of Death and the evolution of that awareness.

While there is an albeit small contemporary literature on Death and Death Anxiety (subjects largely not considered by psychoanalysts except occasionally[2] as they pertain to mourning and terminal illness) a subject that it generally fails to consider is Suicide. Psychiatrically and sociologically, it is mostly treated as an untreated symptom of depression—refractory or otherwise—to be approached psychopharmacologically with added offers of the contact information for suicide hotlines. Its consideration in terms of anything but a therapeutic failure has been limited. Philosophy in general and Existentialism in particular have not been included in these discussions and the exploration of suicide in the intellectual and philosophical circles of *fin de siècle* Vienna ignored. We will address these deficits here.

My Appointment in Samarra

I debated about this section for some time. Did I really want to reveal so much of myself? Over the years I had described my subjective experiences of death and death anxiety in composite case vignettes drawn from my practice, some of them appearing in previous chapters. The answer to my question, I decided, was that if I truly wanted to describe my views of the impact of Death on the Self and the Psychoanalysis (self or two-person) to deal with it, I had no choice. I have also seen many examples of colleagues handling (or refusing to handle) their own approaching deaths in ways that damaged their patients. So, with this as a background let me begin.

On a pleasant June afternoon in 1979, I was completing a daily five-mile run when I felt what seemed to be a golf ball hitting me in the chest. After seeing that I felt too faint to walk or run, I flagged down a passing motorist who drove me the few blocks to my home. I continued to feel weak and (finally) went to the hospital that evening. (The physician on call for my internist, upon hearing that I was a psychiatrist, was convinced that "it was all in my head." I have to say that his differential diagnosis fitted well with my wishes.) It turned out that I had suffered a small heart attack. I was 34 years old and in my fourth year of what would be six years of psychoanalytic training. I was unable to be aware of just how frightened by it I was; on a practical level, I had a wife, an infant son, and no assets to speak of. I relied on denial to deal with it; it was a blip, and a heart-healthy lifestyle would take care of it. This was 1979; diagnostic and therapeutic tools were nothing like we have today, and I was discharged without further treatment. I told my patients I had had a "heart problem"; beyond wanting to know that I was "all right" (I answered in the affirmative) they said nothing and I did not ask for their thoughts or questions about the heart problem.[3] The driving force behind my reticence was my fear that if my patients knew I'd had a heart attack they would stop seeing me and that the financial consequences would have been disastrous. The thoughts of my colleagues in our then small psychoanalytic community—San Diego—on the subject were quite clear had my anxiety allowed me to see them: I received no further referrals.[4]

I decided to solve the referral problem at least by moving to Minneapolis, a community with a shortage of psychoanalysts, not patients. It was also a way, I imagined, to leave my medical history behind me. I developed a large, successful, practice and, in due course, became a Training and Supervising Analyst. I also suffered two major heart attacks during my first years there, the consequences of which were largely mitigated by the use of intracardiac clot-dissolving enzymes. I was otherwise physically healthy, had told my patients more about my health, and a cocktail of medications had put an end to subsequent heart attacks. I observed that my medical issues did not impact my practice and I continued to have a waiting list—I was amazed that *nobody cared*! For a few years I suffered some vague sensations in my chest that terrified me but were never diagnosed. I was convinced that each of the frequent episodes foretold a crippling heart attack until the cardiologist I sought out at the Harvard medical complex assured me they did not. It is important to note that I believed him; I was able to end these few years of being, I have to say it, a cardiac cripple. Once again, I thought I had escaped my "appointment." I was then ready to explore the concept of my own Death and my feelings about it. (The work of the Existentialists on the subject (Leffert, 2021) was unknown to me at that time.) I knew that the dying itself, the transition, terrified me. I researched reincarnation and the then (ca. 1990) popular belief in past lives but found none of the anecdotal descriptions to be at all convincing; those who found them to be true, I thought, did so because they wished to believe them to be.

As the millennium approached it became clear to both my wife and I that, although Minnesota had been good to both of us professionally and a good place to raise our children, it was not where we wanted to live out our lives. With our sons going off to college we decided to return to California, and, seeking a location that would replicate our lifestyle there in the 1970s, we ultimately moved to Santa Barbara, a small beach city without a psychoanalytic institute but only two hours from Los Angeles, where I became active in psychoanalytic circles. The move I made to Minneapolis was determined by the professional support I expected and received there; The move to Santa Barbara, as I was nearing 60, was determined entirely by lifestyle considerations. I realize now, looking back, that I was in some denial about Death; it seemed far off, and I didn't even think about it (it was three or so years before I sought medical care in my new home).

A happy and productive decade (both personally and professionally) ensued for us both but, inevitably perhaps, my heart rejoined the conversation at the end of it. I had begun writing in 2002 and was starting my third book (Leffert, 2016) when this took place. During a fairly minor surgery in which my anesthesia was mismanaged, I developed acute congestive heart failure (CHF). There were perhaps a couple of signals of it that both my cardiologist and I had ignored. Five days later I was home, well stabilized on medications, trying to get my bearings in this new heart-world I found myself living in. I had had considerable experience as a medical student and later an intern in internal medicine treating patients hospitalized for CHF. Typically, they had stopped taking their meds and abused salt in their diets. It was a relatively straightforward matter to diurese them, restart their meds, monitor their fluid loss, and send them home in a few days. They usually repeated the pattern several months later. I had not thought much of it. So, after I got home, I got out my *Merck Manual* and looked up CHF in it. Imagine my surprise when I read that what I had considered to be a simple chronic medical condition was indeed a serious, potentially terminal illness, and that, should I require hospitalization for it in the next year, my prognosis would be poor indeed. It should come as no surprise that, when I saw my cardiologist for my first follow-up visit, I asked him what my prognosis was (I asked the same question of all my doctors at that point). Imagine *my* surprise when he shook his head and said he didn't know. I got the same answer from everyone along with some mentions of an absence of crystal balls. I had not realized that CHF was in fact a vicious killer and that it was not, as I had imagined it to be, simply a convenient catchall diagnosis that could be listed as a cause of death. I enlarged my already large library to include books on cardiology and heart failure and found a heart failure specialist to see in nearby Los Angeles. There was no question that I would fight this thing, and I also investigated the options for a heart transplant should it become necessary. Absent my prior denial, I did not doubt for a moment that I might lose the battle.[5] My Death had become a subject for serious reflection, one I had to "do philosophy" about in order to really understand.

So, at age 68, I was again dealing with the prospect of my own death, this time not a sudden death from a failed resuscitation following another heart attack but a slower process that occurred as my heart failed me.

I found that I had become both flexible and open in my communications with my patients about my health. If something occurred that interfered with my being able to be in the office, a rare event (twice in several years), I spoke with my patients immediately about it via cellphone. When I was hospitalized this past summer with diverticulosis, I promptly communicated with them, including letting them know when I had to revise how long I would be out for. Back in the office, I asked all of them how much they wanted to know about my illness—nothing other than that I had recovered, a little information, or the whole story. They fell equally into the last two categories (they may well have felt able to ask for information because I was, unlike with that first heart attack, unconflicted about giving it to them).

All of this left me an agnostic, viewing physical death as a finality, but with some sense that we continued to exist for a time in the social networks (including the internet) that we had belonged to (Christakis & Fowler, 2009) while physically alive. This hypothesis, although I still think it, correct, did not help much. My experiences with an illness that, striking me at so young an age and certainly threatening death, offered me credentials for exploring the subject.

With help, I ascertained that my terror of dying, the transition[6] to Being dead if you will, could be traced back by standard psychoanalytic means to the trauma of anesthesia for a tonsillectomy suffered at age 4½. It is one of my earliest memories, of being held down while I screamed and a spinning blackness overcame me as ether was applied, along with its suffocating chemical odor of course. The whole experience was accompanied by a terrible aloneness. The recovery of this memory pretty much cleared the anxiety that accompanied the future death-transition (future travel, Schacter, Addis, & Buckner, 2008) and left me grappling instead with the idea of ceasing to exist and, less so, what would happen then to my physical body. It made me into a sort of folk-Cartesian (for lack of a better term); something was lost, my Soul, if you will, while something else remained. The obvious choices for what would be done with my body disturbed me: I realized that the disturbance originated in a premise that I would be alive in *some way* to consciously experience it. (Most people I have observed either have a particular mortuary practice that they want to partake of or don't particularly care.) This had more to do, I think, with future-travel, an aspect of consciousness that blurred into my perceptions of reality, than with what I actually felt to be the case. I am able to imagine both my world with me absent from it and my body (dead) in it. Future travel makes all these things more real.

I realize that, in writing this, I have left out the role of personal therapy or analysis in my dealing with my health and my explorations of death and dying. The reason, I have to understand, at this writing, is that, unfortunately, they played no role. I was in analysis at the time of my first heart attack. Neither I nor my analyst knew anything about Existentialism or Phenomenology. Beyond suggesting a few neurotic possibilities—I was identifying with the illnesses of two older and beloved uncles or a fear of being punished by my now dead father—he had little to say on the subject. I wanted to believe him because it offered the potential for retaining some control over my body, but I just couldn't. (Perhaps two years after termination, my analyst died at the young age of 62 of a massive heart attack. I believe that he, like me, also suffered from a chronic heart condition which he never mentioned.). To the extent that my heart became a subject of analysis in my second analysis, it was to have my symptoms and some physical limitations interpreted as neurotic; I wasn't buying it. When my third MI occurred during that analysis I simply left and didn't return. I came to deal with this in a self-analysis that took place roughly between 1995 and 2002. I felt better here and, as I interpreted it, thought that the successful work I did on myself enabled me to move on in my life: I began writing and I became a sculptor as well as an analyst. I had a third analysis with a much more sensitive and understanding analyst (I would now say he operated existentially but I know he would not use the term) and I used the work to integrate and consolidate the gains I had made on my own.

I am now 78 years old, in half time practice and, as you see, still writing. As I have aged, my practice has aged with me (I see patients in active old age, but also some young adults). I find that they want very much to talk about death as a kind of existential crisis, a phenomenological entity. Neurotic elements do come up, but we have not found that they add much explanatory power to the conversations we have about it. It is particularly common, for example, for men to believe that they will die at or before the chronological age at which their own fathers died. (Freud (Schur, 1972) himself was much concerned with his father's death and what he termed *critical periods* in his life, seemingly a kind of oedipal punishment that played out over the course of his life.) In past decades, I never heard such material but, as Yalom's (1980) work suggested to me, I had not previously asked for it. I had to be open to the conversation and, many? most? therapists are not, except in the uncommon situation in which the patient is terminally ill or the more common one in which the patient is in mourning. When I asked about it, patients usually were both willing and eager to talk about Death. Children, in particular, are particularly interested in talking about it: They consider it, along with adult sex and the fertilizing function of sperm, to be one of life's great mysteries—just as their parents do not and instead supply them with obvious misinformation.

My willingness to consider my own death and its inevitability resulted in my being able to offer my patients a secure base from which to talk about their feelings about losing me. My age, as it had not been in the past, was clearly a factor here. In thinking about patients' experiences of or responses to that inevitability, I realized that I had been thinking about my *current* patients and, what little consideration the analyst's death has been given in the literature, it too refers to the patients in therapy or analysis at the time. What easily emerged now was that patients in their 20s, 30s, and 40s, were only partly concerned with the forced, premature ending of our *work*, but were much more involved with loosing me *whether or not they were seeing me regularly at the time*. Patients talked about what it would be like to lose me in the future or to find out about my death in that future. This was a loss on multiple levels: loss of a [real] relationship with a [real] object (I hate the unemotional quality of this term here), the loss of a working alliance, and, least importantly, a transference loss. The transference loss part did provide an opportunity to work through previous losses—parents, siblings, mentors, others—that a patient had been unable to or lacked the opportunity to deal with in the past.

What is unusual about considering the meaning and experiencing of death at the present time—the 2020s—is that we are in the midst of the great COVID Pandemic.[7] In my own experience neither I, my family, friends, nor my patients have had any direct experience of death from COVID (there is some experience at two degrees of separation). Some patients and some of their friends and family (and mine!) have had COVID but none required hospitalization. I have not had (although I have colleagues who have) patients who do not "believe in" COVID and refuse vaccination. Most of the people I have contact with, my patients among them, do not respond with a fear of dying so much as with depression at the curtailment of their lives that safety requires. I have felt my own safety to be largely in my own hands although, given my chronic health issues, there is, I think, some denial here. Unlike the response to the Influenza Pandemic there has been an early outpouring of papers on COVID in the psychoanalytic journals. They mostly involve trying to apply the usual psychoanalytic tools, uninformed by Existentialism, to understand this Pandemic. I would expect this literature to become broader and more powerful as time goes on.

The effect of my life history, and the dealings with chronic illness[8] that it has required, has meant that, for most of my life I have had to deal with Death Anxiety, its presence, or questions of denial in its absence. Death Anxiety is one of the tertiary elaborations of the primary affect FEAR (Panksepp, 2009). Let's first consider Death itself, followed by Death Anxiety.

Death

Death is Life's ultimate Absurdity. It bestows both Meaninglessness and Meaning on us and our lives *at the same time*. Who we are and what we have accomplished is an expression of transience and an ephemerality. They do not last. Yet without death the endlessness of life would rob anything we did of meaning and we would lapse into a terminal boredom of Everydayness. We would exhaust possibility. The way forward from this is that meaning is to be found in what we do for others. In other words CARE (Panksepp & Watt, 2011) and the way we change people like ourselves for the better. Yalom (2009) uses the term *ripples* to describe the effects we have on others and how those ripples spread out through degrees of separation. (We also possess the power to do the reverse—to do injury and change people for the worse; this is how I would define Evil.)

To understand this Absurdity, I am drawn to the legend (Homer, 1998) of the "great warrior" Achilles and his role in the Trojan War. Achilles was born to the Nereid Thetis. As the story goes, he was offered a choice of two lives. He could have a rich long life, beloved by family and friends. When he died, he would be mourned and remembered for perhaps 50 years or so. Then memory of him would fade completely and it would be like he had never been. Or, he could lead a short life as a famed warrior and would be remembered for thousands of years. He chose the latter. To make him invulnerable, Thetis dipped him in the river Styx, but the heel she held him by was not protected. The war progresses, Achilles kills the crown prince Hector and is killed by Hector's brother, Paris. But the two things he is remembered for down through the ages are not his successes but his failings. It is commonly remembered that Paris kills him by shooting an arrow into his *weak* and *vulnerable* heel, his Achilles Heel. Less commonly known is that when Achilles killed Hector (in revenge for Hector's slewing his friend Patroclus—this is a log story) he desecrates his body, first by dragging it behind his chariot and then ripping out his eyes so he will be forever blind in the underworld. King Priam, Hector's father is forced to enter the Greek camp in disguise and beg Achilles for his son's body so he can give it a proper burial. Achilles seems oblivious to the gross dishonor he has committed. This is so very much a "be careful what you wish for" sort of legend and Achilles ends up as a tragic figure in the Sophoclean rather than the Shakespearean sense of the term.

It is clear from these ancient stories and the mortuary practices that precede them, sometimes by millennia (Pettitt, 2010), that we have been trying for a very long time to find our ways around the inevitability of Death. In some cultures, Dynastic Egypt's for example, such practices were systemized by a ruling religious order whose priesthood turned them into expressions of power relations. It is, however, impossible to know how much belief in life in an afterworld was really present in a culture that was unable to put a stop to systematic grave-robbing. All of these practices (including the 80% of people who *believe* in some sort of afterlife) can be subsumed under the rubric of "hoping for the best."

If we are looking for an approximate date in prehistory for the appearance of reflective consciousness of Death, I would posit that it coincides, in Europe at least, with the birth of symbolic cognition in the Upper Paleolithic revolution (Mellars, 2005); the transition from the Middle to the Upper Paleolithic occurring around 50,000 BCE. Reflective Consciousness of Death entails the awareness that, as others have died in the past, more others and, ultimately, we will die in the future.

Phenomenologically, Death and Death Anxiety can be engaged in any of the three ways of Being—Thrown, Fallen, or Everyday. The appearance of Death on the horizon of Being can shift us from one to the other. One may move from Everyday to Thrown in a search for Meaning or can collapse into the Fallen by a failure to engage the task. There is a particular literature on Being-toward-Death, *Sein-zum-Tode* (Kasket, 2012; Mandíc, 2008). Mandíc is focused on Heidegger's differing concepts of Being-ahead-of-itself and Being-a-whole involving an inauthentic stance toward Death versus an authentic Being-toward-Death on the other. Death reveals *authentic possibility* to those who seek it out. It is a first-person human response, not a third-person studied, "objective" response. Heidegger posits that Being-toward-Death is essentially an anxiety response. It is Heidegger's use of the *hyphen* that measures our mortality and increases our attention on *Meaning*. Dasein can either be lost in the Everydayness of what he calls the they-self or to Be itself in the freedom-toward-death. In claiming responsibility, we become an authentic (*eigentlich*) self, no longer an everyday they-self. To do so is to also accept *mortality*. It is part of the "thereness" of Dasein. Being-a-whole involves grasping our existence in terms of our finite, whole life. This involves *interpretation*, an intensely personal process, as opposed to *explaining*, a natural science they-process.[9] This is a state of mind (Heidegger's important *Befindlichkeit*, a kind of how-you are-ness or how you find your Self to Be) through which we understand ourselves. It highlights a focus on *having a life* versus merely living. One deals with an openness toward Death, an authenticity, its certainty, as opposed to its concealment.

Heidegger (1959/1966) develops the idea of freedom, or releasement (*Gelassenheit*) toward Death and posits that this is a part of our experience of joy connected with the authentic Being-toward (Heidegger, 1927/2010), with potentiality. I find this concept of a joyful freedom toward Death doubtful. It is consistent with Phenomenological theory concerning the relevance of Death to our meaningful Being and resonates with Camus' (1942/1989) existentialist hero, Meursault, in *The Stranger* who finds Meaning in anticipating his public guillotining as public punishment for a meaningless murder. This is a theoretical topic that philosophers' write about but living and dying folk don't actually experience. Death requires us to search for Meaning in a way that immortality does not (or instead brings us meaninglessness by obviating Time). It is a call to search for Meaning and, while there can be joy in the finding of it, the meaning is not in the joy. One finds peace in Death following a painful and disabling terminal illness, but I have never clinically seen joy in this context and plenty of anxiety as such a death approaches. The COVID epidemic, which has been playing out as I have been writing this book (we are currently in the second Omicron spike) has no joy connected with it. It has been complex and frightening, depending on an individual's beliefs about it and its realities. An epidemic, or, for that matter, a terminal illness can threaten to suck the meaning out of life, making our mortality a real-world event. Like other epidemics, wars, and the civil unrest pervading parts of the United States, it is a very different way of Being when Being-with-Death is literally in the air. Mandíc (2008) posits that Heidegger would assert, based on the world we live in, that life is an outrageous horror and that this is "precisely what we have to live with, and to do so is to live an authentic Being-towards-death" (p. 263). This ignores the existence of and search for Meaning and does not recognize that that Meaning is a subjective matter. It is what Camus struggled with in his "three Absurds (1944/1958, 1942/1989, 1942/1991a)," particularly in *The Myth of Sisyphus* (1942/1991a). Mandíc is implicitly critical of this Existentialist position, that life has meaning in the subjective importance we attach to it and is only meaningless if we fail to do so.[10] He would be unable to deal with the whole subject of Absurdity, insisting instead that a *higher* Meaning (not subjective Meaning) is the goal we must strive for.

Mandíc (2008) identifies, as do I, addressing an individual's Being-toward-Death as a task that any psychoanalytic therapy must engage in. He coins a phrase—to "living dyingly" (p. 264)—that I find particularly apt here. We know that finding one's Meaning in a review of a whole life is of importance to us, to many of the people we know, and to the people who come to us for help—*even if they have never identified it as such.* The many people for whom this is not the case are those that Phenomenology identifies as the Fallen. Sometimes they can be rescued from this state but often not.

When I look at my own [eventually] terminal illness, CHF, I struggle to keep an [accurate] eye on the certainty of my Being-toward-Death and to live dyingly. My condition has been stable for 10 years and I'm told that the longer I remain so, particularly without any hospitalizations, the more likely I will continue to be (as opposed to other illnesses in which survival time seems to get used up). It's a little like a cancer in remission: There is no reliable date range here, so it's hard for me to be clear about what constitutes denial and what, for lack of a better term, hypochondriasis. I have a patient with metastatic lung cancer with whom I've focused on navigating this same divide. He, like many of my patients, is generally aware of my medical condition and I use it in my work with him, bridging what would otherwise limit his acceptance of my empathy.

Kasket (2012) posits that Being-toward-Death has been irrevocably changed by what she would call the "Digital Age," and what we would call a decade later, the *Metaverse.* "Not only are we increasingly telepresent with one another[11] in life, but we leave behind a digital legacy when we die, often to include detailed co-constructed representations of ourselves" (p. 249) in this new part of lifespace. In phenomenological language we are talking about an extension of the there, the *da*, in Dasein. This presence is in a dynamic space that increases and decreases, one in which—varying with how present we are in the Metaverse—most of us undergo a second, digital death. Sometimes fragments of us survive and for a (fortunate?) few, there is a digital immortality to be had. Depending on where you get your statistics, there are 1.69 billion active users whose digital profiles reside on the social networking site. Scattered among them are what have become the digital headstones of dead users. To the Heideggerian being of nature (*res extensa*) and the being of mind (*res cogitans*), we must now add a third being, *res digitalis*. It is important to remember that, on a human scale, our presence and being in the digital age exists as the equivalent of a premature infant. It is such early days that we truly can have no idea what our digital presence in the metaverse will look like five or ten years from now. It is possible that some new way of being in the metaverse, not even imagined now, will have taken over; this is more likely than not.

Kasket (2012) studies how and why people build digital profiles on Facebook. She wonders if building a lasting digital biography offers the author an opportunity to exercise denial of Being-toward-Death. She then considers what I would phrase as how our interacting with deceased others in the Metaverse affects our awareness of our Being-toward-Death. Let's take Kasket's Being-toward-Death out for a test drive in the in the wider world of the internet where one encounters, in addition to what we post and construct about ourselves, what other people and organizations post about us. I have seen no consideration of the internet in the analytic or therapeutic literature and almost none in the Existentialist/Phenomenological literature. Yalom and Yalom (2021) do not mention the internet or the Metaverse in their work on death and dying.

We all search for old friends, colleagues, former classmates, and acquaintances on the internet. We usually aren't interested in contacting them so much as finding out where they have gotten to. By the time we have reached our 50s—and perhaps our 40s—we are particularly interested in finding out if they are still alive, that is, are they dead? There are many reasons for wanting to find this out, depending on whether we had positive or negative feelings about the person in question. We can be surprised and grieved to find out someone we cared about has died. I have felt warmed when I find out that someone I lost touch with or cared about had a good life.

When someone dies who is on Facebook their profile is "memorialized," it is fixed, and nobody can change it. These profiles become virtual cemeteries. People can still post on the "Wall" and "friends" can continue to interact with it. If a close relative requests that the memorial be taken down, the request is currently honored by Facebook. Mourners can create an in-memory-of group where they can share memories and comments. Someone who is expecting to die may appoint an executor to supervise their Facebook materials and the in-memory-of site. Kasket (2012) first studied five of these in-memory-of groups that memorialized a homogenous group: late adolescents who lived in the English-speaking West and died in car crashes.[12] These groups were involved, essentially, in the social construction of reality (Altheide, Coyle, DeVriese, & Schneider, 2008) around the Death of the individual. She used quantitative document analysis (QDA) to study 943 "Wall" posts which she found "well suited to analyzing content from the 'mass-mediated' world" (p. 252). Unfortunately, this takes us far away from people and patients. She went on to interview the executors (three of the five consented) about their interactions with the groups and with the dead person's in-life profile. For this, she used interpretative phenomenological analysis (IPA) (Smith, Flowers, & Larkin, 2009) a qualitative method that looks at the ways individuals experience and construct the Meaning of things they find significant.

She found that many (?) of the people using the sites believed that they provided one-way communication with the deceased, while the deceased either could not respond or responded through coded events in the participant's life. The site was felt as providing a continuing bond with the lost person and was sometimes used to update them on the participant's life. As one participant wrote, it allowed a piece of a deceased Human Being to live on for friends and family. Reading other users' posts provided succor to members of the mourning group. Is this different from a visit to a bricks and mortar cemetery where a friend or loved one is buried? We have seen from the history of burial practices (Pettitt, 2010) that they originated in prehistoric attempts to keep the dead present and with us (some early burials were in the floor of a family's living area). The living, as part of the experience of their own eventual deaths could expect to be kept with the family in this way, instead of expecting some horrible disappearance. This experience existed fairly uniformly across ancient social groups. So then, is the Facebook memorial site simply what we get if we scroll forward 50,000 years or so? It has yet, however, to spread across the digital universe (this may look different ten years from now). We need to recognize, as other authors do not, that these practices occur in social networks and are best understood in the context of social network theory (Barabási, 2003; Christakis & Fowler, 2009).

Now we come to the really tricky part. What exactly is the ontology of these memorial sites, these *profiles*, that contain something of the self in them? Has the nature of the Facebook profile changed when someone dies? Kasket (2012) suggests a number of possibilities. It can be a *thing*, or an extension of Dasein, a *res digitalis*. (I would add the question: Has its nature been changed by Dasein's Death? I would posit that it has.) The profile has durability (but not permanence!), it is unchanging, it can be acted on again and again, we can return to it again and again and act (if not interact) on it again and again. It can be forever but, *at the same time*, it can disappear (cease to be) from the world in an instant without a trace, the victim of a keystroke at the hands of a Facebook employee. Heidegger described three kinds of representations (1979/2009). In the first a thing simply stands for itself:

A physically present chair is a chair. This is *bodily presence.* The second is when we are someplace else, remembering the chair. This is *empty intending.* The third kind of representation Heidegger called the *perception of a picture,* which involves being given a postcard picturing the chair. The profile has some properties of all three.

As we have discussed, the Facebook profile of a living person is a component of the Self; it is a Digital Being (Kim, 2021), an extension of our physical Being (I mean both in the noun and the verb sense of the word), a *thing.* So, what happens when we die, what happens to the profile then? It retains an embodiment for the other Daseins that related in life to the deceased; it is a kind of surrogate for the persons cadaver going back into prehistory. Perhaps it is related to the display of the perfectly dressed and embalmed cadaver prior to burial or cremation. (We are again reminded of the elaborate mortuary and burial practices that in ancient Egypt sent the deceased on to a new life, provided they could afford the bill.) It has, however, undergone a change in nature from the interactive to the acted upon or, grammatically, from subject to object.

Is the goal of producing a durable structure (here a profile) in the metaverse a denial of Being-toward-Death? Is this what people are doing today (it has to be today since the metaverse and its customs are in such rapid flux)? We would have to say at present mostly "no" or "not yet." A possible exception might be what people terminally ill and facing their own approaching death might do along with other acts such as making a will, making selfies or videos, etc. Kasket (2012) comments on the experience of having the deceased on their Facebook "friends" list where they keep coming up. It keeps them present in our lives along with the manner of their dying. Does this make Death less final for us and our own Being-toward-Death less real? I think not. It does make remembrance more real (akin to the prehistorically burying beloved dead in the floors of living areas) and fosters a more matter of fact attitude toward death and dying that can lessen Death Anxiety. This has not yet been much thought about or studied.

Heidegger (1979/2009)[13] equates Death with Dasein's "being finished or finished Being." He sees care as fundamentally involved with Everyday Being, in Heideggerian German involving *Sorge* (care) and *Sein-bei,* (being with in the *Mitwelt*). Death stands *before* Dasein (Being *there* in space and time)—it is always impending. Death thus belongs to Dasein, even when it is not dying. "Death is understood as a character of Dasein only when it is conceived from the structure of the being of Dasein, from care, from the *being-ahead-of-itself*" (p. 313).[14] Care is most about the caring about the Being of Dasein, an integral part of which includes Dasein's having the potential of being-no-more, anticipating a future time without Dasein. Death is the utmost possibility of Dasein's Being.

Dasein's Everydayness (as opposed to its Thrownness or Fallenness) (Heidegger, 1975/1982) is emersed in Everyoneness in which encounters with Death in being-with-one-another (*Mit-Sein*) are a full part of everyday Being. Everyone is both the Everyday group and what is true of all of us as Everyday individuals. This gives rise to the paradox "Everyone Dies" which refers to us as individuals and Everyone the group in which the group never dies, driving away Death.[15] "In not wanting to think about Death, the everydayness of Dasein is in constant *flight in the face of death*" (p. 317). This is an attempt to engineer an *estrangement* from Death and to deny the *indefiniteness* of Being in which Death can come at any moment. Let's see what Yalom (Yalom, 1980, 2009; Yalom & Yalom, 2021) makes of this very dense Heideggerian writing. For this, we must turn from Death to its anticipation: Death Anxiety.

Death Anxiety

What makes us uniquely human is our self-reflective consciousness, our awareness of our selves and the world around us, past present and future. This is a special kind of awareness, sometimes, as we have seen, called autonoetic consciousness (Tulving, 1985/2003). Speaking in terms of Evo-Devo (Leffert, 2018), these abilities had enormous evolutionary value, but they came with a price. In biblical terms it is a blessing and a curse. The price of general awareness is a unique awareness—the awareness of our own mortality, the inevitability of our own deaths, the manner of our dying: Being-toward-Death. While an Existential engagement with Death may mitigate against Death Anxiety, it does not eliminate it.

Yalom (Yalom, 1980, 2009; Yalom & Yalom, 2021) has been a major contributor, perhaps *the* major contributor, to the Existential work on Death Anxiety. He has brought the classical Greek philosopher Epicurus (Warren, 2009b), a sort of proto-existentialist, into this conversation. Like many of what I would call the interdisciplinary philosophers of Greece and Rome, it was relatively easy (compared to its impossibility today) for Epicurus to be well-grounded across philosophy, psychology, and the natural sciences, given the limited knowledge base available in those times (ca. 300–400 BCE). In particular, Yalom has, over much of his long career, specifically offered psychotherapy aimed at treating Death Anxiety.

Folk psychology enhances the denial of Death, asserting in effect that we don't think much about Death or experience much anxiety about it until the final decades of life, except in special and unusual circumstances, such as developing a chronic or terminal illness, the death of a loved one or of a prominent figure. Yalom (2009) instead offers what Anna Freud would term a Developmental Line (1963) of Death Anxiety. He posits Death Anxiety in early childhood and a lack of comprehension surrounding the child's sense of the impermanence of life and adult grief. It wanes in middle childhood and reappears in adolescence probably around the experience of the catastrophic (seemingly) changes in the teenage body. It is then pushed aside by the developmental tasks of marriage, starting a family, and establishing a vocation. (In my own life, this was the point at which a potentially fatal illness appeared and kept my focus on Death and its accompanying anxiety.) Midlife and the ensuing ages of man (Erikson, 1950/1963) return the active consideration of Death to our self-reflective narratives.

Death Anxiety also appeared as a feature of the Upper Paleolithic revolution (Mellars, 2005). It, along with joy are the ultimate cognitive-emotional regulators of homeostasis (Fotopoulou & Tsakiris, 2017). They distinguish us as Human Beings, *H. sapiens sapiens*. They are hard-wired into us as tertiary affective states; living things that do not possess Autonoetic Consciousness nevertheless experience the primary affective components of them (Panksepp & Biven, 2012). The primary affect from which Death Anxiety is derived is FEAR; it has neuroanatomically defined roots in the midbrain. I wonder if there is a secondary affect component best termed EXISTENCE-FEAR. It is a part of the experience that prey have of predators, the Vagus Nerve's response (Porges, 2011) to the imminence of Death.[16] Death Anxiety and its terrors, as a tertiary affect, is a part of the Upper Paleolithic package that led to the innovation of religion, a response to the (then) unknowable parts of life and world (*Eigenwelt* and *Umwelt*). Religion, or more accurately in Evo-Devo terms, proto-religion, offered the reassurance contained in the idea of a higher power that one could appeal to in times of terror or loss or uncertainty. The Evo-Devo of religion—from proto-religion, to polytheism, to monotheism—forms a Developmental line from an ill-formed-higher power, to gods being like us (Homer, 1998) (polytheism), to the capacity to experience these supernatural powers as residing in a single being (monotheism) These early Existentialists were struggling with some of the very same things that we continue to face as the young 21st century continues to unfold. These external failures of homeostasis, manifest on the levels of the *Mitwelt* and the *Umwelt*, increase in contemporary times, with the former driving the latter. The result is a species of existential anxiety as seen in the past when the four horsemen of the apocalypse—Death, War and Pestilence, Famine (*Revelation* 6)—have ridden (we might want to now add a fifth, Climate Change). We are looking at a potential failure of our government and decent into an anocracy (Walter, 2022) (our American *Mitwelt*) in the results of the 2024 elections. We already have the disputed 2020 election and the Capital Riots (now named January 6 as the destruction of the World Trade Center is known as 9/11) that almost succeeded. A literature on this potential failure (Marche, 2022; Walter, 2022) is already beginning to appear and has made its way onto media and social media. Climate change is largely experienced discontinuously as something episodic we must bear and recover from with each disaster; it is not yet perceived as something that will fundamentally affect the world population of Human Beings driving the numbers down from the present seven billion to possibly less than half of that. Friends, relatives, patients, and colleagues are very much caught up in and frightened and depressed by the political issues and the endless Pandemic. They are now dealing with the soft version of Climate Change (for the low countries of Europe and the South Pacific it is something much more, how much it is felt is as yet unclear),[17] a picture that will change in a decade or two. Peoples' reactions to these national and global catastrophes fuel still-latent Death Anxieties.

There is now a large body of work on Death Anxiety to which psychoanalysts and psychotherapists have not contributed and of which they remain largely unaware. They often tend to take the position (erroneously) that it is simply a displacement from neurotically based anxieties. Contrary to the expectations of these non-existential therapists (Thorson & Powell, 1992), Death Anxiety researchers find it to be not at all unusual and a part of the emotional makeup of Human Beings. Vaillant (2002), in his work on the Harvard Adult Development Study, takes his lead from Erikson (1950/1963) and the developmental task of the last of the latter's eight ages of man—being able to maintain *Integrity* in the face of physical and mental decline (that is, approaching Death). He mistakenly confines Death Anxiety to Erikson's eighth and last stage of life—we will review the empirical evidence that this is not the case. Most clinicians and theoreticians fail to consider the fact that maintaining integrity does not mean an absence of Death Anxiety, nor that it is a factor in most of the other seven developmental stages. It is stronger in some of the earlier stages than in the later ones. I have attempted here and in my most recent work (Leffert, 2021) to change that. Of clinicians working in an Existential vein, Yalom (Yalom, 2009; Yalom & Yalom, 2021), Frankl (1959/2006) and May (May, Angel, & Ellenberger, 1958) are the most prominent, with their work being richly enhanced by personal narrative (I have followed that path here). They oppose Death Anxiety with Personal Meaning.

Existential clinicians continue to study Death Anxiety. Yalom begins his work (2009) quoting Gilgamesh from the 4,000-year-old *Gilgamesh Epic*, "Sorrow enters my heart. I am afraid of death." One only hears about Death Anxiety if we listen for it or ask after it; Yalom's experience is that many patients seek him out precisely because they are much concerned by the two—Death and Death Anxiety—and know he will give them a fair hearing. It is important to recognize that an individual's leading a meaningful life and coming to terms with death does *not* mean that they are also devoid of Death Anxiety. Meaning and dying are separate; it may, or may not, be easier to end a meaningful life then to end an empty or a fallen one.

There is, if we seek it out, a considerable empirical literature on Death Anxiety and a clinical literature growing out of Existential psychotherapy. As I have observed, "it is when Death becomes a pathological focus of Being or when the anxiety is rampant throughout one's existence, one's dream's and one's hopes for the future that Death should become a focus of therapeutic inquiry" (Leffert, 2021, p. 185). Death and Death Anxiety can become a focus in any of Heidegger's three modes of Being: the Thrown, the Everyday, and the Fallen.

Empirical researchers have found that Death Anxiety is, perhaps surprisingly, *a stable personality trait*. It consists of a group of negative cognitive reactions to Death and dying. Templer (1970) began studying Death Anxiety over 60 years ago and developed a Death Anxiety Scale (DAS) that is still in use today. It consists of 15 items (e.g., "I fear dying a painful Death" and "The sight of a dead body is horrifying to me") to which the subject was asked to respond "true" or "false." These were modernized with the substitution of the usual five-point scale going from "strongly disagree" (1) to "strongly agree" (5). The appearance of the DAS heralded the onset of an era in which Death and dying could be studied instead of being treated as a taboo subject (like cancer or mental illness), an attitude that Kübler-Ross (1964/2014) described when she began studying Death and dying in the 1950s.

The most often cited definition of Death Anxiety remains Templer's (1970) as "an unpleasant emotional state precipitated by contemplation of one's own death." The idea of the universality of the fear of Death goes back at least to the work of Hall in 1896 (Thorson & Powell, 1992). Lonetto and Templer (1986) offer a four-dimensional approach to Death Anxiety: (1) it ties together cognitive and emotional reactions to death; (2) it describes reactions to real or imagined changes in the physical body in its Being-toward-Death; (3) an awareness of the unstoppable nature of time that subjectively expands the past and compresses the future;[18] (4) the pain and stress, actual or anticipated, brought about by chronic or terminal illness or our fears of them. In particular, they studied Death Anxiety as it appears in childhood and adolescence—something we did not think existed.

The most common image of Death is as a formless black entity (Lonetto & Templer, 1986). This image is not necessarily associated with anxiety, as when it replaces images of burial and decay. In talking about children's feelings about death in 1986, it's like these authors feel they are on the defensive and have to justify the data. Lonetto (1980) quotes a child,

> ... scarry, frightening, disturbing, dangerous, unfeeling, unhearing, or silent. It takes you away but if you can see death coming at you in time, you can escape. Death can be invisible like a ghost, or ugly like a monster, or it can be a skeleton. Death can be a person, a companion of the devil, a giver of illness, or even an angel.
>
> (p. 92).

Phenomenologically, these constructs and fantasies are real; they are experiences as a part of Dasein's Being *there*, in World. Among 6-year-olds, they (Lonetto & Templer, 1986) found that 22 out of 100 people get taken away by death monsters, with the numbers of people dying rising as Middle Childhood progresses. Young children—3- to 5-year-olds—tend to see it as a temporary state of living under different circumstances. This progresses into the Middle Child's explorations of Death involving attempts to understand and quantify it, a process that will continue across the entire life cycle. It can best be understood as a Developmental Line (A. Freud, 1963). Sometime between ages 9 and 12 children surmount the developmental task of concluding that Death is inevitable, a *biological* event, with the subsequent denial of that reality moving from the realms of the Thrown and Everyday to the Fallen.

The measurement of Death Anxiety has proved very hard to validate or quantify. An exception is the Threat Index (of Death Anxiety) or TI (Krieger, Epting, & Hays, 1979; Neimeyer, 1994/2015). It grows out of the, sadly, little remembered foundational theories of George Kelly (1955/1963), contained in his psychology of personal constructs. I have called him (Leffert, 2021) a proto-dialectical constructivist whose work anticipated by a half-century modern relational theory and dialectical constructivism (Hoffman, 1979/1998, 1998). Kelly posited that life involves the representation and construction of reality: His fundamental postulate is that we "anticipate events by construing their replications." He posited that, by construing replications, Human Beings literally construct the Meaning in their lives. Camus (Camus, 1942/1989, 1942/1991a; Leffert, 2021) would have approved. His postulate anticipates both Hoffman and, some decades later, that of Tversky and Kahneman (Kahneman, Slovic, & Tversky, 1982; Tversky & Kahneman, 1974/1982). Kelly's work established a replicable basis for construing an individual's constructs about Death and Dying. The takeaway for Existential Psychotherapists exploring Death Anxiety in their patients is that we all construct our own social reality around Death, Dying, and Death Anxiety and that we need to engage patients around their personal constructs, instead of automatically substituting our own (as we therapists often do).

Neimeyer (1994/2015) criticizes current research on Death Anxiety as "intellectually impoverished" in their definitions of death attitudes. It relies on instruments of doubtful validity and reliability. In particular, it fails to engage existential concepts such as that the experience of Death Anxiety also constitutes an affirmation of life, and that one's own Death has a valid meaning of its own. The TI devised by Krieger and colleagues (Krieger, Epting, & Leitner, 1974), based on Kelly's core constructs which define identity and existence, "represents the best validated measure of death attitudes in the literature, with a 20 year history of psychometric refinement that has continued to the present" (Neimeyer, 1994/2015, p. 62). They make it possible to identify an individual's core concepts around Death. When these constructs are challenged, people experience a Threat with Death being the "prototypical challenging event."

The TI in its original form took 60–90 minutes and was individually administered as a structured interview. It was cumbersome but rich in data. There were two parts to the TI, first a construct elicitation phase and then an element placement phase. The subject is offered three cards. One card always says *Death* (to keep the subject focused on Death) but the other two describe specific situations. Neimeyer (1994/2015) offers a list of 19 cards that have been used in previous studies; for example, a card might say, "Your grand-mother dies in her sleep" (p. 64) or "You ran over and killed a young child" (p. 64). The administrator then asks the subject "to state some important ways in which any two situations are alike and different from the third, e.g., these two seem unpredictable, but this one seems predictable" (p. 63). Their answer is then recorded as one of the ways that they construe death. Different triads of the 19 are used until 30 constructs are elicited.

In the element placement phase, the subject is then asked to consider each of the constructs in turn and describe which side they most identify with in themselves or their life, their ideal self, or their ideal life, and their death. With our example, the administrator might ask the subject, "Do you see yourself or your life more as predictable or unpredictable?" The administrator then goes on to ask the subject questions to elicit how they see their ideal life, their ideal self, and their death. The extent of the Death Threat is assessed by how often the subject cognitively splits the self and life from Death as oppo-sites. The higher the percentage of these splits occurring in the subject's con-structs, the higher the Threat Index is. The TI was found to possess internal consistency and test-retest reliability. It wasn't confounded by social desir-ability response bias and proved consistent with other self-reported Death Anxiety measures. The TI met criteria for construct validity and the presence of fewer splits correlated with the subject's being better able to conceive of their own Death. Lastly, this method of eliciting the subject's own constructs yielded intensely meaningful material, much more so than that elicited by standardized semantic scales. The material was useful in a clinical context.

This method of TI administration is of course cumbersome and labor inten-sive. This led Krieger and colleagues (1979) to develop a self-administered, more streamlined form of the test, incorporating some of the most popular constructs (e.g., *predictable-random* and *feels good-feels bad*) that were elicited in the original studies (Krieger et al., 1974). It circumvents the construct elic-itation phase of the test and can be administered in 15–30 minutes. It also eliminates the need for a trained administrator. It lends itself to easily being taken into the clinical setting.

Wong and colleagues (Wong, 2012; Wong, Reker, & Gesser, 1994/2015) have observed that the focus on Death Anxiety research has resulted in a lessening of work on other attitudes toward Death. They posit that both Death Anxiety and Death Acceptance are related to the pursuit of personal meaning (Frankl, 1959/2006; Leffert, 2021). They posit three kinds of Death Acceptance: Neutral, Approach, and Escape. (There is also Death Avoidance.) Neutral Acceptance is an Existential acceptance; Approach Acceptance involves beliefs in an afterlife or reincarnation; Escape Acceptance involves relief from pain and suffering. Both anxiety and acceptance are, to an extent, always present. Death Acceptance involves cognitively the acknowledgement that life is finite and death inevitable accompanied emotionally by some degree of equanimity in the face of that certitude. It represents both confrontation and integration. Both Death Anxiety and Death Acceptance are complex, multidimensional processes that, while referencing common themes, are unique to the personal subjectivity of the individual. An aspect of fear of death is the fear that one will not be able to find personal meaning in life. In terms of Erikson's (1950/1963) developmental stages we are talking about the eighth and last developmental challenge: the struggle between *integrity* and *despair.* This stage is assumed to play out in the decades of late life and old age but, in the case of someone suffering from a terminal illness, their time frame is condensed.

If we are looking at the Evo-Devo (Carroll, 2005; Hofer, 2014) of Death Anxiety going back from tertiary to secondary to primary affective states, we find it to be a normative tertiary process that is, however, subject to pathological exaggeration. It traces back to Panksepp's primary affective state of FEAR and the secondary assessment of danger that is found at least in vertebrates.[19] What is available at a tertiary level is Autonoetic Consciousness and a conceptualization of Death that exists in us and, in some form, in mammals and birds.

I had treated Joan, a single academic in her 50s, for a decade when she was discovered to have a stage iv metastatic carcinoma. A new research protocol offered her a survival time measured in years rather than months. She suffered from a chronic depression surrounding an inability to form a love relationship and unfulfilled academic goals. In the moment of receiving her diagnosis, these items shifted from her "to do" list to impossibility. She hated herself for her failure to achieve them and blamed her cancer, with uncertain validity, on her own dubiously bad behavior. As an Existentially grounded clinician, I moved to both engage her feelings about Death and to help her redefine Meaning in her life. I treated these as problems best addressed in the present rather than in the infantile past addressed by genetic interpretations.[20] We identified two Meaningful goals for the present: shepherding their only daughter through college and, hopefully, attending her graduation, and completing a research project she had been working on for several years. Death and Death Anxiety have been worked and reworked over the past year and these goals have fallen in and out of Meaning as she has cycled between Neutral Acceptance, Avoidance, and Rage. I did decide to share my medical history (as described earlier in the chapter) with Joan. She had encountered bits of it over the years, but I decided to show why I could claim a seat at the table, so to speak. I recognize that this was a controversial decision that could easily be criticized (or even interpreted) but I felt it to be right and consistent with my reading of other authors' clinical work (e.g., Yalom, 1980, 2009) on Death and Dying. It resulted in Joan's being able to maintain a connection to me in what had previously been a highly ambivalent transference situation.

Existentially informed therapists (Firestone & Catlett, 2009; Yalom, 2009) who work with Death and Death Anxiety do not structure it as a replacement for the other threads of exploratory, psychodynamic psychotherapy and psychoanalysis but rather as a supplement that is necessary but not sufficient. It is necessary because we can't just deny or avoid Human Beings' awareness of Death and Death Anxiety over it from our search to locate the Meaning that we find in life. Firestone and Catlett posit that the core pathological defense against Death Anxiety is what they describe as the *fantasy bond*. It offers an idealized connection to an idealized intimate other in the person's life that vanquishes Death. Like other such pacts, it comes at a price. It is a form of bondage in that it makes it impossible for the individual to conceive of their own Death. It also crowds out the other real connections with intimate others and the intimacy that these connections produce. They posit that the fantasy bond is hidden beneath other defenses like denial and enactment that must first be interpreted and worked through. If the therapist doesn't know of or acknowledge this deeper and more primitive defense, it cannot be worked with to free up authentic relationships and an Existential engagement of Death. It leads instead to fantasied gratification and a *fallen* life.

Yalom (1980) devotes the first third of his textbook, *Existential Psychotherapy*, to Death and Death Anxiety. He argues that Life and Death are interdependent, and that Death is a "primordial source of anxiety" and the genetic source of psychopathology. There is a clear biological boundary between Death and Life, but no such *psychological* boundary exists. Life fades, *we* fade, and the task we face is to integrate this immutable fact into our personal sense of Meaning. Put a different way, Death is not a problem for the Everyday (Heidegger, 1975/1982) where Being is not a consideration; it is a problem for the Thrown and the Fallen with the latter being about flight and the former meaningfulness. The necessity for the truly engaged and authentic Dasein to engage Death to find Meaning flies in the face of Death Anxiety: We find it hard to swallow. The corollary to it, endless life, is life without Meaning.[21] Close encounters with Death, on the other hand, can enhance either Meaning or Flight. As I have lived through a half-century of mortal illness, including, early on, a near-death experience, I have been repeatedly thrown into periods of both, but from almost the beginning, I knew I had to keep Death in my sights if I was to truly live. My intimate relationships, my writing, my work in caring for patients, and indulging my insatiable curiosity became the fonts from which I drew personal meaning.

Death is a terror (a more meaningful and emotion-rich term than *anxiety*), and our first impulse is to meet it with denial. The Evo-Devo of death-terror led to the earliest huddling together of mammals and birds that underwent a qualitative change with the advent of autonoetic consciousness or self-awareness. The heard or flock became a group, originally the prototypical group of 150 or so—Dunbar's (1993) number. Yet what confounds us is that, while we live our lives together, we, existentially, are born and die alone. If we look at the particular fears that can make up Death Anxiety, we find they come in two sorts: fear of how our death would affect our social group and our intimate others, and, individually, fear of the process of dying itself and what happens to us after Death. Our attempts to deny Death Anxiety often take the form of (unconsciously) breaking it down into more mundane, everyday fears or even disabling phobias. I am positing here a very different, phenomenological explanation of anxiety as arising out of our deepest Being rather than some putative psychodynamic roots (A. Freud, 1936/1966; S. Freud, 1926/1959). These roots do shape our anxieties and must be clinically dealt with in the usual manner but must be understood as a Developmental Line (A. Freud, 1963) starting out with childhood or early childhood Death Anxiety. What follows from Yalom's position is the premise that therapeutic action must focus on healing and care (Leffert, 2016) rather than conflict resolution or deficit amelioration.

What further sets contemporary experiences of Death Anxiety apart is that, going back to the Early Modern period (1500–1800) and before, the possibility of Death was much more present across all the life cycle: It was frightening but not unusual. Paradoxically, with the exception of war, terrorism, and natural disaster, medical science has made death relatively rarer until the end of the life cycle. As a result, after the death-exploratory time of early and middle childhood, its relative uncommonness (in contemporary Europe and North America) both facilitates denial and heightens terror when the "Appointment in Samarra" does appear.

Yalom (Yalom & Yalom, 2021), over his long career, has seen hundreds of patients suffering from Death Anxiety. He writes about the fulfilled life in opposition to the life unlived—that of a person who has not lived their goals or leaves so much on the table that they have never done. In his clinical experience, the amount of a life that is unlived is directly proportional to the amount of Death Anxiety that an individual suffers. This can also occur through no fault of their own when someone faces an unseasonable death; when a life is shortened through a terminal illness. This was particularly painful for a patient in their 50s who was a smoker and was diagnosed with stage iv lung cancer and attributed their cancer to their smoking. Many of us who deeply value our minds and intellects singularly fear decline and dementia (myself included). I have come to believe that this is a displaced form of Death Anxiety. Yalom doesn't take this a step farther from the Existential to the Phenomenological: that an unlived life is a Fallen life (Heidegger, 1927/2010) and a fully lived life is a Thrown life. The amount of life lived in the Everyday[22] can also lead to Death Anxiety if someone is trapped in it. Yalom, however, also comes at Death Anxiety from the perspective of unmetabolized Trauma. He observes that his dying wife, Marilyn, seemed to experience little or no Death Anxiety while he is overwhelmed by it as she approaches her death from multiple myeloma. He attributes this to the lack of Trauma in her early years, growing up from what we would call a Secure Base (Bowlby, 1988) while Trauma and its accompanying anxiety was so much a part of his own childhood. Trauma can then be reprocessed much later into Death Anxiety.

Yalom (2009) draws on the work of the ancient Greek philosopher Epicurus (Warren, 2009a), who posited that the primal source of human misery is *"our omnipresent fear of death"* (Yalom, 2009, p. 77). Epicurus offered three arguments to alleviate Death Anxiety which I find, shall we say, less perfect than Yalom does, and certainly not so Existentially defensible:

1. The mortality of the soul. This is a formulation that still has not penetrated Folk Psychology and religion: that the soul (we could substitute the Self here) is linked to the body and perishes with it. This contrasted with the position of Socrates that the putative immortality of the soul was a comfort that later found its way into Judeo-Christian traditions of an afterlife. Epicurus was perhaps the first to criticize the actions of religious leaders and clergy (of whatever sort) that act to enhance Death Anxiety as a way of increasing their power. Death and consignment to Hell became a punishment for religious transgressions. If we are mortal and we perish body and soul, then there is no need to fear an afterlife. He did not dare to assert that the gods did not exist (we are sometimes braver today) but only that they were oblivious to us humans and our actions. He saw them as models to aim for; however, as described by the Ancient Greeks, they seem to have had all of our failings and weaknesses.

2. The ultimate nothingness of Death. Epicurus argued that if we are, at our Deaths, dispersed, body and soul, then we cannot perceive and, if we cannot perceive, there is nothing to fear. If we are dead, we won't know we are and there is again nothing to fear. This one, from an Existential point of view, I can't really accept, and my criticism reflects partially on the first argument. It works if one fears hell and damnation at the hands of a judgmental god. It doesn't address the problem; What if what I fear is that very Nothingness (or, phenomenologically, no-thing-ness)? Speaking personally, as someone who accepts the first argument, I grant you that I will know nothing and feel nothing after I die. But my problem is that it is this very nothingness[23] that I understand but also dread in the present, and the fact that it can only bother me now, when I'm alive, doesn't help.

3. The argument of symmetry. Simply put, we did not exist before birth and will not exist after we die, there wasn't a problem before so there won't be after. Nabokov describes life as a brief interval between two entities of darkness (nothingness) and notes that most people find the second one harder to deal with than the first. The Existentially troubling aspect of this argument is the premise that life changes nothing, it doesn't matter overmuch to the *Umwelt* and the *Mitwelt*, but it certainly matters to *us*.

Where this leaves me, and should, I think, leave all of us is that, while Death Terror is problematic and, we would say, an object of therapeutic action, Death Anxiety is more normative and, in modest dosages, should not be considered pathological. There is a range here. While many people in Erikson's eighth age seem to approach Death without anxiety, Nuland (1993) described 20% of people screaming in terror as they died. A further problem for us is that while Death Terror is an object of therapy for some of us, it is, for others, it is an object of religion or of pastoral counseling.[24] I don't think we can argue that, outside the realms of philosophy, one or the other is intrinsically better, however much we might like to do so, but only that one is more suited to a given individual than another.[25]

Epicureanism (Warren, 2009b) does suggest meaningful possibilities. Consistent with ancient Greek philosophy, it is based on the premise that what philosophy had to offer was a path to the maximization of happiness and the relief of pain (Tsouna, 2009; Warren, 2009a). I reached similar expanded conclusions (Leffert, 2016, 2017) and criticized standard psychoanalytic thought for not prioritizing these goals and, instead, viewing therapeutic action in terms of gained insight and freedom. The Greeks saw unhappiness and fear as diseases of the Soul, and Epicurus in particular viewed "therapy" as a purging of the soul. (The soul exists still in folk psychology; we, however, would instead label it the *Self*.) Epicurus was the first to compare philosophy to medical science and the philosopher to a medical doctor. Since their knowledge of disease, physiology, and pathophysiology was limited and often wrongheaded, there is not much to be had here; I would consider these philosophers to be early psychologists whose theories of diseases of the soul were much more amenable to an effective treatment (most importantly to remove or neutralize pain, suffering, and unhappiness) that the philosopher-as-therapist could deliver.

I would have hoped to have come to a more [philosophically] satisfying conclusion about Death Anxiety other than its being normative. It is entirely consistent, however, with Becker's (1973) conclusions arrived at a half-century ago. Becker argued that Death Anxiety was transformed into Terror through a child's conflicts and trauma on which were superimposed historical and sociocultural factors (COVID-19 offers an at-hand example). Firestone (2015) similarly posits that, in response to early frustrations, deprivations, and trauma, the infant develops a fantasy bond with the mother that is transformed into the core defense against Death Anxiety. He sees neurosis as the transformation of a real fear based on Death into the neurotic misery of a well-known plethora of defenses. To reprise, the primary affect FEAR (Panksepp, 2009) is processed up from the midbrain to the secondary and tertiary affective state of Death Anxiety.

Suicide

The first question you might ask is: Given the vast amounts that have been written about suicide over the years, why would I imagine that I have anything of significance to add to it in a brief section of a chapter? The answer is that I want to say something about its Postphenomenological properties, as a particular strand of Being-toward-Death (Kasket, 2012; Mandíc, 2008). Perhaps the first thing to say about suicide, from an Existential point of view, is that it is not what it seems. It is particularly not simply a neurobiological entity arising in conditions of severe depression and psychosis and encompassed by the tag line accompanying many media presentations: "If you are thinking about harming yourself, call [this or that Help Line]." Instead, it is a highly complex piece of thought and behavior with diverse meanings and ontologies. Epidemiologically speaking, the most frequent cause of suicide *is* untreated, inadequately treated, or deeply refractory depression.[26] Severe depression is accompanied by a pain so terrible that when treatments fail, death offers the only relief. Psychosis is a distant second.

Suicide isn't only Depression gone awry; it is a surrender to the *possibility* of Death and makes it a reality. There is more. Suicide and Death have, for some, a strange magnetic appeal, like Baudelaire's *Fleur du Mal*, published in 1857 (1857/2008), and embodying the fused themes of eroticism, decay, and death that would reach fruition in *fin-de-siècle* Vienna. As various times, historically and geographically, suicide has become a source of meaning that paradoxically makes life significant and consequential. This has been true of imperial Japan over the centuries but, for our purposes, *fin-de-siècle* Vienna offers more of an opportunity to explore this meaning-through-death.

Fin-de-siècle Vienna manifested a particular episteme embedded in time-place-culture. A group of perhaps 70 thinkers—Freud was one—gathered in its coffee houses (Johnston, 1972) and came to a series of understandings that would dominate 20th-century thought. The Viennese episteme portrayed a *City of Dreams* that embodied a brilliant, shining surface (like the famous *Schlag*, the whipped cream that the cafés ladled on their *Strudels*) layered over another Vienna, the gritty impoverished center of a rotten and dying empire. The coffeehouses shown so brightly in part because housing was terrible: The intellectuals left their grim, unheated rooms for the light, the conversation, and the *central heating* of the cafés. Vienna was also the center of the dying 1,000-year-old Austro-Hungarian Empire plagued by its decay and languishing under the 60-year rule of its emperor Franz Joseph.

Aestheticism, impressionism, and therapeutic nihilism all revealed the Austrian attitude toward Death (Johnston, 1972): "Austrians cultivated a Baroque vision of death as the fulfillment of life" (p. 165). *Jung Wien* a particular group of young Viennese intellectuals, for whom the author Hermann Bahr (1863–1934) became a sort of spokesman, viewed Death not as a savior but as a consummator. *Fin-de-siècle* authors wrote of life as ephemeral and death as evanescent. This fit with Viennese impressionism, the changeable, ephemeral, and nervous fluctuations of life in the City of Dreams. Bahr wrote of dark latent contents beneath a changing surface. "For the unemployed youth of the middle and upper classes, Death was a remedy for the weariness and ennui of life and suicide *the envied means of achieving it*" (Leffert, 2013,

p. 167 italics added). Authors both in and beyond *Jung Wien* offered a warm, positive view of Death. Johnston called them the "poets of Death" the most celebrated of whom was the Viennese-born Arthur Schnitzler.

Schnitzler, a Jewish doctor and son of a doctor who turned playwright, portrayed Death as comforting and "assuaging the wounds of the living" (Johnston, 1972, p. 171). His characters engage in illicit sex devoid of Meaning that reflects a crisis of the individual. Death brings them a reckoning, an awakening, and a liberation. Both Johnston and Janik and Toulmin (1973/1996) comment on the high suicide rate among Austrian intellectuals in the decades before and after 1900. The suicides among intellectuals often had to do with their work not being appreciated or ridiculed. Suicide was found among the children of successful and renowned parents who, unable to live in their shadows, could not find a place, intellectually or professionally, in this decaying society. Unlike in our contemporary episteme, suicide was accepted as a matter of course in Austria, similar to an epidemic (social contagion (Christakis & Fowler, 2009) across the Viennese Social Network in this *fin-de-siècle* episteme should not be underestimated as a cause). The most famous of these suicides was that of Prince Rudolph and a woman who agreed to die with him in the lodge Myerling in 1989. Suicide fit with the culture's therapeutic nihilism in which treatment of illnesses of whatever variety was judged useless and the body should be left to heal on its own, or that Death healed the living. The culture's appreciation of Death made suicide attractive and natural. Taken together, this range of factors lent suicide a kind of magnetic appeal.

If we move ahead to the early 21st-century United States, we find differences and similarities with *fin-de-siècle* Vienna. They were unchanged by the availability of successful (and unsuccessful) antidepressant treatments. Medically assisted suicide in the face of a painful or debilitating terminal illness has been legalized in 12 countries and 11 states in the United States. Although controversial, it has also gained moral purchase. In other cases, however, associating suicide with untreated depression would relieve us of the necessity of exploring its meaning and magnetism.

Where Vienna offered a dense social network in which suicidal thought and action could percolate, the United States demonstrates much higher geographical diversity. The internet, however, has strengthened its social networks and conquered this dispersity. Suicide has become a Postphenomenological entity. Suicide and self-harm communities abound in the metaverse (Mitchell, Wells, Priebe, & Ybarra, 2014) in 2022. These communities do not aim to oppose or treat suicide potential but rather to enhance or support it. Members exchange information about suicide methodologies, how to obtain the materials that allow one to painlessly end one's life, and advice on the hows and wheres of doing so. It is true that these communities also serve people with untreated depressions who want to end their lives: They are peripheral outliers at two or three degrees of separation from the active network core for whom suicide has meaning and is a positive value. The internet also offers suicide "supplies," accompanied by a hotline number, that are available for second day delivery. Amazon offers sodium nitrite (a chemical used to cure meat that is said to provide a painless suicide) and books (Humphrey, 1991/2002; Kilian, 2021)[27] that supportively consider suicide, death, and the how-to to bring it about. An example of how these communities operate involves a woman who takes an overdose of sodium nitrite and becomes frightened. She makes contact on the web and says she is scared and connects with someone who talks to her and encourages her until she loses consciousness.

If we are to consider suicide Existentially we must start out from Camus' *The Myth of Sisyphus and Other Essays* (Camus, 1942/1991b). In the book's early essays Camus observes, "*The fundamental subject of "The Myth of Sisyphus" is this: it is legitimate and necessary to wonder whether life has a meaning: therefore, it is legitimate to meet the problem of suicide face-to-face*" (p. v) and "There is only one truly serious philosophical problem and that is suicide. Judging whether life is or is not worth living amounts to answering the fundamental question of philosophy … These are facts the heart can feel: yet they call for careful study before they become clear to the intellect" (p. 3). Camus argues at the start of *The Myth* that, if a life is without meaning and *cannot be made to develop it*, then, as surely as night follows day, suicide is the only solution, the only response to an Absurd life (Leffert, 2021). Camus (Camus, 1942/1991b; Zaretsky, 2013) argues that this cannot and must not be the case. He contended that revolt gives life its value. Paradoxically, Meursault, the protagonist in *The Stranger* (Camus, 1942/1989), reaches a similar conclusion when he seeks Meaning through his being publicly guillotined, both a revolt *and* a suicide. Suicide is at the cusp of the battle between Meaning and Absurdity. *Jung Wien* was certainly caught up in this problem.

If Camus offers a philosopher's take on suicide, we must now come to the COVID pandemic which reads like a Peoples' History of Absurdity. At the time of writing this, we are at the point in the winter of 2022, certainly a winter of discontent, in which we are an exhausted depressed people immersed in futility. The symptoms are everywhere. The Great Resignation in which people simply refuse to work at underpaid jobs and walk away in search of better work or in search of nothing at all is just one symptom. The fact that there are now vast political cleavages and social unrest (Walter, 2022) that many authors (e.g., Marche, 2022; Walter, 2022) see as the beginnings of a new Civil War is another. In our country we have been in the midst of a class struggle between the upper 1% that own 50% of the United States' wealth and the lower 50% of it that own 2.5%. The country is neatly divided between the Red and the Blue but, if you look past the divisive rhetoric that becomes a group psychosis, you find that the people on both sides have the same social and economic complaints, they only misunderstand them differently. We come again to the cusp of the battle with Absurdity—self-medication with alcohol, marijuana, and opiates—and the overdose cum suicide deaths they produce. Camus is alive and well in the midst of folk psychology.

Roberts and Lamont (2014) observe, correctly, I think, that suicide is one of the primary concerns of the mental health profession: The literature there focuses on diagnosis and prevention of a mental illness. They posit that framing the subject in this way does not allow for its critical reexamination. They too saw Camus as offering a particular perspective on suicide as a uniquely human attempt to make sense out of "the struggles and sorrows of life." They challenge attempting to understand suicide exclusively in a context of mental illness and a literature that focuses on suicide prevention; they offer an Existential reconceptualization of it instead. Suicide cannot be understood without considering the historical and sociopolitical context upon which it is contingent. Its "framing" determines how it is thought about and whether its rightful purview is medicine or philosophy or, most powerfully, both. The framing very much determines how mental health workers, at whatever level, think about suicide and how they respond to a suicidal patient.

Camus, in his discussions of suicide, does not, separate those suicides that grow out of mental illness, usually untreated depression with a bio-psycho-social base, from suicides that grow out of an Existential problem of Meaning and Meaninglessness. He sees the person who suicides as having made a judgment about the value of life, about the very value of Existence which is now in question. The "Da"—the *there*—of Dasein has changed. For such people, all of life has become irreversibly Absurd. When suicide becomes an Existential problem, it requires an Existential therapy to address it as opposed to an antidepressant. Sometimes the problem can be bypassed by a "grand narrative" (Roberts & Lamont, 2014), or metanarrative, such as religion, philosophy, or politics (e.g., communism). Such an approach requires first of all faith and belief. Kierkegaard (1849/1980, 1843/1983)[28] attempted to shore up these metanarratives Existentially, but postmodernity has fractured the faith and belief necessary to maintain them. In his retelling of the Sisyphus myth, Camus' (1942/1991a) response to the Existential challenge of Absurdity is that *"even within the limits of nihilism, it is possible to find the means to proceed beyond nihilism"* (p. v). Roberts and Lamont (2014) posit that even when there is no overarching concept that can make sense of life's struggles,

> there exists an opportunity to engage in a collaborative exploration of what those struggles can come to mean in the unique context of that individual's life, an opportunity to respond to life's challenges in a manner that enables the construction of a system of personal meaning that promotes new growth, development, and direction in that individual's life.
>
> (p. 13).

This is just what Camus' Sisyphus does in each hour he walks down the mountain to reengage the boulder and push it to the top one more time. We have a reconceptualization of (I would say some) suicides as Existential crises rather than mental illness.

O'Dwyer (2012) observes, accurately I believe, that the *thought* of suicide passes through most people's minds at some point in their lives. In her discussions of the prevalence of suicide in contemporary Western society, she unknowingly draws a parallel to *fin-de-siècle* Vienna. The difference is that, in Vienna, suicide was more of a failed young intellectual's or a professional's game, whereas in 2022 it is more a failed blue collar or rural matter. What they have in common is that they originate in despair and a sense of hopelessness that they will ever find Meaning, however the torn souls may choose to define it. Camus, throughout his life, was intensely concerned with the plight of his fellow Human Beings, a plight that ultimately came together around the polarities of Existential suicide and the search for Meaning. What stands out about this struggle is that it is a solitary one; it is the task of the therapist to penetrate that solitude. Camus (1942/1991b) views the Absurdity that would make suicide an Existential choice as growing out of a number of causes: if life is only an unintegrated series of events, the transient nature of Existence, a sense of futility of effort or struggle, and the inevitability of Death. A life lived *exclusively* in the boredom of the Everyday (Camus, 1942/1989) is a life without Meaning, an Absurd life. For some Human Beings, suicide is the only perceived solution to such pain and despair (others choose, explicitly or not, to sink into the Everyday).

Camus (1942/1991b) stresses that Absurdity is an aspect of life, an aspect of Dasein. An *Existenz* that will be wiped away with all its connections by Death must be seen, by its very nature, as, to a degree, an Absurd kind of Being. In his retelling of the myth of Sisyphus, Camus wishes to solve the original problem: that, if a life lacks meaning, then suicide becomes the only response to it. Taking Sisyphus as an extreme case he shows us that, even in his circumstances, it is possible to find Meaning.

In this chapter, I have divided an Existential inquiry into Death into three categories: Death, Death Anxiety, and Suicide. Each addresses a different aspect of the end-of-life experience. Perhaps the most important thing to take away from these discussions is that discourse in these areas has a place in *any* Psychoanalysis and *most* Psychotherapies, not just those in which a patient is facing a terminal illness, mourning, or is actively planning suicide. By and large, with the exception of Existentially (e.g., May et al., 1958; Yalom, 2009) or Phenomenologically (e.g., Boss, 1963) informed psychotherapists, clinicians confine their explorations precisely to these circumstances. I'm hoping that I've given the reader good reasons to widen that discourse.

Notes

1   To wit that Mind and Body are separate things that, in Descartes words there is a separation between willing my arm to rise and its actually rising.
2   Yalom (2009) and Frankl (1959/2006) are the standout exceptions here.
3   At the time, the manifest content of my treatment of the problem was not unusual. Most analysts would have said nothing: Abend (1982) argued that an analyst's giving

the patient *any* information about himself was a manifestation of countertransference acting out. (Dewald (1982) described a for-the-times courageous disclosure of his own serious illness to his patients.) How many psychoanalysts and psychotherapists use theory of technique to hide feelings such as I experienced, I don't know.

4 The explosive growth of the population of psychoanalysts in our small community only made matters worse and there remains, to this day, a sparsity of psychotherapy or psychoanalytic patients.

5 The piece of good news that I got was that, unlike cancer, when you were always rolling the dice about a recurrence, the longer you lived with CHF and, better, yet, stayed out of the hospital for it, the longer you were likely *to* live (I'm approaching 10 years).

6 Woody Allen's comment, "I'm not afraid of death: I just don't want to be there when it happens," is relevant here.

7 Interestingly, if one looks at the psychoanalytic literature during and after the Influenza Pandemic of 1918–1920 there is biographical writing and correspondence about Influenza and who contracted it but there is no writing about its psychological meaning in terms of trauma and loss for the analysts or their patients. There is nothing about what patients made of it or their grief connected to it. Obviously, a pandemic that probably killed 100 million worldwide must have affected everyone in treatment during the period and the decades that followed it. There is no evidence, for example, that Freud had anything to say about the psychological loss of his daughter Sophie, who died after a 4-day illness with influenza, and its meaning (or the meaning of his own bout with influenza) to him.

8 I have never cared for the use of the term *battle* in this context; we have little choice in the matter except whether to retain our dignity in the face of inevitable struggle. I similarly question the Jewish burial tradition of referring to the deceased as a woman or man of valor.

9 This brings us back to Eissler (1968).

10 This does not address the critique that such subjective meaning can be a horror in the eyes of others, but that is an issue subject to analysis outside the disciplines of Phenomenology and Existentialism.

11 If Facebook were a country, it would be the largest country on earth.

12 This is an elegant research design that yields clean data. However, as I have commented elsewhere (Leffert, 2010), producing clean data in the service of controlling variables limits what we can learn about a wide range of people. We find ourselves, with the best of research intentions, only learning more and more about less and less.

13 The *Appointment in Samarra* at the start of the chapter is relevant to what follows.

14 This is a very hard sentence. Heidegger seems to be attempting to tie Death intimately to Dasein's Being, to care, and to its always being before Dasein and its Being. The italics in the text here are Heidegger's.

15 This is seen when Daseins are willing to sacrifice themselves (e.g., wars) for the group of Daseins.

16 This is also the biological reality of S. Freud's (1920/1955) otherwise debatable theory of a Death Instinct.

17 My personal views of the climate disaster, and those of some of the people I encounter is that, at my age of 77, I am unlikely to experience much of it. It will, however, certainly damage the ripples of myself I'd expected to leave behind.

18 I have noticed as I have moved into my 70s that the days of the week seem to fly by. Patients and friends observe the same thing. I have thought that we measure our sense of time by comparing present time with our stored memories. As we age, a week becomes a much smaller percentage of our total memories and is experienced accordingly.

19 Even single cell organisms demonstrate avoidances.

20 Some sense of how Death was experienced *throughout the life cycle* was useful but not as a focus of therapeutic action. In a patient for whom Death was associated with the early/earlier loss of parents or significant others, genetically focused work would certainly be more of a part of the treatment.

21 Imagine even centuries of life, endless time in which authenticities loose Meaning again and again as life becomes ever more forced and empty. In more Everyday terms, how much chocolate can you eat?

22 In my own work, I draw a distinction between the Everyday and the Fallen that Phenomenologists (and Heidegger) do not; Everyday is not a fallen state if the individual can also move in and out of the Thrown.

23 There is indeed the old Sartrian joke (Bakewell, 2016). Jean-Paul Sartre walks into a café and orders coffee without cream. The waiter returns after a bit and says, "I'm sorry, M. Sartre, we are all out of cream, will milk do (to be withouted)?"

24 Extreme Unction in Catholicism is just one example of such intervention.

25 Years ago, a colleague of mine developed a rapidly terminal ocular melanoma. Although he identified himself as (culturally?) Jewish, he and his wife were in no way observant. In the last weeks of his life, however, what he seemed to find most comforting were the visits of a rabbi I had put him in touch with when he asked for a rabbi to conduct his burial service. That same rabbi had told me that how he conceptualized his vocation was to help his congregants through the various transitions of life. He described an airline pilot who he had converted to Judaism, officiated at his wedding to a Jewish woman, conducted a naming ceremony for their child, and, later, conducted his funeral service after his death from cancer.

26 Virginia Woolf was either bipolar or suffered from major depressive disorder (MDD) throughout her life. She had at least two episodes of depression (Rose, 1979) lasting several months for which there was, at that time, no effective treatment (she tried psychoanalysis, which was common in her circle at the time but, without adjunct treatment with modern mood stabilizers, it could not be of much help). At age 59 in 1941, when she felt another episode beginning, she felt she simply couldn't bear the pain and drowned herself. Sylvia Plath, also bipolar, seemed to use serious suicide attempts as a way of diving into Death to fuel her creativity (Alvarez, 1971/1990). In 1963, at age 31, she again attempted suicide but the arrangements she had made to be found in time failed and she ended her life.

27 *Humphrey's book is number 17 on Amazon's best seller list of books on medicine and law. Both books bear the hotline notice about suicide.*

28 Sartre (1947/2007) demolished Kierkegaard's argument with his Existentialist "battle cry": *Existence precedes Essence.*

References

Abend, S. M. (1982). Serious illness in the analyst: Countertransference implications. *Journal of the American Psychoanalytic Association, 30*, 365–379.

Altheide, D., Coyle, M., DeVriese, K., & Schneider, C. (2008). Emergent qualitative document analysis. In S. N. Hesse-Biber, & P. Leavy (Eds.), *Handbook of emergent methods* (pp. 127–154). New York, NY: The Guilford Press.

Alvarez, A. (1990). *The savage God: A study of suicide.* New York, NY: W. W. Norton & Co. (Original work published in 1971).

Bakewell, S. (2016). *At the existentialist café: Freedom, being and apricot cocktails.* New York, NY: Other Press.

Barabási, A.-L. (2003). *Linked.* London, England: Plume Books.

Baudelaire, C. (2008). *The flowers of evil (Oxford World's Classics) (English and French edition)* (J. McGowan, trans.). Oxford, England: Oxford University Press. (Original work published in 1857).

Becker, E. (1973). *The denial of death*. New York, NY: Free Press.

Boss, M. (1963). *Psychoanalysis and Daseinanalysis*. New York, NY: Basic Books.

Bowlby, J. (1988). *A secure base: Parent-child attachment and healthy human development*. New York, NY: Basic Books.

Camus, A. (1958). Caligula. *Caligula and 3 other plays* (pp. 1–74). New York, NY: Vintage Books. (Original work published in 1944).

Camus, A. (1989). *The stranger* (M. Ward, trans.). New York, NY: Vintage Books. (Original work published in 1942).

Camus, A. (1991a). The myth of Sisyphus. In J. O'Brien (Ed.), *The myth of Sisyphus and other essays* (pp. 3–138). New York, NY: Vintage Books. (Original work published in 1942).

Camus, A. (1991b). *The myth of Sisyphus and other essays* (J. O'Brien, trans.). New York, NY: Vintage Books. (Original work published in 1942).

Carroll, S. B. (2005). *Endless forms most beautiful: The new science of Evo-Devo*. New York, NY: W. W. Norton & Co.

Christakis, N. A., & Fowler, J. H. (2009). *Connected: The surprising power of our social networks and how they shape our lives*. New York, NY: Little, Brown and Company.

Dewald, P. A. (1982). Serious illness in the analyst: Transference, countertransference, and reality responses. *Journal of the American Psychoanalytic Association, 30*, 347–363.

Dunbar, R. (1993). Coevolution of neocortex size, group size and language in humans. *Behavioral and Brain Sciences, 16*, 681–735.

Eissler, K. R. (1968). The relationship of explaining and understanding in psychoanalysis. *Psychoanalytic Study of the Child, 23*, 141–177.

Erikson, E. (1963). *Childhood and society* (2nd ed.). New York, NY: W. W. Norton & Co. (Original work published in 1950).

Firestone, R. W. (2015). Psychological defenses against death anxiety. In R. A. Neimeyer (Ed.), *Death anxiety handbook: Research, instrumentation, and application* (pp. 217–241). London, England: Routledge.

Firestone, R. W., & Catlett, J. (2009). *Beyond death anxiety*. New York, NY: Springer.

Fotopoulou, A., & Tsakiris, M. (2017). Mentalizing homeostasis: The social origins of interoceptive inference. *Neuropsychoanalysis, 19*, 3–28.

Frankl, V. E. (2006). *Man's search for meaning* (I. Lasch, trans.). Boston, MA: Beacon Press. (Original work published in 1959).

Freud, A. (1963). The concept of developmental lines. *Psychoanalytic Study of the Child, 18*, 245–265.

Freud, A. (1966). *The ego and the mechanisms of defense revised edition*. New York, NY: International Universities Press. (Original work published in 1936).

Freud, S. (1955). Beyond the pleasure principle. In J. Strachey (Ed.), *Standard edition* (Vol. XVIII, pp. 7–64). London, England: Hogarth Press. (Original work published in 1920).

Freud, S. (1959). Inhibition, symptom, and anxiety. In J. Strachey (Ed.), *Standard edition* (pp. 87–178). London, England: Hogarth Press. (Original work published in 1926).

Heidegger, M. (1966). *Discourse on thinking* (J. M. Ansderson & E. H. Freund, trans.). New York, NY: Harper & Row. (Original work published in 1959).

Heidegger, M. (1982). *The basic problems of phenomenology* (A. Hofstadter, trans. Rev. ed.). Bloomington: Indiana University Press. (Original work published in 1975).

Heidegger, M. (2009). *History of the concept of time: Prolegomena (Studies in phenomenology and existential philosophy* (T. Kisiel, trans.). Bloomington: Indiana University Press. (Original work published in 1979).

Heidegger, M. (2010). *Being and time* (J. Stambaugh & D. J. Schmidt, trans.). Albany: State University of New York. (Original work published in 1927).

Hofer, M. A. (2014). The emerging synthesis of development and evolution: A new biology for psychoanalysis. *Neuropsychoanalysis, 16*, 3–22.

Hoffman, I. Z. (1998). Death anxiety and adaptation to mortality in psychoanalytic theory. In *Ritual and spontaneity in the psychoanalytic process* (pp. 31–67). New York, NY: The Analytic Press. (Original work published in 1979).

Hoffman, I. Z. (1998). *Ritual and spontaneity in the psychoanalytic process*. Hillsdale, MI: The Analytic Press.

Homer. (1998). *The Iliad* (R. Fagles, trans.). New York, NY: Penguin Books.

Humphrey, D. (2002). *Final exit: The practicalities of self-deliverance and assisted suicide for the dying* (3rd ed.). New York, NY: Dell Publishing. (Original work published in 1991).

Janik, A., & Toulmin, S. (1996). *Wittgenstein's Vienna*. Chicago, IL: Ivar R. Dee. (Original work published in 1973).

Johnston, W. M. (1972). *The Austrian mind: An intellectual and social history 1848–1938*. Berkeley: University of California Press.

Kahneman, D., Slovic, P., & Tversky, A. (Eds.). (1982). *Judgement under uncertainty: Heuristics and biases*. Cambridge, England: Cambridge University Press.

Kasket, E. (2012). Being-towards-death in the digital age. *Existential Analysis: Journal of the Society for Existential Analysis, 23*, 249–261.

Kelly, G. A. (1963). *A theory of personality: The psychology of personal constructs*. New York, NY: W. W. Norton & Co. (Original work published in 1955).

Kierkegaard, S. (1980). *The sickness onto death* (H. V. Hong & E. H. Hong, trans.). Princeton, NJ: Princeton University Press. (Original work published in 1849).

Kierkegaard, S. (1983). Fear and trembling (H. V. Hong & E. H. Hong, trans.). In H. V. Hong, & E. H. Hong (Eds.), *Fear and Trembling/Repetition*. Princeton, NJ: Princeton University Press. (Original work published in 1843).

Kilian, B. (2021). *Suicide: Methods for a safe and peaceful death*. Charleston, SC: CreatSpace.

Kim, G. (2020). Metaverse: Digital earth, the world of rising things. *Hwaseong: Plan-B Design*.

Krieger, S. R., Epting, F. R., & Hays, L. H. (1979). Validity and reliability of provided constructs in assessing death threat. *Omega, 20*, 87–95.

Krieger, S. R., Epting, F. R., & Leitner, L. M. (1974). Personal constructs, threat, and attitudes towards death. *Omega, 5*, 299–310.

Kübler-Ross, K. (2014). *On death and dying*. New York, NY: Scribner. (Original work published in 1964).

Leffert, M. (2010). *Contemporary psychoanalytic foundations*. London, England: Routledge.

Leffert, M. (2013). *The therapeutic situation in the 21st century*. New York, NY: Routledge.

Leffert, M. (2016). *Phenomenology, uncertainty, and care in the therapeutic encounter*. New York, NY: Routledge.

Leffert, M. (2017). *Positive psychoanalysis: Aesthetics, desire, and subjective well-being*. New York, NY: Routledge.

Leffert, M. (2018). *Psychoanalysis and the birth of the self: A radical interdisciplinary approach*. London, England: Routledge.

Leffert, M. (2021). *The psychoanalysis of the absurd: Existentialism and phenomenology in contemporary psychoanalysis*. London, England: Routledge.

Lonetto, R. (1980). *Children's conception of death*. New York, NY: Springer.

Lonetto, R., & Templer, D. I. (1986). *Death anxiety*. New York, NY: Taylor & Francis.

Mandíc, M. (2008). Being-towards-death and its relevance to psychotherapy. *Existential Analysis: Journal of the Society for Existential Analysis, 19*, 254–266.

Marche, S. (2022). *The next civil war: Dispatches from the American future.* New York, NY: Avid Reader Press/Simon and Schuster.

May, R., Angel, E., & Ellenberger, H. F. (Eds.). (1958). *Existence: New directions in psychiatry and psychology.* New York, NY: Simon & Schuster.

Mellars, P. (2005). The impossible coincidence. A single-species model for the origins of modern human behavior in Europe. *Evolutionary Anthropology, 14,* 12–27.

Mitchell, J. M., Wells, M., Priebe, G., & Ybarra, M. L. (2014). Exposure to websites that encourage self-harm and suicide: Prevalence rates and association with actual thoughts of self-harm and thoughts of suicide in the United States. *Journal of Adolescence, 37,* 1335–1344.

Neimeyer, R. A. (2015). The threat index and related methods. In R. A. Neimeyer (Ed.), *Death anxiety handbook: Research, instrumentation, and application* (pp. 61–101). London, England: Routledge. (Original work published in 1994).

Nuland, S. B. (1993). *How we die: Reflections on life's final chapter.* New York, NY: Alfred A. Knopf.

O'Dwyer, K. (2012). Camus' challenge: The question of suicide. *Journal of Humanistic Psychology, 52,* 165–177.

Ogas, O., & Gaddam, S. (2022). *Journey of the mind: How thinking emerged from chaos.* New York, NY: W. W. Norton & Co.

Panksepp, J. (2009). Brain emotional systems and qualities of mental life: From animal models of affect to implications for psychotherapeutics. In D. Fosha, D. J. Siegal, & M. F. Solomon (Eds.), *The healing power of emotion: Affective neuroscience, development, and clinical practice* (pp. 1–26). New York, NY: W. W. Norton & Co.

Panksepp, J., & Biven, L. (2012). *The archaeology of mind: Neuroevolutionary origins of human emotions.* New York, NY: W. W. Norton & Co.

Panksepp, J., & Watt, D. (2011). What is basic about basic emotions? Lasting lessons from affective neuroscience. *Emotion Review, 3,* 1–10.

Pettitt, P. (2010). *The Paleolithic origins of human burial.* London, England: Routledge.

Porges, S. W. (2011). *The polyvagal theory: Neurophysiological foundations of emotions attachment communication self regulation.* New York, NY: W. W. Norton & Co.

Roberts, M., & Lamont, E. (2014). Suicide: An existentialist reconceptualization. *Journal of Psychiatric and Mental Health Nursing, 21,* 873–878.

Rose, P. A. (1979). *Woman of letters: A life of Virginia Woolf.* Oxford, England: Oxford University Press.

Sartre, J.-P. (2007). *Existentialism is a humanism* (C. Macomber, trans.). New Haven, CT: Yale University Press. (Original work published in 1947).

Schacter, D. L., Addis, D. R., & Buckner, R. L. (2008). Episodic simulation of future events concepts, data, and applications. *Annals of the New York Academy of Science, 1124,* 39–60.

Schur, M. (1972). *Freud: Living and dying.* New York, NY: International Universities Press.

Smith, J., Flowers, P., & Larkin, M. (2009). *Interpretive phenomenological analysis.* London, England: Sage Publications.

Templer, D. I. (1970). The construction and validation of a Death Anxiety Scale. *The Journal of General Psychology, 82,* 165–177.

Thorson, J. A., & Powell, F. C. (1992). A revised Death Anxiety Scale. *Death Studies, 16,* 507–521.

Tsouna, V. (2009). Epicurean therapeutic strategies. In J. Warren (Ed.), *The Cambridge companion to epicureanism* (pp. 249–265). Cambridge, England: Cambridge University Press.

Tulving, E. (2003). Memory and consciousness. In B. J. Baars, W. P. Banks, & J. B. Newman (Eds.), *Essential sources in the scientific study of consciousness* (pp. 575–591). Cambridge, MA: MIT Press. (Original work published in 1985).

Tversky, A., & Kahneman, D. (1982). Judgment under uncertainty: Heuristics and biases. In D. Kahneman, P. Slovic, & A. Tversky (Eds.), *Judgment under uncertainty: Heuristics and biases* (pp. 3–20). Cambridge, England: Cambridge University Press. (Original work published in 1974).

Vaillant, G. E. (2002). *Aging well*. New York, NY: Little, Brown and Company.

Walter, B. (2022). *How civil wars start; and how to stop them*. New York, NY: Crown.

Warren, J. (2009a). Removing fear. In J. Warren (Ed.), *The Cambridge companion to epicureanism* (pp. 234–248). Cambridge, England: Cambridge University Press.

Warren, J. (Ed.). (2009b). *The Cambridge companion to epicureanism*. Cambridge: Cambridge University Press.

Wong, P. T. P. (Ed.). (2012). *The human quest for meaning: Theories, research, and applications* (2nd ed.). London, England: Routledge.

Wong, P. T. P., Reker, G. T., & Gesser, G. (2015). Death Attitude Profile—Revised: A multidimensional measure of attitudes toward death. In R. A. Neimeyer (Ed.), *Death anxiety handbook: Research, instrumentation, and application* (pp. 121–148). London, England: Routledge. (Original work published in 1994).

Yalom, I. D. (1980). *Existential psychotherapy*. New York, NY: Basic Books.

Yalom, I. D. (2009). *Staring at the sun: Overcoming the terror of death*. New York, NY: Jossey-Bass.

Yalom, I. D., & Yalom, M. (2021). *A matter of death and life*. Stanford, CA: Redwood Press.

Zaretsky, R. (2013). *A life worth living: Albert Camus and the quest for meaning*. Cambridge, MA: Belknap Press.

Afterword

In this book, I have offered what has proven to be a complex integration of Interdisciplinary Studies dealing with Existentialism and Phenomenology, then moving on to the relatively new discipline of Postphenomenology. The latter takes up the radical Evo-Devo of the Internet and the Metaverse. I have, these past few years (Leffert, 2017, 2018, 2021), been writing on subjects in such a state of flux that they literally change as I write about them. This process can only continue in the 6 months or so that it will take to get this book into print and then on into the future. The only answer I have found to this conundrum has been to continue the development of ideas into a subsequent volume. My writing has always aimed at offering complex Interdisciplinary accounts of our work that aim at weaving together different epistemological threads into a whole that I hope to be greater than the sum of its parts.

As I have continued to Evolve and Develop my ideas over the last two decades, there have been major shifts in World that I have found to be particularly urgent. Sometimes events such as the COVID pandemic and the rise of global unrest (Walter, 2022) have overtaken clinical work, must be taken into account, and frequently aren't. In particular, I have moved away from the elaboration of comfortable psychoanalytic ideas showing their great age. This has involved a shift from Metapsychology to Philosophy and Interdisciplinary Studies. Metapsychology is a curious creature. It was defined early in Psychoanalysis (a century or so ago) and purported to offer increasing powers of explanation with increasing (clinically distant) levels of abstraction. I have argued that what metapsychologies—they are *always* multiple—offer is a system of Heuristics and Biases (Kahneman, Slovic, & Tversky, 1982; Kahneman & Tversky, 1979/2000) that increase speed and comfort in thinking at the price of a loss of uncertainty. What can be most hampering here is the use of the Representativeness Heuristic in which (in Psychoanalysis) a clinical moment is taken to be a representative of a class of moments and is then treated uncritically as having *all* the properties of that putative class. May (May, 1958; May, Angel, & Ellenberger, 1958), in particular, has been deeply critical of such circular reasoning. As a candidate,

DOI: 10.4324/9781003349556-7

a half-century ago, I found great comfort (we all experience this and must try, very hard, to not be *too* comfortable) in learning these rules and feeling the presence of implicit standing in the process. Twenty years later (Leffert, 2003), I was able to begin to question them and have never looked back. I found that there were *many* singular contributors in other fields who offered their conclusions as temporary and lacking the near-religious orthodoxy that one often finds in Psychoanalysis as a single discipline.

It is a mistake to consider the epidemiology of COVID as an exercise in virology, and DNA analysis; it is a social disease. In Latour's (1991/1993) terms, it merges, interreferentially, the Social and the Scientific into a large and complex hybrid. The simplest example to be found in COVID is vaccination where the synthesis of vaccines—which went incredibly quickly—buts heads against the social problem of who can get vaccinated and who chooses to get vaccinated (or doesn't). Mask-wearing is another such conflictual item. We are dealing with a mix of science and social politics.

Social Network Theory (Christakis & Fowler, 2009) offers a relational perspective on how groups of people behave. Dunbar (2016) has studied the limits of small group size (called Dunbar's number of 150); it is a stable measure, showing validity from prehistoric times through the present. Christakis and Fowler describe the way information, called *contagion*, moves through these groups and the way individuals, called *nodes*, are wired into social networks through degrees of separation. Social Network Theory offers a way of understanding social relations and how they impinge on the individual. Unfortunately, most Psychoanalysts and Psychotherapists are unfamiliar with this work or the fact that it externally influences (for good or ill) behavior, affect, and, for our purposes, transference and countertransference. It is a driver of affects, Consciousness, and Unconsciousness that has also not been considered by Panksepp (Panksepp & Biven, 2012) in his seminal work on affect. For all of these reasons I have been discussing it in my work of the past decade.

But there is more. Christakis and Fowler (2009) have also described the existence of very large social networks that, borrowing from the study of insect societies, they have called *Superorganisms*. These networks are often country-sized or, looking at the United States, can fracture into two Superorganisms, pretty much evenly split between red states and blue states. There is not much writing on Human Superorganisms (Aunger, 2017; Zambonelli, 2012, are exceptions) or how they dictate human behavior, thoughts, and affects. The internet and the attendant metaverse profoundly facilitate and amplify contagion in superorganisms, also for good or ill.[1] These are all part of the social "soup," if you will, that we and our patients are emersed in. There is more work to be done here. There are other questions about the nature of contagion and what kind of information it transmits. There is, for example, a growing interest in telepathic dreams (e.g., Mayer, 2001) that is increasingly seen as legitimate. That literature tends to focus on the dreams themselves. It has not looked at these dreams as the outcome of a process, the telepathy, nor raised questions about the nature of that process. I believe that it involves contagion, both on the level of Dunbar-sized groups and that of Superorganisms. We must conclude that we are all wired together more tightly than we had ever imagined and that what we experience as our*selves* is really much more about the Social Networks we are members (or nodes) of.

There is still another frame of reference for the concept of Human Superorganisms referring to the individual. This involves the fact that we humans represent homes to symbiotic colonies of micro-organisms—bacteria, viruses, protozoans—inhabiting the gut, the skin and, internally, even the brain, that effect how we function physically and mentally (Dietert, 2016; Roberts, Farmer, & Walker, 2018). We are talking here, literally of *kilograms* of living microorganisms.

The cultural currency of social contagion involves the function of memes and influencers (Brodie, 1995/2011; Dawkins, 1976/2016; Mauricio & Castaño, 2013). They too operate outside of awareness and surface as affects.[2] This is much enhanced by social media and the metaverse. We are, as a result, profoundly different beings than we were even a decade ago, and the process of change can only accelerate as the metaverse continues to evolve and develop. These things need to be taken up in the therapeutic process; we and our patients are different creatures than we were before the metaverse came along (perhaps birthed itself is a better term). Heuristics and Biases also provide a kind of social currency for the expression of these tendencies in the individual. A chapter integrating these threads would be very useful in a subsequent volume.

Finally, Complexity Theory (Leffert, 2008, 2010) offers a way of understanding how these various elements interact. They function as basins of *attractors* that resist change and, when distorted by events, will tend to return to their steady state after the pressure on the system has relaxed. It is only when enough external pressure is applied to the system that a tipping point is reached and a change of state occurs for the system. Complexity Theory tells us when a system has been over-perturbed in this way—think earthquake faults—but cannot predict *when* the tipping point is reached and a change in state will occur.

All of these issues have clinical relevance and bear on Therapeutic Action. Taken as a whole, they describe powerful systems that are not conscious and resist change. They blunt the force of interpretations and the power of the therapeutic relationship to effect change, again acting outside of the realm of conscious awareness. The uninformed therapist will not understand these systemic behaviors (labeling them as resistance) that are, in fact, probably describing the need for working through that *is* clinically noticed.

The internet, social media, and the metaverse they make possible are now in exponential flux. I have offered, in the present volume, what must be considered a preliminary account of their development. By the time I look at them in the next volume they may well have come to be all but unrecognizable as their universe continues to expand. They produce a radical restructuring of the Self and its Being, a new Dasein if you will, that includes a virtual presence in these new Worlds. We have to consider and perhaps rename the modifications they engender in the *Mitwelt* and the *Umwelt*. Perhaps a change in signifiers will be called for.

It becomes necessary, I think, to reconsider our perceptual connections to reality and the external world they link us to. Take the perception of the color *yellow* as a simple example. I can identify yellowness in certain objects in the world, but wait, what I mean is in *my* world. I know what I mean when I say, "something is yellow." I also know that, if my perception is valid, it will coincide with what someone else identifies as yellow. Pretty obvious, but do I know if our *experience* of yellow is the same? We identify the same thing as yellow but don't know if it's the same. Calling it a *quale* (Dennett, 1992), an individual, subjective, conscious experience, certainly identifies it, but doesn't help much with our experience. This brings us back to the famous question, "What is it like to be a bat?" (Nagel, 1970), and how can we ever know? Yellow *may* or may not be the same across individuals; we can't say for sure. If, however, we get to more complex experiences and the most complex of all experiences, "what is it like to be a conscious Human Being?" we are on firmer ground to say it is different from one to the other of us. We can, I think, quantify the *parameters* of that differentness, shaped by memory, perception, and the changing ways we experience World. I would posit that, if we wish to be effective clinicians, we need to periodically remind ourselves of this differentness as it pertains to how we see our patients over the course of a therapy.

The Simulation Hypothesis (Bostrom, 2003, 2005; Chalmers, 2022) belongs to a branch of philosophy that deals with skeptical hypotheses. Simply put, it states that what we experience as existence (that is, Dasein) is not a measure of the physical measure of World but rather a simulation of it. Currently that would be a computer simulation. The most prominent illustration is the classic 1999 science fiction film, *The Matrix*, in which humans are all plugged into a super-supercomputer that pipes a simulated experience of reality directly into our central nervous systems. Chalmers, who writes about virtual worlds, believes that there is perhaps a 25% chance that that's how we are living now. Even if this is not the case, and I'm inclined to think it is not, as we venture into the metaverse, for recreation or work, we are consciously moving into simulations that will become ever more realistic.

A simple example (Sugura, 2022) is H2, a Sony-backed startup company that is developing an armband that senses the movement of muscles and conveys the information to the user's Avatar in the metaverse. The technology employs electrical stimulation to mimic feelings of weight or pain like being pecked by a bird. Pain sensations act to turn the metaverse world into more of a real-world experience.

It is not necessary to buy the Simulation Hypothesis outright in order to see how simulations mold Human Experience. We form our own kinds of simulations. All of Heidegger's modes of Being—Thrownness, Everydayness, and Fallenness—apply to our own individual experiences, our own *simulations* of reality. In the *Eigenwelt*—our internal world, the other two being the *Mitwelt* and the *Umwelt*—we form these simulations and use Memory to keep track of them. Another term for the outcome of this process is Irreducible Subjectivity, a process with great clinical relevance (Renik, 1993). Self-reflective or narrative or episodic Memory (Schacter, 1996; Schacter, Addis, & Buckner, 2008) is a volatile ever-changing thing. If we tell a story about some event (narrative Memory) and then tell it again a day later, we find that it is not quite the same story, and we then find that the telling of the story *changes* the Memory permanently. It is not quite the same either. Freud (1900/1953) applied this observation to his technique of dream interpretation.

Simulation and its outcomes are also important to keep in mind clinically. They dictate that we and our patients live in different simulated worlds and experience what we say to each other differently. We have no idea, for example, how a patient experiences *their* world and what Meaning they derive from the interpretations we offer them. Some patients make good use of them, whether they agree with them or not, whereas others hardly listen to them, waiting for us to stop talking so they can get on with their monologue. This process is affective as well as cognitive: Transference and Countertransference are just gross examples of it. Over time, the therapeutic relationship may influence both partners to change their experience of the therapeutic world (a species of *Mitwelt*) to be more like each other's. If we approach these observations with different language tools, we see that what we are talking about is Intersubjectivity, or, from still another perspective, the Analytic Third (Ogden, 1994). When we are in a reflective mode—another term is the Default Mode—as opposed to an experiencing mode, it is worth keeping all of this in mind some of the time. The experiencing mode has its limits, however: Much of what we have been talking about is unconscious, we may become conscious of it or try to make it conscious, but it is discontinuous.

By its very nature, this leads us back to the whole question of what Consciousness is as it pertains to these questions of experience, Being, and what exactly is happening in our heads. It has an Evo-Devo going back hundreds of millions of years (Ogas & Gaddam, 2022). I have already considered Consciousness a number of times, including as recently as in Chapter 4 of this volume. There are ample reasons for taking it up again in the light of all of this; whether it merits another chapter of its own or needs simply to be discussed in the context of these various issues remains to be seen.

I have been a Psychoanalyst for nearly 50 years. Over that span of time, the definition of who a Psychoanalyst is and what constitutes a Psychoanalysis have greatly expanded. There was not then, however, and there is not now, a sharply defined consensus of the territory, intellectual and ontological, encompassed by the terms. The observations, flung out at meetings, conferences, or private discussions, that so-and-so is not an analyst, or that so-and-so's presented case is not an analysis, still remain expressions of perhaps the ultimate contempt and depreciation to be leveled at one colleague by another. It makes sense to try and address definitional concerns with the caveat: as long as one can do so without recourse to Metapsychology. Metapsychology is, unfortunately, precisely what analysts and psychoanalytic psychotherapists privilege in these discussions. I have argued (Leffert, 2010) that these become discussions not of clinical theory, but rather discussions of power and politics that, from Freud's day on, have led to *colleagues* (I particularly choose this term) being ejected from psychoanalytic institutions. The politics and power relations (Lukes, 2005) have become more moderate over the decades—to a degree due to simple exhaustion—as we have had to accept clinical and theoretical pluralities. We have, over the years, been subject to waves of theory and practice that sometimes resemble tsunamis. The most recent wave in the United States derives from a revival of the mid-century work of Wilfred Bion that, over the last decade or two, has come to captivate many colleagues. What's different about this today is that the "Bionians" and the more usual Relational/Intersubjective and Contemporary Ego Psychologists[3] seem to coexist quite happily in diverse psychoanalytic institutes, although they strongly but courteously disagree with each other. What still needs to be addressed here, given that the effort will not and perhaps should not please everybody, are the dual questions: What is Psychoanalysis and what is a Psychoanalyst?

We cannot address either the ontology or the epistemology of the terms *Psychoanalyst* and *Psychoanalysis* without first providing an all-important four-dimensional account of context. This includes a sociocultural-locational account of the Self, and its maintenance of a sense of external and internal reality, while accepting Neuroscience and Postmodern critiques of the distinction that require an acknowledgement of a degree of blurring between the two. The old concept of being able to maintain at least a fairly stable distinction between the two as opposed to the inability to do so led to one of the early Psychoanalytic definitions of psychosis. The final dimension of such an account is its historicity or temporality (Heidegger, 1979/2009) in Phenomenological terms or, in Postmodern terms, the Archaeology of the Self (Foucault, 1969 & 1971/1972, 1966/1994).

Archaeology and the Archaeology of the Self are Postmodern concepts that I have written about (Leffert, 2013, chapter 2) at some length. As the reader may be unfamiliar with them, some explication is worthwhile here. For the reflective person, Archaeology and Memory are intimately caught up with each other. The former offers a processual and post-processual approach to understanding the latter and its dependence on a contextual rather than a content-based reading of historicity. Context is so powerful that it can determine whether specific content can even be perceived, let alone discussed. Archaeology is not about narrative construction. Rather, it constitutes an epistemological inquiry into the discursive and non-discursive practices that lie beneath the content and construction of narratives. Discursive practices are stable ways of describing how things *are*. They are present in a particular social system at a particular time. Taken together, they constitute a *Discursive Formation*. The term neurosis is an example of a discursive formation that came into being at the beginning of the last century. What I added to this (Leffert, 2013) was the premise that an individual had their own set of discursive practices that were influenced by the social and sociative groups they were members of. Discursive practices led to Linguistic practices that were not noticed and shaped discourse; Lukes (2005) wrote about the power relations implications of such practices, that they were designed to make certain discourses challenging power elites impossible. Foucault (1969 & 1971/1972) describes non-discursive practices as arising out of domains that include institutions, political events, economic practices and processes. He seeks out the relations between the discursive and the non-discursive that can lead to *rapprochements* between the two.

Archaeologies are unconscious; they offer the rules of knowledge in existence historically when an event occurred and contrast them with those existing in the moment when a narrative was being subsequently constructed. Taken together, these rules constitute an Episteme with Foucault positing that a single Episteme could describe a particular time in history. For example, the Episteme of the Classical Age—the 17th and 18th centuries—was mathematics and taxonomy. A specialized Episteme of that age involves a discourse on madness (Foucault, 1961/2006). In the present, Epistemes can apply to decades rather than centuries or millennia. They can exist, I posit, for an individual, a small group (up to 150 individuals or so), or a superorganism. Enclose this in an *Epoché* for the moment; we shall come back to it.

Connected to this account is another complex account, an account of identity that entails Diversity. Contemporarily, Diversity signifies discourses on race, religion, gender, and sexual identity. They are intense, volatile, and often involve, understandably, strong emotions. There is currently there is so much writing on them that I can't possibly cover or add anything to in a chapter-length essay. I would suggest, however, that Diversity is a narrowed discourse drawn, explicitly or implicitly, from a wider Postmodern discourse on *Différance* (Derrida, 1978, 1972/1991). Derrida conceptualizes a sheaf of *Différence* in which various strands are woven together in a state of tension and at times oppositeness. There are a number of relevant things for us to say about this. The problem is that these issues are so intensely emotional and political that it is difficult to have conversations about them. The only thing that can ease this problem is the passage of time, the same thing that has made these issues more prominent (certainly the current understandings about race and the events that have pushed them—the George Floyd murder, for example—have dramatically changed the thinking of our superorganism). My son, now in his 40s, tells me that for his generation—a California generation born to liberal parents, however—sexual orientation is not something anyone even thinks about anymore.

The thing about *différance* is that it must be understood foundationally in terms of a particular historicity and its Archaeology. These are post-structural arguments that indeed serve to deconstruct the discourses of diversity. They are accompanied by the neo-pragmatist[4] arguments concerning race and religion such as those developed by Edward Said (1979, 1994), particularly on "Orientalism." The latter is, in effect, a form of racism. It states that a putative geographic East (the location of which moves ever-more eastward with the passage of time) exists, whose people are very different from us—that is Caucasian, Christian Europeans.[5] They are, to put it bluntly, described as decadent, corrupt, childlike, and non-Christian. The argument went (in the last three centuries) that it was appropriate, even beneficial to these "Easterners," to be colonized by the superior West, with the exploitation, contempt, and infantilization being denied. This led to the post-colonial, global era in which we now exist, in which some former colonies remain damaged as a result of the colonial experience.

Différance has, however, a wider context, beyond Diversity, that is relevant to our work. It refers to the fact that, as Human Beings we are all different; we think and feel very differently from one another. The factors that contribute to this *différance* are social, cultural, developmental, historical, and heredity—wiring differences. The way to manage *différance* clinically is to keep it in mind when we are reflecting, as opposed to experiencing, with a patient and to treat it as something to be specifically learned about a patient. This is still another point of view from which to understand a patient. The potential for error here is to implicitly think that our patients are like ourselves—although in some ways they obviously are—but rather to maintain our sense of their *différance* and alikeness in a state of dynamic tension. Malabou and Derrida (1999/2004) describe such a process in their book, *Counterpath*. If we apply this kind of thinking to individuals who are now subsumed under the term *diverse*, we have an opportunity to view and experience their *différance* from both inside and outside. This is much harder to do from a perspective of *sameness*.

Finally, and this would require a chapter in the next volume, living in these very difficult times brings with it changing perceptions of social reality. An easy example is to be seen in the 2020 Presidential Election in which huge numbers of people—members of different superorganisms really—believe the outcome was either fair or stolen. I am a member of the former group, and I can cite actual scientific data to prove it. The *Guardian* tells us, however, that 40% of Americans belong to the latter group.[6] They do not accept this data, insisting that it is corrupted. (Kellyanne Conway, a former advisor to the former president invokes the concept she coined—*alternative facts*—to explain the difference.) The fact is that both groups are equally sincere in their beliefs, except for people, often politicians, who don't believe anything, and are simply exploiting the groups for their own gain. By the way, the two groups view each other from a perspective of hatred and contempt. (Similar issues exist globally, such as Putin's attempts to control and shape the Russian peoples' reality of the Ukraine war.) We have moved into a particularly dark, Postmodern world, dominated by Post-structural and Neo-pragmatic Epistemologies. It is an era best described as one of Post-Truth and Post-Empathy. Members of differing social groups of whatever size—ranging in size from Dunbar's Number to superorganisms—*can* be empathic with each other and have shared belief-truths, for lack of a better term, *but not with those who inhabit a different group.*

This book has turned out to offer an often intense, and sometimes strange, ride into a possible future for Psychoanalysis. It is only a reflection of just how strange the world has gotten to be as we've entered into the 21st century. What I've tried to do in it is to document these complexity driven shifts and to consider how they drive, or should drive, what we do as Psychoanalysts and Psychotherapists. At the same time, our brand, as the name for a kind of Psychotherapy, has become tarnished, seemingly old-fashioned, and less relevant to this world. The brand does still have relevance, particularly as a discipline to be taught, expanded through research and discourse, and brought closer to interdisciplinary studies. Its uses, particularly to the culture at large, as a label for a kind of therapeutic process, have declined—most of us now call ourselves, in the community at large, Psychotherapists—and it is probably best to tacitly accept this trend. Ironically, as our thinking has Evolved and Developed over the last half-century, we have more to offer our patients today than we have ever had. I am left with the realization that I have more to say about these issues and will need another volume in which to say it.

Notes

1 The red state-blue state split in the United States certainly could not have happened without it.
2 Fashion comes to mind. In mid-20th century, the La Coste alligator on knit shirts just *seemed* right. By the end of the century, it was the Polo horse and rider that *seemed* right.
3 I don't subscribe to any of these metatheories unless they demonstrate some kind of interdisciplinary validation coming from *outside* of psychoanalysis.
4 Post-structuralism and Neo-pragmatism are two of the four categories of Postmodernism, the other two being Neo-Marxism and Difference, the postmodern term encompassing issues of gender, race, religion, and sexual identity.
5 One could add cis-gender, male to this.
6 The divide extends to other issues as well, such as Global Warming.

References

Aunger, R. (2017). Moral action as cheater suppression in human superorganisms. *Frontiers in Sociology*, *2*, 1–19.

Bostrom, N. (2003). Are we living in a computer simulation? *The Philosophical Quarterly*, *53*, 243–255.

Bostrom, N. (2005). In defense of human dignity. *Bioethics*, *19*, 202–212.

Brodie, R. (2011). *Virus of the mind*. New York, NY: Hay House, Inc. (Original work published in 1995).

Chalmers, D. J. (2022). *Reality+: Virtual worlds and the problems of philosophy*. New York, NY: W. W. Norton & Co.

Christakis, N. A., & Fowler, J. H. (2009). *Connected: The surprising power of our social networks and how they shape our lives*. New York, NY: Little, Brown and Company.

Dawkins, R. (2016). *The selfish gene: 40th anniversary edition*. Oxford, England: Oxford University Press. (Original work published in 1976).

Dennett, D. C. (1992). *Consciousness explained*. New York, NY: Little Brown & Co.

Derrida, J. (1978). *Writing and différence* (A. Bass, trans.). Chicago, IL: University of Chicago Press.

Derrida, J. (1991). Différance. In P. Kamuf (Ed.), *A Derrida reader: Between the blinds* (pp. 59–79). New York, NY: Columbia University Press. (Original work published in 1972).

Dietert, R. (2016). *The human superorganism: How the microbiome is revolutionizing the pursuit of a healthy life*. New York, NY: Dutton.

Dunbar, R. (2016). *Human evolution: Our brains and behavior*. Oxford, England: Oxford University Press.

Foucault, M. (1972). *The archeology of knowledge & the discourse on language* (A. M. S. Smith, trans.). New York, NY: Pantheon. (Original work published in 1969 & 1971).

Foucault, M. (1994). *The order of things: An archeology of the human sciences*. New York, NY: Vintage Books. (Original work published in 1966).

Foucault, M. (2006). *History of madness* (J. Murphy & J. Khalfa, trans.). London, England: Routledge. (Original work published in 1961).

Freud, S. (1953). The interpretation of dreams. In J. Strachey (Ed.), *Standard edition* (Vols. IV & V). London, England: Hogarth Press. (Original work published in 1900).

Heidegger, M. (2009). *History of the concept of time: Prolegomena (Studies in phenomenology and existential philosophy* (T. Kisiel, trans.). Bloomington: Indiana University Press. (Original work published in 1979).

Kahneman, D., Slovic, P., & Tversky, A. (Eds.). (1982). *Judgement under uncertainty: Heuristics and biases*. Cambridge, England: Cambridge University Press.

Kahneman, D., & Tversky, A. (2000). Prospect theory: An analysis of decisions under risk. In D. Kahneman, & A. Tversky (Eds.), *Choices, values, and frames* (pp. 17–43). Cambridge, England: Cambridge University Press. (Original work published in 1979).

Latour, B. (1993). *We have never been modern* (C. Porter, trans.). Cambridge, MA: Harvard University Press. (Original work published in 1991).

Leffert, M. (2003). Analysis and psychotherapy by telephone: Twenty years of clinical experience. *Journal of the American Psychoanalytic Association*, *51*, 101–130.

Leffert, M. (2008). Complexity and postmodernism in contemporary theory of psychoanalytic change. *Journal of the American Academy of Psychoanalysis and Dynamic Psychiatry*, *36*, 517–542.

Leffert, M. (2010). *Contemporary psychoanalytic foundations*. London, England: Routledge.

Leffert, M. (2013). *The therapeutic situation in the 21st century*. New York, NY: Routledge.

Leffert, M. (2017). *Positive psychoanalysis: Aesthetics, desire, and subjective well-being*. New York, NY: Routledge.

Leffert, M. (2018). *Psychoanalysis and the birth of the self: A radical interdisciplinary approach*. London, England: Routledge.

Leffert, M. (2021). *The psychoanalysis of the absurd: Existentialism and phenomenology in contemporary psychoanalysis*. London, England: Routledge.

Lukes, S. (2005). *Power a radical view* (2nd ed.). New York, NY: Palgrave Macmillan.

Malabou, C., & Derrida, J. (2004). *Counterpath* (D. Wills, trans.). Stanford, CA: Stanford University Press. (Original work published in 1999).

Mauricio, C., & Castaño, C. (2013). Defining and characterizing the concept of internet meme. *Revista CES Psicologia, 6*, 82–104.

May, R. (1958). Contributions of existential psychotherapy. In R. May, E. Angel, & H. F. Ellenberger (Eds.), *Existence* (pp. 37–91). New York, NY: Simon & Schuster.

May, R., Angel, E., & Ellenberger, H. F. (Eds.). (1958). *Existence: New directions in psychiatry and psychology*. New York, NY: Simon & Schuster.

Mayer, E. (2001). On "telepathic dreams?" *Journal of the American Psychoanalytic Association, 49*, 629–657.

Nagel, T. (1970). What is it like to be a bat? *Philosophical Review, 83*, 435–450.

Ogas, O., & Gaddam, S. (2022). *Journey of the mind: How thinking emerged from chaos*. New York, NY: W. W. Norton & Co.

Ogden, T. H. (1994). The analytic third: Working with intersubjective clinical facts. *The International Journal of Psychoanalysis, 75*, 3–19.

Panksepp, J., & Biven, L. (2012). *The archaeology of mind: Neuroevolutionary origins of human emotions*. New York, NY: W. W. Norton & Co.

Renik, O. (1993). Analytic interaction: Conceptualizing technique in light of the analyst's irreducible subjectivity. *Psychoanalytic Quarterly, 62*, 553–571.

Roberts, R. C., Farmer, C. B., & Walker, C. (2018). *The human brain microbiome; there are bacteria in our brains!* Paper presented at the Annual meeting for the Society for Neuroscience, November 2018.

Said, E. W. (1979). *Orientalism*. New York, NY: Vintage Books.

Said, E. W. (1994). *Culture and imperialism*. New York, NY: Vintage Books.

Schacter, D. L. (1996). *Searching for memory*. New York, NY: Basic Books.

Schacter, D. L., Addis, D. R., & Buckner, R. L. (2008). Episodic simulation of future events concepts, data, and applications. *Annals of the New York Academy of Science, 1124*, 39–60.

Sugura, E. (2022, March 21). Metaverse start-up seeks gain from pain. *Financial Times*, p. 11.

Walter, B. (2022). *How civil wars start; and how to stop them*. New York, NY: Crown.

Zambonelli, F. (2012). Toward sociotechnical urban superorganisms. *Computer, 45*, 76–78.

Index

For Product Safety Concerns and Information please contact our EU
representative GPSR@taylorandfrancis.com
Taylor & Francis Verlag GmbH, Kaufingerstraße 24, 80331 München, Germany

www.ingramcontent.com/pod-product-compliance
Lightning Source LLC
Chambersburg PA
CBHW050648280326
41932CB00015B/2830

9 7 8 1 0 3 2 3 9 4 0 1 5